WOMAN'S WEEKLY
Knitting Book

WOMAN'S WEEKLY
Knitting Book

edited by Marion Smith

HAMLYN
London · New York · Sydney · Toronto

The designs in this book were originally featured
in *Woman's Weekly* magazine.

First published in 1983 by
The Hamlyn Publishing Group Limited
London · New York · Sydney · Toronto
Astronaut House, Feltham, Middlesex, England

Filmset in England by Servis Filmsetting Limited,
in 8 on 9pt Monophoto Plantin 110.

Printed in Hong Kong
ISBN 0 600 35344 3

Contents

Aran-style Slipover (see page 65)

Introduction

Our Knitting Correspondence Department at Woman's Weekly receives hundreds of letters each week and reading and dealing with these has made the job of compiling this book very much easier for me.

The majority of these letters asks for copies of published patterns because, perhaps, a friend has made a garment which has been much admired, or during the process of knitting either the baby or the family pet has managed to chew up the instructions. In many cases, the patterns have been used so many times that the print is faded and is no longer legible.

Although much time and hard work is involved answering such requests, we are delighted to receive them as they feed back to us details about the styles and types of garments that are the most popular among our readers. We try to bear all this information in mind when planning for future issues.

For this book I have chosen a variety of patterns that have proved to be popular during the last few years. On the whole, they use the standard types of yarn, but I have included a number requiring speciality yarns that have enjoyed long-standing popularity.

I do hope that you find at least one of your favourite patterns within these pages and others which may be new to you that were perhaps missed at the time of publication and which you may like to try out now. I have also included some knitting and making up hints which should help you to achieve the best results with the least difficulty.

Marian Smith

Helpful Hints

SELECTING YOUR YARN

It is very important to obtain the yarn stated in the pattern, especially when a speciality yarn is used. Unfortunately, much time, effort and money can be wasted if this point is disregarded. Obviously, retailers cannot stock all the yarns and makes available, but do try to find the correct yarn whenever possible as results cannot be guaranteed when a substitute yarn has been used. (I have included a list of spinners' addresses on page oo who will be pleased to supply either a local stockist or a postal service.)

In many cases where standard yarns such as 4-ply, double knitting and some Aran weights are substituted, the results are successful, but it is always advisable to buy just one ball of the proposed yarn and knit a tension sample before buying the full amount the pattern requires. If the correct tension is obtained and the resulting fabric is acceptable, then the garment will knit up to measurements similar to those stated in the pattern. However, do remember that yarn amounts differ, especially if a man-made fibre is used in place of 100 per cent wool, as wool weighs heavier and so has fewer metres to the ball. It is not advisable to substitute speciality yarns as no two yarns are exactly the same in weight or finish and, in many cases, the fabric is very difficult to unravel once it has been knitted up and often the surface of the yarn can be damaged in the process.

TENSION

The way to achieve successful results and a well fitting garment lies in obtaining the correct tension. This term is used to describe the number of stitches and rows which are produced to a certain measurement using a given size of needles, the specified yarn and a particular stitch pattern.

Before starting any pattern, knit up a sample square using the stated yarn and needles and enough stitches to measure at least 10 × 10 cm (4 × 4 in) according to the instructions given at the start of each pattern. If the finished square measures less than it should, it is working up too tightly and you should try again using a size larger needles. If it is larger, then the knitting is too loose and the square should be knitted again with a smaller size of needles. Also check your tension at regular intervals during the process of knitting your garment to make sure that you maintain the same tension throughout.

SIZES

Many of the patterns in this book are given in a range of sizes but this may create a certain amount of confusion, especially where a large number of sizes is included. It is advisable for knitters to first go through the instructions and underline all the figures which relate to the size to be worked.

JOINING NEW YARN

When possible, it is always advisable to join in a new ball of yarn at the beginning of a row. The ends are then woven into the seams when the garment is being made up. If the yarn has to be joined in the middle of the row, the 'splice' method is satisfactory in most cases. Unravel each end to be joined and cut away half of the strands from each end; overlay the remaining strands of the two ends from opposite directions and twist them together to obtain a similar thickness to that of the original yarn. Knit the next few stitches very carefully until the 'join' has been passed.

CHANGING COLOURS

When more than one colour is used in a row, it is necessary to weave in the loose strands at the back unless the colours are changed regularly every three or four stitches. In this latter case remember to strand the yarn not in use lightly across the back or the work will become puckered and will not lie smooth. Also remember when working adjacent blocks of colours to twist the yarn just used round that of the next colour to be used to avoid leaving a gap.

The 'weave in' method is used to avoid long strands on the wrong side of the garment that can easily catch and pull and distort the pattern when more than three or four stitches of one colour are worked before changing to another colour. For right side rows, the yarn not being used is lightly held in the left hand at the back of the knitting. To catch this up, insert the right-hand needle into the next stitch and under this back yarn, then knit the stitch in the usual way. The next stitch is then knitted excluding the back yarn, and you will find that the yarns not in use are neatly held in the back of the knitting. This procedure is repeated every four or five stitches. The same method works equally as well on wrong side rows, when the free yarn is lightly held in front of the work.

When knitting in stripes, strand yarn not in use

up the side of the knitting, by twisting it with the yarn in use every few rows to catch threads to the sides.

PICKING UP STITCHES

This is needed mainly for neck edges but also sometimes for front bands. Work with the right side of the fabric facing, unless otherwise stated. Divide the selected edge into several equal sections using pins as markers, then pick up an equal number of stitches from each section to obtain an evenly spaced edging.

If picking up from a straight edge, insert the needle either between or into the centre of the stitches along the edge of the fabric, take the yarn around the needle and draw a loop through. Continue inserting the needle into the same position along the remainder of the edge to obtain a neat join. A curved edge is worked in a similar way, but the needle is inserted into the centre of each stitch where possible.

PRESSING AND AFTER CARE

If the yarn used requires pressing then block out each piece of the garment with the wrong side of work uppermost, using plenty of pins and taking care to keep the shape of the knitting. Many patterns give information on pressing, but always check carefully with the instructions given by the manufacturers on the ball band, as once a yarn has been pressed wrongly and the fabric has gone 'flat', no amount of work will return it to its original state of elasticity. This also applies to the washing. Many of the modern yarns are machine washable, and easily maintained, but there are also a number of speciality yarns that are hand washable only. It is useful to include a ball band when giving a hand-knitted garment as a gift, so that after-care instructions are passed on for future use.

THE MAKING UP

There are several ways to seam pieces of the garment together and everyone has their own preferences, so I will mention three of the most popular methods. In each case you should use a blunt-ended wool needle and either the original yarn or a finer quality in the same shade.

Back stitch seam This is worked with the two right sides together and about 5 mm ($\frac{1}{4}$ in) from the edges and is ideal for joining shaped edges. Insert the needle down through the two pieces and bring it up two stitches to the left, pulling the yarn through, *take the needle back across the front of the work to the right and insert it at the end of last stitch worked, then bring it up four stitches to the left; repeat from * to end.

Invisible seam This is worked in the centre of or between stitches with the right sides of the work facing and the pieces laid side by side. *Insert the needle under a stitch on one edge and pull the yarn through, then insert the needle under an adjacent stitch on the other edge and pull the yarn through; repeat from * taking a stitch from each side and drawing yarn up tightly between each stitch to form an invisible join.

Invisible seam

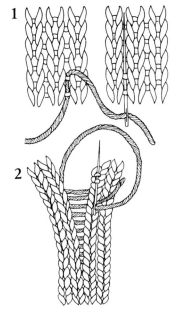

Flat seam This is worked with right sides together. *Insert the needle into an edge stitch of the first side, through the adjacent stitch on the second side and draw the yarn through, insert the needle into the next stitch to the left on the second side and through the adjacent stitch on the first side and draw the yarn through; repeat from * to end.

Babies and Children

Layette in Berry Stitch

Illustrated on pages 15, 18 and 19

MATERIALS: *Allow the following quantities in 50 g balls of Lister/Lee Baby Love 3-ply and 4-ply:* **Shawl:** 6 of 3-ply; *a pair of No. 8 (4 mm) knitting needles.* **Matinee jacket:** 2 of 4-ply; *a pair each of No. 7 (4½ mm), No. 9 (3¾ mm) and No. 10 (3¼ mm) knitting needles; 1 metre of lacy frilling; 4 buttons.* **Dress:** 2 of 4-ply; *a pair each of No. 7 (4½ mm) No. 9 (3¾ mm) and No. 10 (3¼ mm) knitting needles; 1 metre of lacy frilling; 80 cm of narrow ribbon; 4 buttons.* **Cardigan:** 2 of 4-ply; *a pair each of No. 7 (4½ mm) and No. 10 (3¼ mm) knitting needles; 8 buttons.* **Jersey:** 2 of 4-ply; *a pair each of No. 7 (4½ mm) and No. 10 (3¼ mm) knitting needles; 6 buttons.* **Vest:** 1 of 3-ply; *a pair each of No. 9 (3¾ mm) and No. 10 (3¼ mm) knitting needles; 1 metre of narrow ribbon.* **Bonnet:** 1 of 4-ply; *a pair each of No. 7 (4½ mm), No. 9 (3¾ mm) and No. 10 (3¼ mm) knitting needles; 50 cm of lacy frilling; 1 metre of ribbon.* **Helmet:** 1 of 4-ply; *a pair each of No. 7 (4½ mm) and No. 10 (3¼ mm) knitting needles; 1 button.* **Bootees:** 1 of 4-ply; *a pair each of No. 7 (4½ mm) and No. 10 (3¼ mm) knitting needles; 80 cm of narrow ribbon.*
For the complete layette: *7 of 3-ply and 9 of 4-ply.*

TENSION AND MEASUREMENTS: *Worked at a tension of 34 stitches and 31 rows to measure 10 × 10 cm, over the berry pattern, using No. 8 (4 mm) needles and 3-ply; 28 stitches and 34 rows to measure 10 × 10 cm, over the stocking stitch, using No. 9 (3¾ mm) needles and 3-ply, and 30 stitches and 30 rows to measure 10 × 10 cm, over the berry pattern, using No. 7 (4½ mm) needles and 4-ply, the layette will fit a 46 cm (18 inch) chest size.* **Shawl:** *106 cm (41¾ inches) square.* **Matinee jacket:** *side seam 18.5 cm (7¼ inches); length 28.5 cm (11¼ inches); sleeve seam 16.5 cm (6½ inches).* **Dress:** *side seam 18.5 cm (7¼ inches); length 27.5 cm (10¾ inches); sleeve seam 3 cm (1¼ inches).* **Cardigan:** *side seam 15.5 cm (6 inches); length 25.5 cm (10 inches); sleeve seam 16.5 cm (6½ inches).* **Jersey:** *side seam 15.5 cm (6 inches); length 25 cm (9¾ inches); sleeve seam 15.5 cm (6 inches).* **Vest:** *side seam 18 cm (7 inches); length 26 cm (10¼ inches); sleeve seam 4 cm (1½ inches).* **Bonnet:** *all round face edge 34 cm (13¼ inches); depth 10 cm (4 inches).* **Helmet:** *all round at brim 36.5 cm (14¼ inches).* **Bootees:** *foot length 8.5 cm (3¼ inches).*

ABBREVIATIONS: To be read before working: *K., knit plain; p., purl; st., stitch; tog., together; k. 2 tog.b., k. 2 tog. through back of sts.; s.s., stocking st. (k. on right side and p. on wrong side); r.s.s., reverse stocking st. (p. on right side and k. on wrong side); y.r.n., yarn round needle; y.fwd., yarn forward; inc., increase (by working twice into next st.); dec., decrease (by taking 2 sts. tog.); up 1, pick up loop lying between needles and k. or p. into back of it; 3 in 1, 3 sts. from 1 st. (k., p. and k. all into front of next st.); single rib is k. 1 and p. 1 alternately; s.k.p.o., slip 1, k. 1, pass slipped st. over.*

THE SHAWL
Illustrated opposite

THE CENTRE: With No. 8 (4 mm) needles and 3-ply, cast on 214 sts. loosely.

   1st pattern row (right side): P. to end.
   2nd row: K. 1, * p. 3 tog., 3 in 1; repeat from * until 1 st. remains, k. 1.
   3rd row: P. to end.
   4th row: K. 1, * 3 in 1, p. 3 tog.; repeat from * until 1 st. remains, k. 1.
   These 4 rows form the pattern. Repeat them 47 times more.
   Cast off loosely.

THE SIDE BORDERS (4 alike): With No. 8 (4 mm) needles and 3-ply, cast on 32 sts. loosely.
   Pattern row: P. 1, * y.r.n., p. 2 tog.; repeat from * until 1 st. remains, p. 1.
   Repeat pattern row, 207 times more.
   Cast off loosely.

THE CORNERS (4 alike): With No. 8 (4 mm) needles and 3-ply, cast on 3 sts.
   1st row (right side): P. 3.
   2nd row: Inc., 3 in 1, inc.
   3rd row: P. 7.
   4th row: Inc., 3 in 1, p. 3 tog., 3 in 1, inc.
   5th row: P. 11.
   6th row: Inc., 3 in 1, * p. 3 tog., 3 in 1; repeat from * until 1 st. remains, inc.
   7th row: P. to end.
   Repeat 6th and 7th rows, 15 times, then 6th row again. Cast off loosely.

THE EDGING: With No. 8 (4 mm) needles and 3-ply, cast on 9 sts.
   1st pattern row: K. 9.
   2nd row: K. 1, y.fwd., * k. 2 tog., y.fwd.; repeat from * twice, k. 2.
   3rd row: K. 10.
   4th row: K. 1, y.fwd., * k. 2 tog., y.fwd.; repeat from * twice, k.3.
   5th row: K. 11.
   6th row: K. 1, y.fwd., * k. 2 tog., y.fwd.; repeat from * twice, k. 4.
   7th row: K. 12.
   8th row: K. 1, y.fwd., * k. 2 tog., y.fwd.; repeat from * twice, k. 5.
   9th row: K. 13.
   10th row: Cast off 4 sts. loosely, k. to end—9sts.
   Repeat last 10 rows, 107 times more.
   Cast of remaining 9 sts.

Opposite *Dress (page 16) and Shawl*

Continued on page 16

TO MAKE UP THE SHAWL: Sew side borders to sides of centre piece, then inset corners, sewing shaped sides of corners to cast-on and cast-off edges of side borders. Join cast-on and cast-off edge of edging together, then sew straight row-ends to outer edge of shawl. Pin out to size and press lightly with a warm iron over a dry cloth.

THE MATINEE JACKET
Illustrated on page 18

THE BACK: With No. 7 (4½ mm) needles and 4-ply, cast on 106 sts. and work the 4 pattern rows of shawl centre, 12 times.

Dec. row: K. 1, * k. 2 tog., k. 2 tog., k. 1; repeat from * to end—64 sts.

Change to No. 9 (3¾ mm) needles and, beginning with a p. row, s.s. 7 rows.

To shape armholes: Continue in s.s. and cast off 7 sts. at beginning of next 2 rows—50 sts.

S.s. 28 rows.

To slope shoulders: Cast off 8 sts. at beginning of next 2 rows, then 7 sts. on the following 2 rows. Cast off remaining 20 sts.

THE LEFT FRONT: With No. 7 (4½ mm) needles and 4-ply, cast on 50 sts. and work the 4 pattern rows of shawl centre, 12 times.

Dec. row: K. 2, k. 2 tog., k. 1, * k. 2 tog., k. 2 tog., k. 1; repeat from * to end—31 sts.

Change to No. 9 (3¾ mm) needles and, beginning with a p. row, s.s. 7 rows—s.s. 8 rows here when working right front.

To shape armhole: Continue in s.s. and cast off 7 sts. at beginning of next row—24 sts.

S.s. 18 rows.

To shape neck: Cast of 5 sts, at beginning of next row, dec. 1 st. at same edge on next 2 rows, then the 2 following alternate rows—15 sts.

S.s. 4 rows.

To slope shoulder: Cast off 8 sts. at beginning of next row.

Work 1 row, then cast of 7 sts.

THE RIGHT FRONT: Work as left front, noting variation.

THE SLEEVES (2 alike): With No. 10 (3¼ mm) needles and 4-ply, cast on 39 sts. and, beginning odd-numbered rows with k. 1 and even-numbered rows with p. 1, work 13 rows in single rib.

Increase row: Rib 1, up 1, * rib 6, up 1; repeat from * until 2 sts. remain, rib 2—46 sts.

Change to No. 7 (4½ mm) needles and work the 4 pattern rows of shawl centre, once then, keeping continuity of pattern and working extra sts. in r.s.s. as they occur, inc. 1 st. each end of next row and the 3 following 8th rows—54 sts.

Pattern 9 rows across all sts.—mark each end of last row to denote end of sleeve seam.

Pattern a further 8 rows.

Cast off fairly loosely.

THE NECK BAND: First join shoulder seams.

With right side facing, rejoin 4-ply and, using No. 10 (3¼ mm) needles, pick up and k. 15 sts. from right front neck,

20 sts. across back neck and 15 sts. from left front neck—50 sts.

K. 4 rows, then cast off.

THE BUTTONHOLE BAND: With right side facing, rejoin 4-ply and, using No. 10 (3¼ mm) needles, pick up and k. 77 sts. from row ends of right front edge, including neckband.

K. 2 rows.

Buttonhole row: K. 1, * k. 2 tog., y.fwd., k. 6; repeat from * 3 times, k. to end.

K. 3 rows. Cast off k.wise.

THE BUTTON BAND: Work as buttonhole band, along left front edge, omitting buttonholes.

TO MAKE UP THE JACKET: Press s.s. parts lightly with a warm iron over a dry cloth. Set in sleeves, setting row ends above markers to sts. cast off at underarms. Join side and sleeve seams. Sew lace frilling to pick up row at neck and lower edge. Add buttons.

THE DRESS
Illustrated on page 15

THE BACK: With No. 7 (4½ mm) needles and 4-ply, cast on 98 sts. and work the 4 pattern rows of shawl centre, 12 times.

Dec. row: K. 2, * k. 2 tog., k. 2 tog., k. 1; repeat from * until 1 st. remains, k. 1 more—60 sts.

Change to No. 9 (3¾ mm) needles.

Beginning with a p. row, s.s. 7 rows.

To shape armholes: Continue in s.s. and cast off 3 sts. at beginning of next 2 rows, then dec. 1 st. each end of the following 3 rows—48 sts. **

S.s. 3 rows.

To divide for opening: Next row: K. 22, k. 2 tog., turn, and work on these 23 sts. for right half back, leaving remaining 24 sts. on spare needle for left half back.

The right half back: S.s. 19 rows—s.s. 20 rows here when working left half back.

To slope shoulder: Cast off 7 sts. at beginning of next row and following alternate row.

Work 1 row, then cast off 9 sts.

The left half back: With right side facing, rejoin yarn to inner end of 24 sts. on spare needles, k. 2 tog., k. to end.

Work as right half back, noting variation.

THE FRONT: Work as back to **.

S.s. 13 rows.

To divide for neck: Next row: K. 18, turn, leaving remaining sts. on spare needle, work on these sts. for left half front.

The left half front: Dec. 1 st. at neck edge on next 2 rows then the 2 following alternate rows—14 sts.

S.s. 3 rows—s.s. 4 rows here when working right half front.

To slope shoulder: Cast off 7 sts. at beginning of next row.

Work 1 row, then cast off 7 sts.

The right half front: Return to sts. on spare needle, slip centre 12 sts. on to a safety-pin, with right side facing, rejoin yarn to inner end of remaining 18 sts. and work as left half front, noting variation.

THE SLEEVES (2 alike): With No. 9 (3¾ mm) needles and 4-ply, cast on 41 sts. and k. 2 rows.

Slot row (wrong side): P. 1, * y.r.n., p. 2 tog., repeat from * to end.

P. 2 rows.

Increase row: K. 2, * up 1, k. 4; repeat from * until 3 sts. remain, up 1, k. 3—51 sts.

Beginning with a p. row, s.s. 5 rows.

To shape sleeve top: Cast off 3 sts. at beginning of next 2 rows, then dec. 1 st. each end of next row and the 2 following alternate rows—39 sts.

P. 1 row, then cast off 7 sts. at beginning of next 2 rows. K. 1 row.

Dec. row: * P. 2 tog.b.; repeat from * 5 times, p. 1, ** p. 2 tog.; repeat from ** 5 times—13 sts. Cast off.

THE NECKBAND: First join shoulder seams.

With right side facing, rejoin 4-ply and, using No. 10 ($3\frac{1}{4}$ mm) needles, pick up and k. 9 sts. from left back neck, 10 sts. from left front neck shaping, k. 12 sts. from safety-pin, pick up and k. 10 sts. from right front neck shaping, and finally 9 sts. from right back neck—50 sts.

K. 4 rows. Cast off k.wise.

THE BACK OPENING BORDER: With right side facing, rejoin 4-ply and, using No. 10 ($3\frac{1}{4}$ mm) needles, pick up and k. 22 sts. from row ends of right back opening, then 22 sts. from row ends of left back opening—44 sts.

Buttonhole row: P. 26, y.r.n., p. 2 tog., * p. 3, y.r.n., p. 2 tog.; repeat from * twice, p. 1.

K. 1 row. Cast off k.wise.

TO MAKE UP THE DRESS: Press as for matinee jacket. Set in sleeves, then join side and sleeve seams. Sew lace frilling to pick up row at neck and lower edge. Sew on buttons. Cut 2 pieces of ribbon 40 cm ($15\frac{3}{4}$ inches) in length and thread through slot rows on sleeves to tie on top.

Cast of 22 sts.

The right half front: With wrong side facing, rejoin 4-ply to inner end of 27 sts. on spare needle and work as given for left half front, noting variation.

THE SLEEVES (2 alike): Work as given for sleeves of matinee jacket.

THE BUTTON BAND: With No. 10 ($3\frac{1}{4}$ mm) needles and 4-ply, cast on 9 sts. and work 80 rows in single rib as given on matinee sleeves.

Break yarn and leave.

THE BUTTONHOLE BAND: Work as for button band until 2 rows in single rib have been worked.

1st buttonhole row: Rib 3, k. 2 tog.b., y.fwd., rib to end.

Rib 7 rows.

Repeat buttonhole row, then rib a further 15 rows.

Repeat the last 24 rows, twice more, then repeat the buttonhole row.

Rib 6 rows, do not break yarn.

THE NECK BAND: Join shoulder seams. With needle holding 9 buttonhole band sts., k. across 6 sts. on safety-pin at right front neck, pick up and k. 10 sts. from row ends of right front neck, 21 sts. across back neck, 10 sts. from row ends of left front neck, k. across 6 sts. on safety-pin, and finally rib across 9 sts. of button band—71 sts.

Rib 1 row, then repeat the buttonhole row.

Rib 2 rows. Cast off in rib.

TO MAKE UP THE CARDIGAN: Do not press. Join sleeve seams. Set in sleeves, sewing row ends above markers to sts. cast off at underarms. Sew down front bands. Add buttons.

THE CARDIGAN
Not illustrated

THE MAIN PART (Worked in one piece to armholes): With No. 10 ($3\frac{1}{4}$ mm) needles and 4-ply, cast on 145 sts. and work 12 rows in single rib given on the matinee jacket sleeves, increasing 1 st. on centre of last row—146 sts.

Change to No. 7 ($4\frac{1}{2}$ mm) needles and work the 4 pattern rows of shawl centre, 9 times.

To divide for back and fronts: Next row: P. 27 and leave on spare needle for right half front, cast off next 16 sts., p. a further 59 and leave these 60 sts. on spare needle for back, cast off next 16 sts., p. to end and work on these 27 sts. for left half front.

The left front: Pattern 20 rows—pattern 21 rows here when working right half front. Break yarn.

To shape neck: Next row: Slip first 6 sts. on to a safety-pin and leave for neck band, rejoin yarn to next st., k. 2 tog., pattern to end—20 sts.

Dec. 1 st. at neck edge on next row—19 sts.

Pattern 3 rows.

To slope shoulder: Cast off 9 sts. at beginning of next row.

Work 1 row, then cast off 10 sts.

The back: With wrong side facing, rejoin 4-ply to inner end of 60 sts. on spare needle and pattern 25 rows.

To slope shoulders: Cast off 9 sts. at beginning of next 2 rows, then 10 sts. on following 2 rows.

THE JERSEY
Illustrated on page 19

THE BACK: With No. 10 ($3\frac{1}{4}$ mm) needles and 4-ply, cast on 73 sts. and work 12 rows in single rib as given on matinee sleeves, increasing 1 st. in centre of last row—74 sts.

Change to No. 7 ($4\frac{1}{2}$ mm) needles and work the 4 pattern rows of shawl centre, 9 times.

To shape the armholes: Cast off 8 sts. at beginning of next 2 rows—58 sts. ***

Pattern 22 rows.

To slope shoulders: Cast off 8 sts. at beginning of next 2 rows, then 10 sts. on following 2 rows.

Cast off 22 sts.

THE FRONT: Work as given for back to ***.

Pattern 14 rows.

To divide for neck: Next row: P. 20, turn and leaving remaining sts. on a spare needle, work on these sts. for left front neck.

The left front neck: Dec 1 st. at neck edge on each of the next 2 rows—18 sts.

Pattern 5 rows—pattern 6 rows here when working right front neck.

To slope shoulder: Cast off 8 sts. at beginning of next row.

Work 1 row. Cast off 10 sts.

Continued on page 20

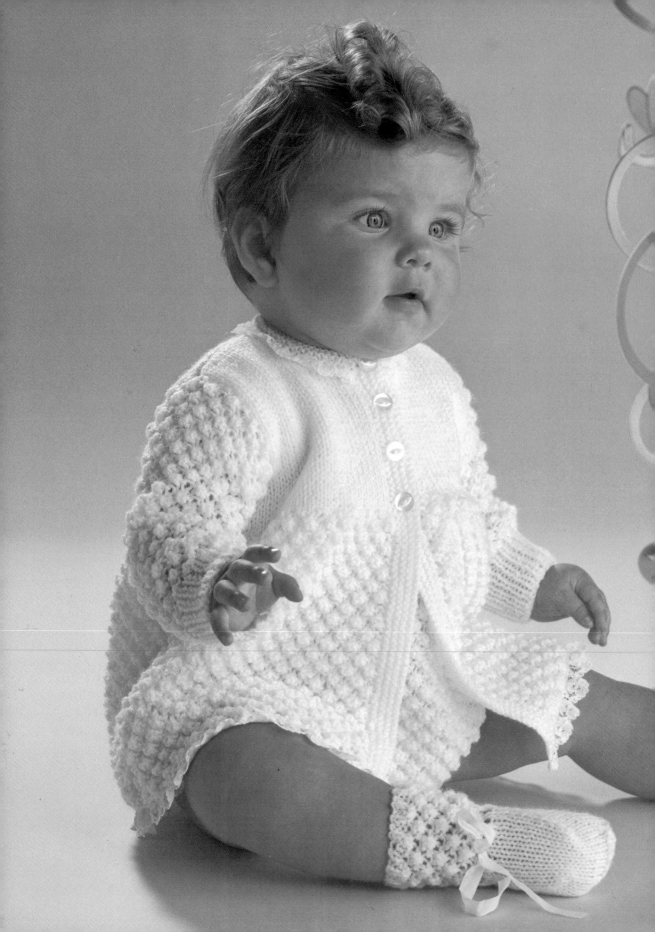

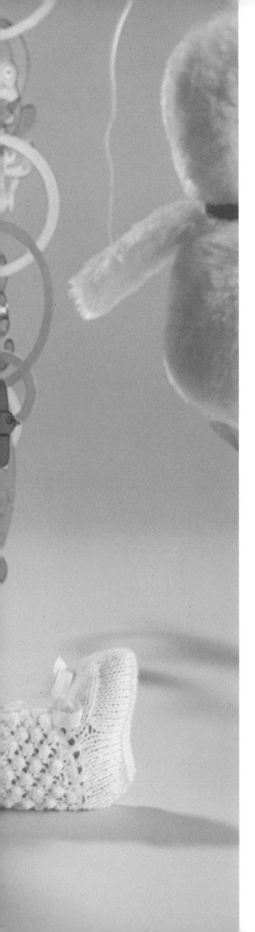

Top *Jersey (page 17)*
Above *Crossover Vest (page 20)*
Left *Matinee Jacket (page 16) and Bootees (page 21)*

The right front neck: Return to sts. on spare needle, slip centre 18 sts. on a safety-pin, with right side facing, rejoin yarn to remaining 20 sts., p. to end, then work as left front neck, noting variation.

THE SLEEVES (2 alike): With No. 10 ($3\frac{1}{4}$ mm) needles and 4-ply, cast on 37 sts. and work 13 rows in single rib as given on matinee sleeves.

Increase row: Rib 3, up 1, * rib 8, up 1; repeat from * until 2 sts. remain, rib 2—42 sts.

Change to No. 7 ($4\frac{1}{2}$ mm) needles and work the 4 pattern rows of shawl centre, once.

Keeping continuity of the pattern and working extra sts. in r.s.s. as they occur, inc. 1 st. each end of next row and the 3 following 8th rows—50 sts.

Pattern 5 rows across all sts.—mark each end of last row to denote end of sleeve seam.

Pattern 10 rows.

Cast off.

THE BACK NECK RIBBING: With right side facing, rejoin 4-ply and, using No. 10 ($3\frac{1}{4}$ mm) needles, pick up and k. 21 sts. across back neck.

Beginning with an even-numbered row, work 4 rows in single rib as given on matinee sleeves.

Cast off in rib.

THE FRONT NECK RIBBING: With right side facing, rejoin 4-ply and, using No. 10 ($3\frac{1}{4}$ mm) needles, pick up and k. 10 sts. down left front neck, k. across centre front sts., increasing in centre, then pick up and k. 10 sts. up right front neck—39 sts.

Work as given for back neck ribbing to end.

THE SHOULDER EDGINGS: First join shoulder seams across 8 sts. from armhole edge.

The left shoulder: With right side facing, rejoin 4-ply and, using No. 10 ($3\frac{1}{4}$ mm) needles, pick up and k. 29 sts. round shoulder opening including row ends of neck ribbings.

Buttonhole row: P. 2 tog., y.r.n., * p. 3, p. 2 tog., y.r.n.; repeat from * once, p. to end.

K. 1 row, then cast of k.wise.

The right shoulder: Pick up as given for left shoulder.

Buttonhole row: P. 17, * y.r.n., p. 2 tog., p. 3; repeat from * once, y.r.n., p. 2 tog.

K. 1 row, then cast of k.wise.

TO MAKE UP THE JERSEY: Do not press. Sew in sleeves, setting row ends above markers to cast-off groups at underarms. Join side and sleeve seams. Add buttons.

THE CROSSOVER VEST
Illustrated on page 19

THE BACK AND FRONTS (Worked in one piece to armholes): With No. 10 ($3\frac{1}{4}$ mm) needles and 3-ply, cast on 148 sts. and k. 7 rows.

Change to No. 9 ($3\frac{3}{4}$ mm) needles.

1st row: K. to end.

2nd row: K. 4, p. until 4 sts. remain, k. 4.

Repeat last 2 rows, 27 times.

To divide for back and fronts: Next row: K. 39 and leave these sts. on a spare needle for right half front, cast off next 6 sts., k. a further 57 sts. and leave these 58 sts. on spare needle for back, cast off next 6 sts., k. to end and

work on these last 39 sts. for left half front.

The left half front: Keeping continuity of 4 st. border at front edge, dec. 1 st. at armhole edge on next row and the 3 following alternate rows—35 sts.

To shape neck: Next row: K. 30 and leave remaining 5 sts. on a safety-pin—30 sts.

Next row: Cast off 5 sts., p. to end—25 sts.

Dec. 1 st. at neck edge on each of the next 13 rows—12 sts. Work 1 row.

To slope shoulder: Cast off 6 sts. at beginning of next row. Work 1 row, then cast off 6 sts.

The back: Return to dividing row and with wrong side facing, rejoin yarn to inner end of 58 sts.

Dec. 1 st. each end of next row and the 3 following alternate rows—50 sts. S.s. 16 rows.

To slope shoulders: Cast off 6 sts. at beginning of next 4 rows. Cast off 26 sts.

The right front: Return to dividing row and with wrong side facing, rejoin yarn to inner end of 39 sts.

Keeping continuity of 4 st. border at front edge, dec. 1 st., at armhole edge on next row and the 3 following alternate rows—35 sts.

To shape neck: Next row: K. 5 and leave on a safety-pin, k. to end—30 sts.

Next row: P. 25, cast off remaining 5 sts. Break yarn.

Turn, rejoin yarn to inner end of remaining sts. and dec. 1 st. at neck edge on each of the next 13 rows—12 sts. S.s. 2 rows.

To slope shoulder: Cast off 6 sts. at beginning of next row.

Work 1 row, then cast off 6 sts.

THE SLEEVES (2 alike): With No. 10 ($3\frac{1}{4}$ mm) needles and 3-ply, cast on 38 sts. and k. 5 rows.

Change to No. 9 ($3\frac{3}{4}$ mm) needles, and working in s.s., inc. 1 st. each end of 3rd row and following 4th row—42 sts.

S.s. 3 rows.

To shape sleeve top: Cast off 3 sts. at beginning of next 2 rows, then dec. 1 st. each end of next row and the 4 following alternate rows—26 sts.

P. 1 row, then cast off.

THE NECKBAND: First join shoulder seams.

With right side facing, slip 5 sts. at right front neck on to a No. 10 ($3\frac{1}{4}$ mm) needle with point to inner end, rejoin yarn and pick up and k. 21 sts. from right front neck, 26 sts. across back, 21 sts. from left front neck and finally, k. across 5 sts. on safety-pin—78 sts.

K. 4 rows, then cast of k.wise.

TO MAKE UP THE VEST: Press lightly with a warm iron over a dry cloth. Join sleeve seams, then set sleeves into armholes. Cross right front over left and sew on 4 lengths of 20 cm (8 inch) ribbon.

THE BONNET
Not illustrated

TO MAKE: With No. 7 ($4\frac{1}{2}$ mm) needles and 4-ply, cast on 102 sts. and work the 4 pattern rows of shawl centre, 3 times then 1st and 2nd rows again, for brim.

Change to No. 10 ($3\frac{1}{4}$ mm) needles.

Dec. row: P. 2, * p. 2 tog., p. 2; repeat from * to end—77 sts.

Work 12 rows in single rib as given on matinee sleeves.

Change to No. 9 (3¾ mm) needles and beginning with a k. row, s.s. 22 rows.

To shape back: Cast off 26 sts. at beginning of next 2 rows—25 sts.

S.s. 6 rows, then dec. 1 st. each end of next row and the 2 following 8th rows—19 sts. S.s. 7 rows. Cast off.

THE NECK RIBBING: Sew row ends of back extension to 26 st. cast-off groups.

With right side facing, rejoin 4-ply and using No. 10 (3¼ mm) needles, pick up and k. 73 sts. along neck edge, omitting pattern rows of brim.

Dec. row: * K. 1, p. 1; repeat from * 10 times, k. 2 tog., ** p. 1, k. 2 tog.; repeat from ** 8 times, * p. 1, k. 1; repeat from this * 10 times—63 sts.

Work 7 rows in rib as set. Cast off.

TO COMPLETE BONNET: Press s.s. parts only with a warm iron over a dry cloth. Sew lace frilling round outer edges of brim pattern. Turn brim to right side and catch down corners. Sew 2 pieces of ribbon 50 cm (19½ inches) in length to ends of neck ribbing.

THE HELMET
Not illustrated

THE BUTTONHOLE FLAP: With No. 10 (3¼ mm) needles and 4-ply case on 1 st.

1st row (wrong side): K. 1, p. 1 and k. 1 all into st.—3 sts.

2nd row: K. 1, 3 in 1, k. 1.

3rd row: K. 1, p. 1, 3 in 1, p. 1, k. 1.

4th row: P. 1, k. 1, p. 1, 3 in 1, p. 1, k. 1, p. 1.
Rib 5 rows.

Buttonhole row: Rib 4, y.fwd., k. 2 tog., rib to end.
Rib 12 rows.

Next (increase) row: Rib 4, 3 and 1, rib 4.
Rib 3 rows.

Repeat last 4 rows, 3 times more, then the increase row again, working 1 st. extra in rib at each end on each repeat of the increase row—19 sts.

Rib 2 rows. Break yarn and leave.

THE BUTTON FLAP: Work as given for buttonhole flap, omitting buttonhole.

THE CROWN: With No. 10 (3¼ mm) needles and 4-ply, cast on 111 sts. and beginning with an even-numbered row, work 11 rows in single rib as given on matinee sleeves.

To join in flaps: Next row: Rib 11, place button flap behind right-hand needle, * working through next st. of crown and next st. of flap together, rib next st. *; repeat from * to * 18 times more, rib 51 sts., place buttonhole flap behind right-hand needle, repeat from * to * 19 times, rib remaining 11 sts. of row—111 sts.

Rib 7 rows, decreasing 1 st. in centre of last row—110 sts.

Change to No. 7 (4½ mm) needles and work the 4 pattern rows of shawl centre, 4 times.

Change to No. 10 (3¼ mm) needles, and k. 2 rows.

To shape top: 1st dec. row: K. 1, * k. 2 tog.b., k. 10; repeat from * 7 times, k. 2 tog.b., k. 9, k. 2 tog.—100 sts.

K. 3 rows.

2nd dec. row: K. 1, * k. 2 tog.b., k. 9; repeat from * to end—91 sts.

K. 3 rows.

3rd dec. row: K. 1, * k. 2 tog.b., k. 8; repeat from * to end.

K. 1 row.

Repeat last 2 rows, 7 times, working 1 st. less between decreases on each repeat of the dec. row—19 sts.

Next dec. row: K. 1, * k. 2 tog.b.; repeat from * 8 times—10 sts.

P. 1 row.

Next dec. row: * K. 2 tog.b.; repeat from * 4 times.

Break yarn, leaving an end. Run end through remaining sts., draw up and fasten off, then join seam. Turn ribbing below flap joining row to right side. Sew on button.

THE BOOTEES
Illustrated on page 18

TO MAKE (2 alike): With No. 7 (4½ mm) needles and 4-ply, cast on 37 sts. and work 2 rows in rib as given on matinee sleeves, increasing 1 st. in 2nd row—38 sts.

Work 4 pattern rows of shawl centre, 3 times. Change to No. 10 (3¼ mm) needles.

Dec. row: P. 1, k. 1, p. 1, k. 1, p. 2 tog., * k. 1, p. 1, k. 1, p. 1, k. 1, p. 2 tog.; repeat from * until 4 sts. remain, k. 1, p. 1, k. 1, p. 1—33 sts.

Next row: K. 1, * p. 1, k. 1; repeat from * to end.

Slot row: P. 1, * y.fwd., k. 2 tog.b.; repeat from * to end. Rib 1 row.

Beginning with a k. row, s.s. 2 rows.

To divide for instep: Next row: K. 22, turn, leaving remaining 11 sts. on a safety-pin.

Next row: P. 11, turn, leaving remaining 11 sts. on a safety-pin.

The instep: On centre 11 sts., s.s. 12 rows. Break yarn.

With right side facing, slip 11 sts. at right side on to a No. 10 (3¼ mm) needle with point to inner end, rejoin yarn and pick up and k. 10 sts. from row ends of instep. Across instep sts. work k. 2 tog., k. 7, k. 2 tog. Pick up and k. 10 sts. down other side of instep, and finally, k. 11 sts. from safety-pin—51 sts. S.s. 7 rows.

To shape for foot: 1st dec. row: K. 1, s.k.p.o., k. 18, s.k.p.o., k. 5, k. 2 tog., k. 18, k. 2 tog., k. 1.

K. 1 row.

2nd dec. row: K. 1, s.k.p.o., k. 17, s.k.p.o., k. 3, k. 2 tog., k. 17, k. 2 tog., k. 1.

K. 1 row.

3rd dec. row: K. 1, s.k.p.o., k. 16, s.k.p.o., k. 1, k. 2 tog., k. 16, k. 2 tog., k. 1.

K. 1 row.

4th dec. row: K. 1, s.k.p.o., k. 15, sl. 1, k. 2 tog., p.s.s.o., k. 15, k. 2 tog., k. 1—35 sts. Cast off k.wise.

Join back and under foot seam. Thread a 40 cm (15¾ inch) length of narrow ribbon through slot row to tie at front.

Layette in a Lacy Stitch

Illustrated on pages 23, 26 and 27

MATERIALS: *Allow the following quantities in 20 g balls of Wendy Peter Pan Darling 2-ply:* **Shawl:** 12 *balls;* **Matinee jacket:** 3 *balls;* **Dress:** 3 *balls;* **Angel top:** 3 *balls;* **Christening robe:** 9 *balls;* **Vest:** 2 *balls;* **Leggings:** 3 *balls;* **Bonnet:** 1 *ball;* **Bootees and Mitts:** 1 *ball; a pair each of No.* 8 *(4 mm), No.* 9 *(3¾ mm), No.* 10 *(3¼ mm), No.* 11 *(3 mm) and No.* 12 *(2¾ mm) needles;* 4 *small buttons for matinee jacket;* 3 *small buttons each for dress and angel top;* 5 *small buttons for Christening robe; shirring elastic for leggings;* 75 *cm of narrow ribbon and* 1.85 *metres of* 2 *cm (¾ inch) wide ribbon for Christening robe;* 1.85 *metres of* 2 *cm (¾ inch) wide ribbon for bonnet;* 1 *metre of narrow ribbon for bootees and mitts and* 1 *metre of narrow ribbon for vest.*

TENSION AND MEASUREMENTS: *Work at a tension of* 26 *stitches and* 34 *rows to measure* 10 × 10 *cm, over the shawl centre pattern, using No.* 8 *(4 mm) needles and* 34 *stitches and* 44 *rows to measure* 10 × 10 *cm, over the shawl centre pattern, using No.* 10 *(3¼ mm) needles, and* 35 *stitches and* 42 *rows to measure* 10 × 10 *cm, over the stocking stitch, using No.* 10 *(3¼ mm) needles to obtain the following measurements:* **Shawl:** 124 *cm* × 123 *cm (48¾ × 48½ inches), including edging;* **Matinee jacket and Angel top:** *length at back neck* 24 *cm (9½ inches); length at underarm,* 15 *cm (6 inches); sleeve seam,* 11.5 *cm (4½ inches);* **Dress:** *length at back neck,* 27 *cm (10½ inches); sleeve seam,* 2 *cm (¾ inch); length at underarm,* 18.5 *cm (7¼ inches);* **Christening robe:** *length at back neck,* 65.5 *cm (25¾ inches); length at underarm,* 58 *cm (22¾ inches); sleeve seam* 13 *cm (5 inches);* **Vest:** *all round fastened,* 41 *cm (16 inches); side seam,* 16.5 *cm (6½ inches); length at back neck,* 26 *cm (10¼ inches);* **Bonnet:** *all round face edge,* 29 *cm (11½ inches);* **Leggings:** *all round at widest part,* 56.5 *cm (22¼ inches); depth at front,* 18 *cm (7 inches); inside leg seam,* 24 *cm (9½ inches);* **Mitts:** *length* 12 *cm (4¾ inches);* **Bootees:** *length* 10 *cm (4 inches).*

ABBREVIATIONS: To be read before working: *K., knit plain; p., purl; st., stitch; tog., together; inc., increase (by working twice into same st.); dec., decrease (by working 2 sts. tog.); y.r.n., yarn round needle to make a st.; y. fwd., yarn forward to make a st.; sl., slip; s.k.p.o., sl. l, k. 1, pass the slipped st. over; p.s.s.o., pass the slipped st. over; g. st., garter st. (k. plain on every row); s.s., stocking st. (k. on the right side and p. on the wrong side); single rib is k. 1 and p. 1 alternately.*

Directions in brackets must be worked the number of times stated after the last bracket.

THE SHAWL

Illustrated on page 27

THE CENTRE: With No. 8 (4 mm) needles, cast on 281 sts.

1st row: K. 1, * y.fwd., s.k.p.o., k. 2 tog., y. fwd., k. 1; repeat from * to end.

2nd and every alternate row: All p.

3rd row: K. 2, * y. fwd., s.k.p.o., k. 3, k. 2 tog., y. fwd., k. 3; repeat from * ending last repeat with k. 2 instead of k. 3.

5th row: K. 3, * y. fwd., s.k.p.o., k. 1, k. 2 tog., y. fwd., k. 5; repeat from * ending last repeat with k. 3 instead of k. 5.

7th row: K. 4, * y. fwd., sl. 1, k. 2 tog., p.s.s.o., y. fwd., k. 7; repeat from * ending last repeat with k. 4.

9th, 11th and 13th rows: K. 1, * s.k.p.o., k. 2. y fwd., k. 1, y. fwd., k. 2, k. 2 tog., k. 1; repeat from * to end.

14th row: As 2nd row.

These 14 rows form the pattern, repeat them 25 times more. Cast off.

THE EDGING: With No. 9 (3¾ mm) needles cast on 18 sts.

Foundation row: K. 6, p. 7, k. 5.

Now work the 8-row pattern as follows:

1st row: Sl. 1, k. 2, y. fwd., k. 2 tog., k. 2, k. 2 tog., y. fwd., k. 5, y. fwd., k. 2 tog., (y. fwd., k. 1) twice.

2nd row: K. 6, y. fwd., k. 2 tog., p. 7, k. 2, y. fwd., k. 2 tog., k. 1.

3rd row: Sl. 1, k. 2, y. fwd., k. 2 tog., k. 1, (k. 2 tog., y. fwd.) twice, k. 4, y. fwd., k. 2 tog., (y. fwd., k. 1) twice, k. 2.

4th row: K. 8, y. fwd., k. 2 tog., p. 7, k. 2, y. fwd., k. 2 tog., k. 1.

5th row: Sl, 1, k. 2, y. fwd., k. 2 tog., (k. 2 tog., y. fwd.) 3 times, k. 3, y. fwd., k. 2 tog., (y. fwd., k. 1) twice, k. 4.

6th row: K. 10, y. fwd., k. 2 tog., p. 7, k. 2, y. fwd., k. 2 tog., k. 1.

7th row: Sl. 1, k. 2, y. fwd., k. 2 tog., k. 1, (k. 2 tog., y. fwd.) twice, k. 4, y. fwd., k. 2 tog., (y. fwd., k. 1) twice, k. 6.

8th row: Cast off 8 sts. k. wise, k. a further 3, y. fwd., k. 2 tog., p. 7, k. 2, y. fwd., k. 2 tog., k. 1.

These 8 rows form the pattern for the edging. Repeat them until edging fits all round outer edges of centre, allowing for gatherings at corners. Cast off.

Join cast-on and cast-off edges of edging, then sew straight row ends to outer edges of centre, gathering edging at corners to keep work flat. Do not press.

THE MATINEE JACKET

Illustrated opposite

THE MAIN PART (worked in one piece to armholes): With No. 12 (2¾ mm) needles cast on 253 sts. and g. st. 7 rows.

Change to No. 10 (3¼ mm) needles.

Work in pattern as follows:

1st pattern row: K. 6, work as given for 1st pattern row of shawl centre, until 6 sts. remain, k. 6.

2nd pattern row: K. 6, work as given for 2nd pattern row of shawl centre until 6 sts. remain, k. 6.

Continued on page 24

Opposite *Matinee Jacket and Leggings (page 28)*

Continue in this way, working in pattern as given for shawl centre, but keeping 6 sts. in g. st. at each end for front borders until 4 complete patterns and 6 rows of 5th pattern have been worked in all.

To divide sts. for back and fronts: Next row: K. 6, pattern 58 and leave these 64 sts. on a spare needle for the right half front, cast off 4 sts. for underarm, pattern a further 116 and leave these 117 sts. on a spare needle for back, cast off 4 sts. for underarm, pattern until 6 sts. remain, k. 6 and work on these 64 sts. for the left half front.

The left half front: Maintaining continuity of the pattern and keeping 6 sts. in g. st. for front border, dec. 1 st. at armhole edge on each of the next 7 rows. Break yarn and leave these 57 sts. on a stitch-holder for yoke.

The back: With wrong side of work facing, rejoin yarn to inner end of 117 sts. on spare needle and dec. 1 st. at each end of the next 7 rows. Break off yarn and leave these 103 sts. on a stitch-holder for the yoke.

The right half front: With wrong side of work facing, rejoin yarn to inner end of 64 sts. on spare needle, then work as given for left half front.

THE SLEEVES (both alike): With No. 12 (2¾ mm) needles cast on 33 sts. and g. st. 3 rows.

Next (inc.) row: K. 2, * inc. in next st.; repeat from * until 3 sts. remain, k. 3—61 sts.

Change to No. 10 (3¼ mm) needles and work in pattern as given for shawl centre until 3 complete patterns and 6 rows of 4th pattern have been worked in all, decreasing 1 st. at the end of the last row—60 sts.

To shape the sleeve top: 1st and 2nd rows: Maintaining continuity of the pattern, cast off 3 sts., pattern to end.

3rd row: Take 3 tog., pattern until 3 sts. remain, take 3 tog.—50 sts.

Repeat the 3rd row, twice more, then dec. 1 st. at each end of the next 2 rows—38 sts.

Pattern 1 row.

Break yarn and leave these sts. on a stitch-holder for yoke.

THE YOKE: With wrong side of work facing, slip all sts. on to a No. 10 (3¼ mm) needle as follows: left front, first sleeve, back, second sleeve, and finally, right front—293 sts.

Next row: Rejoin yarn, then k. 1, k. 2 tog., y.r.n. for buttonhole, k. 3, (k. 2 tog.) 24 times, k. 3 across right front, k. 2 tog., k. 34, k. 2 tog. across first sleeve, k. 3, (k. 2 tog.) 49 times, k. 2 across back, k. 2 tog., k. 34, k. 2 tog. across second sleeve, k. 3, (k. 2 tog.) 24 times, k. 6 across left front—192 sts.

** G. st. 11 rows.

To shape the yoke: 1st dec. row: K. 1, k. 2 tog., y.r.n. for buttonhole, k. 3, * k. 2 tog., k. 1; repeat from * until 6 sts. remain, k. 6—132 sts.

G.st 11 rows.

Next row: Repeat 1st dec. row—92 sts.

G. st. 7 rows.

Next dec. row: K. 7, * k. 2 tog., k. 1; repeat from * until 7 sts. remain, k. 7—66 sts. ******

1st and 2nd turning rows: K. until 18 sts. remain for 1st row, turn, sl. 1, k. until 18 sts. remain for 2nd row.

3rd and 4th rows: Sl. 1, k. until 24 sts. remain for 3rd row, turn, sl. 1, k. until 24 sts. remain for 4th row.

Next row: Sl. 1, k. across all sts. to end of row.

*** Change to No. 12 (2¾ mm) needles and working a

buttonhole as before, at the beginning of the 3rd row, k. 4 rows.

Cast off loosely. *******

TO MAKE UP THE JACKET: Do not press. Join sleeve seams, then join tiny underarm seams.

Add buttons.

THE DRESS
Not illustrated

THE MAIN PART (worked in one piece to armholes): With No. 12 (2¾ mm) needles cast on 241 sts. and g. st. 7 rows.

Change to No. 10 (3¼ mm) needles and work 76 rows in pattern as given for shawl centre – work 62 rows here when working angel top.

To divide sts. for front and backs: Pattern 62 and leave these sts. on a spare needle for left half back, cast off 3 sts. for underarm, pattern a further 110 and leave these 111 sts. on a spare needle for front, cast off 3 sts. for underarm, pattern to end and work on these 62 sts. for right half back.

The right half back: Maintaining continuity of the pattern, dec. 1 st. at armhole edge of each of the next 7 rows. Break off yarn and leave these 55 sts. on a stitch-holder for yoke.

The front: With wrong side of work facing, rejoin yarn to inner end of 111 sts. on spare needle and dec. 1 st. at each end of the next 7 rows. Break yarn and leave these 97 sts. on a stitch-holder for yoke.

The left half back: With wrong side of work facing, rejoin yarn to inner end of 62 sts. on spare needle and work as given for right half back.

THE SLEEVES (both alike): With No. 12 (2¾ mm) needles cast on 41 sts. and g. st. 3 rows.

Next (inc.) row: (K. 1, inc. in next st.) 20 times, k. 1— 61 sts.

Change to No. 10 (3¼ mm) needles and work 6 rows in pattern as given for shawl centre, decreasing 1 st. at the end of the last row—60 sts.

To shape the sleeve top: Work exactly as given for sleeve top of matinee jacket.

THE YOKE: With wrong side of work facing, slip all sts. on to a No. 10 (3¼ mm) needle as follows: right back, first sleeve, front, second sleeve and finally, left back—283 sts.

Next row: Rejoin yarn, then k. 7, (k. 2 tog.) 24 times across left back, k. 2 tog., k. 34, k. 2 tog. across first sleeve, k. 6, (k. 2 tog.) 43 times, k. 5 across front, k. 2 tog., k. 34, k. 2 tog. across second sleeve, (k. 2 tog.) 26 times, k. 3 across right back, turn and cast on 6 sts. for underlap—192 sts.

Work as given for jacket from ** to **.

**** Next 2 rows: K. 18 for 1st row, sl. 1, k. to end for 2nd row.

Next 2 rows: K. 11 for next row, sl. 1, k. to end for following row. ********

Next row: K. across all sts. to end of row.

Repeat from **** to **** once more, then work from *** to *** as given for matinee jacket.

TO MAKE UP THE DRESS: Do not press. Join sleeve seams, then join tiny underarm seams. Join back seam as far as yoke, then catch base of underlap to wrong side. Sew on buttons.

THE ANGEL TOP
Not illustrated

THE MAIN PART: Work as given for main part of dress, noting variation in rows to be worked before dividing for front and backs.

THE SLEEVES (both alike): Work as given for sleeves of matinee jacket, leaving 38 sts. on spare needle.

THE YOKE: Work exactly as given for yoke of dress. Make up and complete as given for dress.

THE CHRISTENING ROBE
Illustrated on page 26

THE MAIN PART (worked in one piece to armholes): With No. 10 (3¼ mm) needles cast on 411 sts. and g. st. 5 rows.

Work 223 rows in pattern as given for shawl centre ending on a 13th pattern row and increasing 1 st. at the end of the last row—412 sts.

Change to No. 11 (3 mm) needles and decrease for waist as follows:

Next row (wrong side): Cast on 6 sts. for button underlap, k. these 6 sts., then * k. 2 tog., k. 3 tog., pass the k. 2 tog. over k. 3 tog. thus decreasing 4 sts. *, (k. 3 tog.) 132 times, repeat from * to * once, k. 6 for buttonhole border—146 sts.

G. st. 2 rows.

Buttonhole and eyelet row: K. 3, y. fwd., k. 2 tog. for buttonhole, k. 2, * k. 2 tog., y. fwd.; repeat from * until 7 sts. remain, k. 7—146 sts.

G. st. 3 rows.

Work the pattern for the yoke as follows:

1st row: K. 6, p. 2, * k. 2, y. fwd., k. 2 tog., p. 2; repeat from * until 6 sts. remain, k. 6.

2nd row: K. 8, * p. 2, y.r.n., p. 2 tog., k. 2; repeat from * until 6 sts. remain, k. 6.

These 2 rows form the pattern for the yoke with 6 sts. in g. st. at each end for button and buttonhole borders. Repeat them 4 times more.

Next (buttonhole) row: K. 3, y. fwd., k. 2 tog., k. 1, p. 2, * k. 2, y. fwd., k. 2 tog., p. 2; repeat from * until 6 sts. remain, k. 6.

To divide sts. for front and backs (wrong side): Maintaining continuity of pattern, k. 6, pattern 28 and leave these 34 sts. on a spare needle for right half back, cast off 8 sts. for underarm, pattern a further 61 and leave these 62 sts. on a spare needle for front, cast off 8 sts. for underarm, work to end and continue on these 34 sts. for left half back.

The left half back: Keeping pattern correct, dec. 1 st. at armhole edge on the next row and 6 following alternate rows, working a buttonhole on the last of these rows—27 sts.

Pattern 18 rows, working a buttonhole on the 14th row —pattern 17 rows here when working right half back.

To slope the shoulder: Cast off 4 sts. at the beginning of the next row and 2 following alternate rows—work 1 extra row here when working right half back. Leave the remaining 15 sts. on a safety-pin for neck border.

The front: With right side of work facing, rejoin yarn to inner end of 62 sts. on spare needle. Keeping pattern

correct, dec. 1 st. at each end of the next row and 6 following alternate rows—48 sts.

Pattern 4 rows.

To divide sts. for neck: Next row: Pattern 18 and leave these sts. on a spare needle for right front shoulder, pattern 12 and leave these sts. on a stitch-holder for neck border, pattern to end and work on these 18 sts. for the left front shoulder.

The left front shoulder: To shape the neck: Dec. 1 st. at neck edge on the next row and 5 following alternate rows—12 sts.

Pattern 1 row—pattern 2 rows here when working right front shoulder.

To slope the shoulder: Cast off 4 sts. at the beginning of the next row and following alternate row. Work 1 row, then cast off the remaining 4 sts.

The right front shoulder: With right side of work facing, rejoin yarn to inner end of 18 sts. on spare needle and work as given for left front shoulder, noting variation in number of rows to be worked.

The right half back: With right side of work facing, rejoin yarn to inner end of 34 sts. left on spare needle and work as given for left half back, omitting buttonholes and noting variations where indicated.

THE SLEEVES (both alike): With No. 11 (3 mm) needles cast on 30 sts. and g. st. 8 rows.

Next (inc) row: K. 1, * inc. in next st., k. 1; repeat from * until 1 st. remains, k. 1—44 sts.

Work in pattern as follows:

1st row (right side): P. 2, * k. 2, y. fwd., k. 2 tog., p. 2; repeat from * to end.

2nd row: K. 2, * p. 2, y.r.n., p. 2 tog., k. 2; repeat from * to end.

These 2 rows form the pattern for the sleeves, pattern a further 40 rows.

To shape the sleeve top: Cast off 4 sts. at the beginning of each of the next 2 rows, then dec. 1 st. at each end of the next row and 6 following alternate rows. Work 1 row, then cast off 2 sts. at the beginning of each of the next 6 rows.

Cast off the remaining 10 sts.

THE NECK BAND: Join shoulder seams. With right side of work facing, rejoin yarn and, using No. 11 (3 mm) needles, k. across 15 sts. of left back neck, pick up and k. 12 sts. down left front neck shaping, k. across 12 sts. on stitch-holder, pick up and k. 12 sts. up right front neck shaping and, finally, k. across 15 sts. of right back neck— 66 sts.

G. st. 7 rows, working a buttonhole as before on the 4th row. Cast off.

THE FRILL: With No. 10 (3¼ mm) needles cast on 6 sts. and k. 1 row.

1st row: K. 2, y. fwd., k. 2 tog., y. fwd., k. 2.

2nd row: K. 2, (y. fwd., k. 1) twice, y. fwd., k. 2 tog., k. 1.

3rd row: K. 2, y. fwd., k. 2 tog., y. fwd., k. 3, y. fwd., k. 2.

4th row: K. 2, y. fwd., k. 5, y. fwd., k. 1, y. fwd., k. 2 tog., k. 1.

5th row: K. 2, y. fwd., k. 2 tog., y. fwd., s.k.p.o., k. 3, k. 2 tog., y. fwd., k. 2.

6th row: K. 3, y. fwd., s.k.p.o., k. 1, k. 2 tog., y. fwd., k. 2, y. fwd., k. 2 tog., k. 1.

Continued on page 26

7th row: K. 2, y. fwd., k. 2 tog., k. 2, y. fwd., sl. 1, k. 2
tog., p.s.s.o., y. fwd., k. 4.

8th row: Cast off 7 sts., k. 2, y. fwd., k. 2 tog., k. 1.

These 8 rows form the pattern for the frill. Continue in
pattern until work fits all round lower edge of skirt, casting
off after an 8th pattern row.

TO MAKE UP THE ROBE: Do not press. Join sleeve
seams, then set into armholes. Close back seam as far as
waist, then catch base of underlap to wrong side. Add
buttons. Thread narrow ribbon through eyelet holes at
waist and catch ends together. Make a bow with wider
ribbon, leaving ends to hang. Sew to centre front at waist.
Join cast-on and cast-off edges of frill and attach to wrong
side of lower edge, sewing straight edge of frill to last row
of g. st. edging on skirt, leaving g. st. free.

THE VEST
Not illustrated

TO MAKE: With No. 10 (3¼ mm) needles cast on 72 sts.
for lower edge of back and g. st. 5 rows.

Beginning with a k. row, s.s. 58 rows.

To shape for sleeves: Inc. 1 st. at each end of the next
row and 3 following alternate rows, p. 1 row, then cast on
10 sts. at the beginning of next 2 rows—100 sts.

Next row: K. to end.

Next row: K. 4, p. until 4 sts. remain, k. 4.

Repeat the last 2 rows, 14 times, then work the 1st row
again.

To work the border for back neck: 1st row: K. 4, p.
33, k. 26, p. 33, k. 4.

2nd row: K. to end.

Repeat the last 2 rows, twice.

To divide for fronts: Next row: K. 4, p. 33, k. 4 and
leave these 41 sts. on a spare needle for left front, cast off
18, k. a further 3 sts., p. 33, k. 4 and work on these last 41
sts. for right front.

Continued on page 28

The right front: 1st row: K. until 6 sts. remain, inc., k. 5.

2nd row: K. 4, p. until 4 sts. remain, k. 4.

Maintaining continuity of the 4 sts. in g. st. at each end, s.s. 10 rows.

To slope front edge: 1st row: K. until 6 sts. remain, inc., k. 5.

2nd row: K. 4, p. until 4 sts. remain, k. 4.

Repeat these 2 rows, 12 times—55 sts.

** To shape for sleeves: Cast off 10 sts. at the beginning of the next row, then dec. 1 st. at the same edge on each of the 4 following right-side rows, *at the same time*, continue to inc. at front edge as before on every right-side row until a further 8 inc. rows have been worked—49 sts.

Still working 4 sts. in g. st. at front edge, s.s. 52 rows. K. 5 rows, then cast off.

The left front: With right side of work facing, rejoin yarn to inner end of 41 sts. left on spare needle.

1st row: K. 4, inc., k. to end.

2nd row: K. 4, p. until 4 sts. remain, k. 4.

Keeping 4 sts. in g. st. at each end, s.s. 10 rows.

To slope front edge: 1st row: K. 4, inc., k. to end.

2nd row: K. 4, p. until 4 sts. remain, k. 4.

Repeat these 2 rows, 11 times, then work the 1st row again—55 sts.

Work as given for right front from ******.

TO MAKE UP THE VEST: Do not press. Join side and sleeve seams. Sew 2 lengths of narrow ribbon to straight front edge of right front. Fold right front over left front, then sew 2 lengths of ribbon to left front to correspond.

THE LEGGINGS
Illustrated on page 23

THE RIGHT LEG: With No. 12 (2¾ mm) needles cast on 88 sts. and work 12 rows in single rib, increasing 1 st. at the end of the last row—89 sts.

Change to No. 10 (3¼ mm) needles and, beginning with a k. row, s.s. 2 rows—s.s. 3 rows here when working left leg.

To shape the back: 1st and 2nd rows: S.s. 11 for 1st row, turn, sl. 1, s.s. to end for 2nd row.

3rd and 4th rows: S.s. 18, turn, sl. 1, s.s. to end for 4th row.

Repeat 3rd and 4th rows, 4 times more, working 7 sts. more on each successive repeat of the 3rd row.

Continuing in s.s. on all sts., inc. 1 st. at the beginning—back edge—on the 3rd row and at the same edge on 9 following 6th rows—99 sts.

S.s. 7 rows straight—mark each end of the last row for crotch.

To shape the leg: Dec. 1 st. at each end of the next row and every following 3rd row until 26 dec. rows have been worked—47 sts.

S.s. 2 rows – work 1 row here when working left leg. ******

To shape the instep: Next row: K. 40, turn and leave remaining 7 sts. on a safety-pin, p. 18, turn and leave remaining 22 sts. on a stitch-holder.

S.s. 16 rows on remaining 18 sts. Break off yarn.

With right side of work facing, rejoin yarn and pick up and k. 16 sts. from row ends at one side of instep, k. across 18 instep sts., pick up and k. 16 sts. from other side of instep and finally, k. 7 sts. from safety-pin.

Next row: K. to end, then k. 22 sts. from stitch-holder—79 sts. ******* K. 12 rows—k. 13 rows here when working left leg.

To shape the foot: 1st dec. row: K. 5, k. 3 tog., k. 4, k. 3 tog., k. 25, k. 3 tog., k. 13, k. 3 tog., k. 20.

K. 1 row.

2nd dec. row: K. 4, k. 3 tog., k. 2, k. 3 tog., k. 23, k. 3 tog., k. 11, k. 3 tog., k. 19.

K. 1 row.

3rd dec. row: K. 3, (k. 3 tog.) twice, k. 21, k. 3 tog., k. 9, k. 3 tog., k. 18.

K. 1 row, then cast off remaining 55 sts.

THE LEFT LEG: Work as given for right leg to ******, noting variations.

To shape for instep: Next row: K. 25, turn and leave remaining 22 sts. on a stitch-holder, p. 18, turn and leave the remaining 7 sts. on a safety-pin.

S.s. 16 rows on 18 sts. Break off yarn.

With right side facing, rejoin yarn and pick up and k. 16 sts. from row ends at one side of instep, k. across 18 instep sts., pick up and k. 16 sts. from other side of instep and finally, k. 22 sts. from stitch-holder.

Next row: K. to end, k. 7 sts. from safety-pin—79 sts.

Work as given for right leg from ******* to end, noting variation in rows to be worked.

TO MAKE UP THE LEGGINGS: Join back and front seams as far as markers, then join leg seams. Beginning at centre of toe end, join underfoot seam. Run 5 rows of shirring elastic through wrong side of waist ribbing.

THE BONNET
Not illustrated

TO MAKE: With No. 10 (3¼ mm) needles cast on 91 sts. and g. st. 5 rows.

Work 14 rows in pattern as given for shawl centre.

Beginning odd-numbered rows with k. 1 and even numbered rows with p. 1, work 9 rows in single rib.

Beginning with a k. row (thus reversing the work), s.s. 40 rows.

Change to g. st. and work 4 rows.

To shape the crown: 1st row: (K. 7, k. 2 tog.) 10 times, k. 1—81 sts.

2nd row: K.

Repeat the last 2 rows, 7 times, working 1 st. less before the dec. on each successive repeat—11 sts.

Break off yarn leaving a long end. Run end through remaining sts., draw up and fasten off, then join row ends across crown shaping only.

TO COMPLETE THE BONNET: Fold back the pattern rows to form a brim, sew into place at both ends.

With No. 12 (2¾ mm) needles rejoin yarn and pick up and k. 80 sts. along row ends of bonnet – working through double thicknesses at brim – and work 6 rows in single rib. Cast off in rib. Cut ribbon into 2 pieces and, forming 1 end of each into a rosette, sew this end to each side of face edge.

THE BOOTEES
Illustrated on page 27

TO MAKE (both alike): With No. 10 (3¼ mm) needles cast on 41 sts. and g. st. 5 rows.

Work 14 rows in pattern as given for shawl centre, then beginning with a k. row, s.s. 4 rows, decreasing 1 st. at the end of the last row—40 sts.

Next (eyelet) row: * K. 2, y. fwd., k. 2 tog.; repeat from * to end.

Next row: All p. **

Next row: K. 6, (k. 2 tog., k. 11) twice, k. 2 tog., k. 6—37 sts.

Next row: All p.

To divide for instep: Next row: K. 24, turn and leave remaining 13 sts. on a safety-pin, then p. 11 and leave remaining 13 sts. on a safety-pin.

On 11 sts., s.s. 16 rows. Break off yarn.

With right side of work facing, rejoin yarn and pick up and k. 12 sts. from row ends at one side of instep, k. across 11 instep sts., pick up and k. 12 sts. from row ends of other side of instep and finally, k. 13 sts. from safety-pin.

Next row: K. to end, then k. 13 sts. from other safety-pin—61 sts.

G. st. 12 rows.

To shape foot: 1st dec. row: K. 2 tog., k. 23, k. 2 tog., k. 7, k. 2 tog., k. 23, k. 2 tog.—57 sts.

K. 1 row.

2nd dec. row: K. 2 tog., k. 22, k. 2 tog., k. 5, k. 2 tog., k. 22, k. 2 tog.—53 sts.

K. 1 row.

3rd dec. row: K. 2 tog., k. 21, k. 2 tog., k. 3, k. 2 tog., k. 21, k. 2 tog.—49 sts.

K. 1 row.

4th dec. row: K. 2 tog., k. 20, k. 2 tog., k. 1, k. 2 tog., k. 20, k. 2 tog.—45 sts.

K. 1 row, then cast off.

TO MAKE UP THE BOOTEES: Folding cast-off edge in half, join underfoot and back seam. Thread ribbon through eyelets.

THE MITTS
Not illustrated

TO MAKE (2 alike): Work as given for bootees to **.

Continuing in s.s. work 22 rows.

To shape the top: 1st row: (K. 2, k. 2 tog.) 10 times—30 sts.

2nd row: All p.

3rd row: (K. 1, k. 2 tog.) 10 times—20 sts.

4th row: All p.

5th row: (K. 2 tog.) 10 times—10 sts.

Break yarn. Run end through remaining sts., draw up and fasten off, then join seam. Thread ribbon through eyelet holes.

Hooded Jumpsuit
Illustrated on page 31

MEASUREMENTS	*in centimetres (and inches, in brackets)*			
To fit chest sizes	51	(20)	56	(22)
Leg seam, from eyelet row	19	(7½)	23	(9)
Length, from back neck to crotch	31	(12¼)	34	(13½)
Sleeve seam	15.5	(6¼)	18	(7)

MATERIALS: *Allow the following quantities in 20 g balls of Emu Treasure D.K.:* 12 *for* 51 *cm size;* 14 *for* 56 *cm size. For either size: a pair each of No. 9 (3¾ mm) and No. 11 (3 mm) knitting needles; a 3.50 crochet hook; a cable needle; a slide fastener of appropriate length.*

TENSION: *Work at a tension of 24 stitches and 40 rows to measure 10 × 10 cm, over the garter stitch and 31 rows to measure 10 cm in depth over the pattern, using No. 9 (3¾ mm) needles, to obtain measurements given.*

ABBREVIATIONS: To be read before working: *K., knit plain; p., purl; st., stitch; tog., together; inc., increase (by working twice into same st.); dec., decrease (by working 2 sts. tog.); k. 2 tog. b., k. 2 tog. through back of sts.; up 1, pick up loop lying between needles and k. into back of it; y.fwd., yarn forward to make a st.; c. 4 b., cable 4 back (slip next 2 sts. on to a cable needle and leave at back of work, k. 2, then k. 2 from cable needle); c. 4 f., cable 4 front (slip next 2 sts. on to cable needle and leave at front of work, k. 2 then k. 2 from cable needle); g.st., garter st. (k. plain on every row); single rib is k. 1 and p. 1 alternately.*

NOTE: *The instructions are given for the* 51 *cm (20 inch) size. Where they vary, work figures within the brackets for* 56 *cm (22 inch) size.*

THE LEFT LEG: With No. 9 (3¾ mm) needles cast on 39 (43) sts.

K. 1 row.

To shape foot: 1st row (right side): K. 5 (6), up 1, k. 1, up 1, k. 19 (21), up 1, k. 1, up 1, k. 13 (14).

2nd row: All k.

3rd row: K. 6 (7), up 1, k. 1, up 1, k. 21 (23), up 1, k. 1, up 1, k. 14 (15).

4th row: All k.

5th row: K. 7 (8), up 1, k. 1, up 1, k. 23 (25), up 1, k. 1, up 1, k. 15 (16)—51 (55) sts.

G. st. 11 rows.

To shape instep: 1st row: K. 32 (34), k. 2 tog.b., k. 1, k. 2 tog., k. 14 (16).

2nd row: K. 13 (15), k. 2 tog., k. 1, k. 2 tog.b., k. 31 (33)

Continued on page 30

3rd row: K. 30 (32), k. 2 tog.b., k. 1, k. 2 tog., k. 12 (14).

4th row: K. 11 (13), k. 2 tog., k. 1, k. 2 tog.b., k. 29 (31).

5th row: K. 28 (30), k. 2 tog.b., k. 1, k. 2 tog., k. 10 (12).

6th row: K. 9 (11), k. 2 tog., k. 1, k. 2 tog.b., k. 27 (29).

7th row: K. 26 (28), k. 2 tog.b., k. 1, k. 2 tog., k. 8 (10).

For 56 cm size only: 8th row: K. 9, k. 2 tog., k. 1, k. 2 tog.b., k. 27.

9th row: K. 26, k. 2, tog.b., k. 1, k. 2 tog., k. 8.

For both sizes: On 37 sts., g.st. 3 rows.

Beginning and ending 1st row with k. 1 work 2 rows in single rib.

Eyelet row: K. 1, * y.fwd., k. 2 tog.; repeat from * to end.

Single rib 2 rows, then g.st. 1 (5) row(s).

Continuing in g. st., inc. 1 st. each end of next row, then on the 15 (18) following 4th rows—69 (75) sts.

G.st. 11 rows, marking each end of the last of these rows to denote end of leg seam.

G.st. 4 rows, then dec. 1 st. each end of next row, then on the 2 (3) following 4th rows—63 (67) sts.

K. 1 row. Break yarn and leave sts. on a spare needle.

THE RIGHT LEG: Work as left leg, but reading all shaping rows from right to left instead of from left to right, so that the first row of foot shaping will read: K. 13 (14), up 1, k. 1, up 1, k. 19 (21), up 1, k. 1, up 1, k. 5 (6). Do not break yarn.

Next (joining) row: K. to end, then k. across sts. of left leg, increasing 1 st. at beginning of left leg on 56 cm size only—126 (135) sts.

G.st. 7 (11) rows.

Work pattern as follows: Increase and 1st foundation row: K. 4, * p. 1, up 1 p.wise, k. 8; repeat from * until 5 sts. remain, p. 1, up 1 p.wise, k. 4—140 (151) sts.

2nd foundation row: K. 6, * p. 8, k. 2; repeat from * until 4 sts. remain, k. 4.

1st pattern row: K. 4, * p. 2, k. 8; repeat from * until 6 sts. remain, p. 2, k. 4.

2nd row: K. 6, * p. 8, k. 2; repeat from * until 4 sts. remain, k. 4.

3rd row: K. 4, * p. 2, c. 4 b., c. 4 f.; repeat from * until 6 sts. remain, p. 2, k. 4.

4th row: As 2nd row.

5th and 6th rows: As 1st and 2nd rows.

The last 6 rows form the pattern. Pattern a further 34 (40) rows.

Dec. row: K. 4, * k. 2 tog., k. 8; repeat from * until 6 sts. remain, k. 2 tog., k. 4—126 (135) sts.

G.st. 4 rows.

To divide for back and fronts: Next row: K. 29 (30) and leave these sts. on a spare needle for left front, cast off 5 (7), k. 57 (60) and leave these 58 (61) sts on a spare needle for back, cast off 5 (7), k. to end and work on these 29 (30) sts. for right front.

The right front: To shape armhole: Continuing in g.st., dec. 1 st. at armhole edge on next row, then on the 3 following alternate rows—25 (26) sts.

G.st. 19 (23) rows—g.st. 18 (22) rows here when working left front.

To shape the neck: Cast off 4 (5) sts. at beginning of next row, then dec. 1 st. at neck edge on following 7 rows—14 sts.

G.st. 3 rows.

To slope the shoulder: Cast off 7 sts. at beginning of next row—7 sts.

G.st. 1 row, then cast off.

The back: With right side of work facing, rejoin yarn to 58 (61) sts. on spare needle.

To shape the armholes: Dec. 1 st. each end of next row, then on the 3 following alternate rows—50 (53) sts.

G.st. 29 (33) rows.

To slope the shoulders: Cast off 7 sts. at beginning of next 4 rows—22 (25) sts.

Cast off.

The left front: With right side of work facing, rejoin yarn to sts. on spare needle and work as right front, noting variations.

THE SLEEVES (both alike): With No. 11 (3 mm) needles cast on 36 (38) sts. and work 12 rows in single rib.

Change to No. 9 (3¾ mm) needles.

G.st. 4 rows, then inc. 1 st. each end of next row, then on 6 (8) following 6th rows—50 (56) sts.

G.st. 7 (5) rows.

To shape the sleeve top: Cast off 3 (4) sts. at beginning of next 2 rows, then dec. 1 st. at beginning of the following 8 (12) rows—36 sts.

Cast off 2 sts. at beginning of next 10 rows—16 sts.

Cast off.

THE HOOD: First join shoulder seams. With right side of work facing and using No. 11 (3 mm) needles, rejoin yarn and pick up and k. 20 (21) sts. up right front neck, 22 (25) sts. across back, then 20 (21) sts. down left front neck—62 (67) sts.

G.st. 5 rows.

Inc. row: K. 9 (10), * inc., inc., k. 1; repeat from * until 8 (9) sts. remain, k. to end—92 (99) sts.

G.st. 1 row.

Change to No. 9 (3¾ mm) needles and g.st. 62 (66) rows. Cast off.

TO MAKE UP THE SUIT: Press cable pattern only, using a cool iron over a dry cloth. Using a flat seam, join leg seams as far as markers, then join foot seams. Join small crotch seams. Set in sleeves, then join sleeve seams. Join top of hood seam. Sew in slide fastener. Using 3.50 crochet hook, make 2 lengths of chain to measure 56 cm (22 inches) in length, then thread through each eyelet row to tie at front.

Opposite *Hooded Jumpsuit (page 29)*

Zip-up Hooded Jacket and Pram Cover

Illustrated on page 34

MEASUREMENTS	*in centimetres (and inches, in brackets)*			
To fit chest sizes	46 (18)	51 (20)	56 (22)	61 (24)
All round at underarms	51.5 (20¼)	54.5 (21½)	63.5 (25)	67 (26½)
Side seam	17 (6¾)	19.5 (7¾)	21.5 (8½)	24.5 (9½)
Length	27.5 (10¾)	31 (12¼)	34.5 (13½)	38.5 (15¼)
Sleeve seam	18.5 (7¼)	21.5 (8½)	23 (9)	26.5 (10½)

MATERIALS: *Allow the following quantities in 20 g balls of Littlewoods Keynote Acrylic Nylon 4-ply or Double Knitting: 7 balls 4-ply and a pair each of No. 10 (3¼ mm) and No. 12 (2¾ mm) knitting needles for the 46 cm and 51 cm sizes; 12 balls double knitting and a pair each of No. 8 (4 mm) and No. 10 (3¼ mm) knitting needles for the 56 cm size; 13 balls double knitting and a pair each of No. 8 (4 mm) and No. 10 (3¼ mm) knitting needles for the 61 cm size. For any one size: an open-ended slide fastener of appropriate length; a cable needle.*

TENSION: *Work at a tension of 37 stitches and 38 rows to measure 10 × 10 cm, using No. 10 (3¼ mm) needles and 4-ply, or 30 stitches and 31 rows to measure 10 × 10 cm, using No. 8 (4 mm) needles and double knitting, to obtain measurements given.*

ABBREVIATIONS: To be read before working: *K., knit plain; p., purl; st., stitch; tog., together; inc., increase (by working twice into next st.); dec., decrease (by taking 2 sts. tog.); tw. 2 rt., twist 2 right (slip next st. on to cable needle and leave at back of work, k. 1, then k. 1 from cable needle); tw. 2 lt., twist 2 left (as tw. 2 rt., but leave cable needle at front of work); nil, meaning nothing is worked here for this size; single rib is k. 1 and p. 1 alternately.*

NOTE: *The instructions are given for the 46 cm (18 inch) size worked in 4-ply. Where they vary, work figures within brackets for 51 cm (20 inch) size in 4-ply.*

SPECIAL NOTE: *For 56 cm (22 inch) size, work exactly as given for 46 cm (18 inch) size and for 61 cm (24 inch) size, work exactly as given for 51 cm (20 inch) size, but for either size, use double knitting instead of 4-ply, No. 8 (4 mm) needles instead of No. 10 (3¼ mm) and No. 10 (3¼ mm) needles instead of No. 12 (2¾ mm).*

---

46 cm (18 inch) and 51 cm (20 inch) sizes only.

THE BACK: With No. 12 (2¾ mm) needles and 4-ply cast on 94 (100) sts. and work 14 rows in single rib increasing 1 st. at end of larger size—94 (101) sts.

Change to No. 10 (3¼ mm) needles.

1st pattern row: P. 3, * tw. 2 rt., tw. 2 lt., p. 3; repeat from * to end.

2nd row: K. 3, * p. 4, k. 3; repeat from * to end.

3rd row: P. 3, * tw. 2 lt., tw. 2 rt., p. 3; repeat from * to end.

4th row: As 2nd row.

These 4 rows form the pattern. Repeat them a further 12 (14) times.

To shape the armholes: Keeping continuity of the pattern, cast off 7 sts. at beginning of next 2 rows, then dec. 1 st. each end of next row and 6 (7) following alternate rows—66 (71) sts.

Pattern 21 (23) rows.

To slope shoulders: Cast off 9 (10) sts. at beginning of next 2 rows, then 10 sts. on following 2 rows.

Cast off remaining 28 (31) sts.

THE LEFT FRONT: With No. 12 (2¾ mm) needles and 4-ply cast on 48 (50) sts. and work 14 rows in single rib.

Change to No. 10 (3¼ mm) needles.

1st pattern row: P. 3, * tw. 2 rt., tw. 2 lt., p. 3; repeat from * until 3 (5) sts. remain, tw. 2 rt., p. 1 (tw. 2 rt., tw. 2 lt., p. 1).

2nd row: K. 1, p. 2 (4), k. 3, * p. 4, k. 3; repeat from * to end.

3rd row: P. 3, * tw. 2 lt., tw. 2 rt., p. 3; repeat from * until 3 (5) sts. remain, tw. 2 lt., p. 1 (tw. 2 lt., tw. 2 rt., p. 1).

4th row: As 2nd row.

These 4 rows form the pattern. Repeat them a further 12 (14) times.

** **To shape armhole:** Keeping continuity of the pattern, cast off 7 sts. at beginning of next row.

Work 1 row—omit this row when working right front.

Dec. 1 st. at armhole edge on next row and the 6 (7) following alternate rows—34 (35) sts.

Pattern 10 rows—pattern 11 rows here when working right front.

To shape neck: Cast off 10 sts. at beginning of next row, then dec. 1 st. at same edge on the following 5 rows—19 (20) sts.

Pattern 5 (7) rows.

To slope shoulder: Cast off 9 (10) sts. at beginning of next row.

Work 1 row, then cast off remaining 10 sts.

THE RIGHT FRONT: With No. 12 (2¾ mm) needles and 4-ply cast on 48 (50) sts. and work 14 rows in single rib.

Change to No. 10 (3¼ mm) needles.

1st pattern row: P. 1, then tw. 2 lt. (tw. 2 rt., tw. 2 lt.), p. 3, * tw. 2 rt., tw. 2 lt., p. 3; repeat from * to end.

2nd row: K. 3, * p. 4, k. 3; repeat from * until 3 (5) sts. remain, p. 2 (4), k. 1.

3rd row: P. 1, then tw. 2 rt. (tw. 2 lt., tw. 2 rt.), p. 3, * tw. 2 lt., tw. 2 rt., p. 3; repeat from * to end.

4th row: As 2nd row.

These 4 rows form the pattern. Repeat them a further 12 (14) times, then 1st row again.

Work as given for left front from ** to end, noting variations.

THE SLEEVES (2 alike): With No. 12 ($2\frac{3}{4}$ mm) needles and 4-ply cast on 41 (47) sts. and beginning odd-numbered rows with k. 1 and even-numbered rows with p. 1, work 9 rows in single rib.

Increase row: Rib nil (1), inc., * rib 3, inc.; repeat from * until nil (1) remains, rib nil (1)—52 (59) sts.

Change to No. 10 ($3\frac{1}{4}$ mm) needles and work the 4 pattern rows of back, once.

Keeping continuity of the pattern, and working extra sts. into pattern as they occur, inc. 1 st. each end of next row and the 7 following 6th rows—68 (75) sts.

Pattern 13 (25) rows.

To shape sleeve top: Cast off 7 sts. at beginning of next 2 rows, then dec. 1 st. each end of next row and the 6 (7) following alternate rows—40 (45) sts.

Pattern 1 row, then cast off 5 sts. at beginning of the next 6 rows.

Cast off remaining 10 (15) sts.

THE HOOD: With No. 12 ($2\frac{3}{4}$ mm) needles and 4-ply cast on 143 (157) sts. and work 8 rows in rib as given on sleeves.

Change to No. 10 ($3\frac{1}{4}$ mm) needles and work 32 (36) rows in pattern as given on back.

To shape back: Cast off 50 (57) sts. at beginning of next 2 rows—43 sts.

Pattern 48 (58) rows for back extension.

Cast off for back neck edge.

THE NECK RIBBING: First sew cast off groups of hood to row ends of back extension.

With right side facing, rejoin 4-ply yarn and using No. 12 ($2\frac{3}{4}$ mm) needles pick up and k. 97 (101) sts. all round neck edge and work 7 rows in single rib.

Cast off in rib.

TO MAKE UP THE JACKET: Press with a warm iron over a dry cloth. Join shoulder seams, set in sleeves, then join side and sleeve seams. Sew cast off edge of hood neck band all round neck edge. Insert slide fastener.

For 56 cm (22 inch) and 61 cm (24 inch) sizes only: See "Special Note" after "Note" paragraph.

1st row: K. to within 1 st. of centre st., k. 3 tog., k. to end.

2nd row: K. to end.

3rd row: K. to within 2 sts. of centre st., M.B., k. 3 tog., M.B., k. to end.

4th row: K. to end.

These 4 rows form the repeat of the pattern. Keeping continuity of pattern, work a further 2 rows w., then 2 rows bl., 6 rows w., 2 rows bl., 6 rows w., 2 rows bl, then 2 rows w.

Next row: With w., k. 1, k. 3 tog., k. 1.

Next row: With w., k. 3 tog.

Fasten off.

Make another 23 motifs the same then a further 24 motifs using pk. instead of bl.

TO MAKE UP THE COVER: Join the bl. motifs into 6 squares of 4 motifs each, matching row ends and strips, then join the pk. motifs in the same way. Sew the large squares together in 4 rows of 3 squares each, alternating colours.

THE SIDE BORDERS (2 alike): With right side facing, rejoin w. to one corner and using No. 7 ($4\frac{1}{2}$ mm) needles, pick up and k. 128 sts. along one long edge.

K. 1 row. Drop w.

Join in pk. and k. 2 rows increasing 1 st. each end of 1st row. Break off pk.

Take up w. and k. 2 rows increasing 1 st. each end of 1st row. Drop w.

Join in bl.

Pattern row: K. 3, M.B., * k. 5, M.B.; repeat from * until 2 sts. remain, k. 2.

K. 1 row with bl. Break off bl.

Take up w. and k. 1 row increasing each end. Cast off k.wise.

THE END BORDERS (2 alike): With right side facing, rejoin w. to one corner and using No. 7 ($4\frac{1}{2}$ mm) needles, pick up and k. 98 sts. along one short edge.

Work as given for side borders.

Join row ends of borders. Pin out and press with a warm iron over a dry cloth.

PRAM COVER

MATERIALS: *Allow the following quantities in 20 g balls of Littlewoods Keynote Acrylic/nylon Quicknit; 8 white, 2 blue and 2 pink; a pair of No. 7 ($4\frac{1}{2}$ mm) knitting needles.*

TENSION AND SIZE: *Worked at such a tension that each motif measures 7.5 cm square, the cover should measure 50 cm ($19\frac{1}{2}$ inches) × 65 cm ($25\frac{1}{2}$ inches) when completed.*

ABBREVIATIONS: To be read before working: *K., plain; p., purl; st., stitch; tog., together; y.fwd., yarn forward to make a st.; M.B., make a bobble (pick up loop lying between needles and into back of this st. work k. 1, y.fwd., k. 1, y.fwd., k. 1, turn and p. these 5 sts., turn and k. 3, k. 2 tog., then pass the 3 k. sts. over the k. 2 tog., k. next st. of row, then pass previous st. over this st.); increase (by working twice into next st.); w., white; bl., blue; pk., pink.*

THE MOTIF: With No. 7 ($4\frac{1}{2}$ mm) needles and w. cast on 33 sts.

Foundation row (wrong side): K. 15, k. 3 tog.— mark this resulting st. for centre, k. 15.

Above *Zip-up Hooded Jacket and Pram Cover (page 32).*   Opposite *V-neck Cardigan (page 36)*

V-neck Cardigan

Illustrated on page 35

MEASUREMENTS	in centimetres (and inches, in brackets)					
To fit chest sizes	56	(22)	61	(24)	66	(26)
All round at underarms, fastened	57.5	(22½)	63	(24¾)	68.5	(27)
Side seam	21	(8¼)	23.5	(9¼)	26	(10¼)
Length	32.5	(12¾)	35.5	(14)	40.5	(16)
Sleeve seam	23	(9)	25.5	(10)	28	(11

MATERIALS: *Allow the following quantities in 50 g balls of Emu Superwash Wool 4-ply:* 2 *white for* 56 *cm size;* 3 *white for* 61 *cm size;* 3 *white for* 66 *cm size. For any one size:* 1 *ball of the same yarn in blue and* 1 *in red; a pair each of No.* 10 (3¼ *mm) and No.* 12 (2¾ *mm) knitting needles;* 6 *buttons.*

TENSION: *Work at a tension of* 29 *stitches and* 38 *rows to measure* 10 × 10 *cm, over the stocking stitch, using No.* 10 (3¼ *mm) needles, to obtain measurements given.*

ABBREVIATIONS: To be read before working: *K., knit plain; p., purl; st., stitch; tog., together; inc., increase (by working twice into same st.); dec., decrease (by working* 2 *sts. tog.); s.k.p.o., slip* 1*, k.* 1*, pass the slipped st. over; s.s., stocking st. (k. on right side, p. on wrong side); p.* 2 *tog.b., p.* 2 *tog. through back of sts.; w., white; b., blue; r., red; single rib is k.* 1*, p.* 1 *alternately; nil, meaning nothing is worked for this size.*

NOTE: *The instructions are given for the* 56 *cm (22 inch) size. Where they vary, work figures within first brackets for* 61 *cm (24 inch) size; work figures within second brackets for* 66 *cm (26 inch) size.*

THE BACK AND FRONTS (worked in one piece to armholes): With No. 12 (2¾ mm) needles and b., cast on 161 (177)(193) sts. and, beginning odd-number rows with k. 1 and even-number rows with p. 1, work 18 rows in single rib.

** Change to No. 10 (3¼ mm) needles. Joining and breaking colours as required, work the border pattern, which is entirely in s.s., beginning with a k. row, so only the colour details are given.

1st and 2nd rows: All w.

3rd row: 1 r., * 3 w., 1 r.; repeat from * to end.

4th row: 2 r., 1 w., * 3 r., 1 w.; repeat from * until 2 sts. remain, 2 r.

5th row: All r.

6th row: All w.

7th row: 1 w., * 2 b., 3 w., 2 b., 1 w.; repeat from * to end.

8th row: 1 w., * 1 b., 5 w., 1 b., 1 w.; repeat from * to end.

9th row: 4 b., * 1 w., 7 b.; repeat from * ending last repeat with 4 b.

10th row: 3 b., * 3 w., 5 b.; repeat from * ending last repeat with 3 b.

11th row: 2 b., * 5 w., 3 b.; repeat from * ending last repeat with 2 b.

12th row: 1 r., * 3 w., 1 r.; repeat from * to end.

13th row: 2 r., * 1 w., 1 r., 1 w., 1 r., 1 w., 3 r.; repeat from * ending last repeat with 2 r.

14th row: As 10th row, but using r. instead of b.

15th row: As 11th row, but using r. instead of b.

16th row: 1 r., * 7 w., 1 r.; repeat from * to end.

17th row: 1 w., * 2 r., 3 w., 2 r., 1 w.; repeat from * to end.

18th and 19th rows: 2 r., * 5 w., 3 r.; repeat from * ending last repeat with 2 r.

Break off b. and r.

Continue in w. only. **

S.s. 42 (52) (62) rows.

To divide for back and fronts: Next row: P. 40 (44) (48) and leave these on a spare needle for left front, p. 81 (89) (97) and leave these on a spare needle for back, p. to end and work on these 40 (44) (48) sts. for right front.

The right front: To shape raglan armhole and slope front edge: 1st row: Dec., k. until 4 sts. remain, k. 2 tog., k. 2.

2nd row: P. 2, p. 2 tog., p. to end.

3rd row: All k.

4th row: As 2nd row.

5th row: As 1st row.

6th row: All p.

7th row: K. until 4 sts. remain, k. 2 tog., k. 2.

Repeat last 6 rows, 6 (6) (7) times then the nil (2nd to 6th) (2nd to 4th) rows again—3 (3) (4) sts.

For 56 cm size only: Next row: P. 1, p. 2 tog.

For 61 cm and 66 cm sizes only: Next row: K. 2 tog., k. to end.

Next row: P. to end.

For all sizes: K. remaining 2 (2) (3) sts. tog. and fasten off.

The back: With right side of work facing, rejoin yarn to inner end of 81 (89) (97) sts. on spare needle.

To shape raglan armholes: *** **1st row:** K. 2, s.k.p.o., k. until 4 sts. remain, k. 2 tog., k. 2.

2nd row: P. 2, p. 2 tog., p. until 4 sts. remain, p. 2 tog.b., p. 2.

3rd row: All k.

4th row: As 2nd row.

5th row: As 1st row.

6th row: P. to end. ***

Repeat last 6 rows, 6 (7) (8) times, then the 1st and 2nd (1st and 6th) (nil) rows again—21 (23) (25) sts.

Cast off

The left front: With right side of work facing, rejoin yarn to inner end of 40 (44) (48) sts. on spare needle.

To shape raglan armhole: 1st row: K. 2, s.k.p.o., k. until 2 sts. remain, dec.

2nd row: P. until 4 sts. remain, p. 2 tog.b., p. 2.

3rd row: K. to end.

4th row: As 2nd row.

5th row: As 1st row.

6th row: All p.

7th row: K. 2, s.k.p.o., k. to end.

Repeat last 6 rows 6 (6) (7) times, then the nil (2nd to 6th) (2nd to 4th) rows again—3 (3) (4) sts.

For 56 cm size only: Next row: P. 2 tog.b., p. 1.

For 61 cm and 66 cm sizes only: Next row: K. until 2 sts. remain, s.k.p.o.

Next row: P. to end.

For all sizes: K. remaining 2 (2) (3) sts. tog. and fasten off.

THE SLEEVES (2 alike): With No. 12 ($2\frac{3}{4}$ mm) needles and b. cast on 35 (37) (39) sts. and rib 17 rows as on back and fronts.

Inc. row: Rib 4 (1) (2), inc., * rib 1 (2) (1), inc.; repeat from * 12 (10) (16) times, rib to end—49 (49) (57) sts.

Working in pattern as back and fronts from ** to **, and taking extra sts. into the pattern as they occur, work 8 rows, then inc. 1 st. each end of the next row, then on the 6 (10) (8) following 8th (6th) (8th) rows—63 (71) (75) sts.

S.s. 13 (11) (17) rows.

To shape sleeve top: Repeat from *** to *** on back 7 (8) (8) times, then the nil (nil) (1st to 3rd) rows again—7 sts.

For 56 cm and 61 cm sizes only: Next row: K. 2, k. 3 tog., k. 2.

Next row: P. 1, p. 3 tog., p. 1.

For 66 cm size only: Next row: P. 2, p. 3 tog., p. 2.

Next row: K. 1, k. 3 tog., k. 1.

Next row: P. 3.

For all sizes: K. 3 tog. and fasten off.

THE FRONT BORDER: First join raglan seams. With No. 12 ($2\frac{3}{4}$ mm) needles and b. cast on 8 sts. and work 2 rows in single rib.

1st buttonhole row: Rib 3, cast off 2, rib to end.

2nd buttonhole row: Rib to end, casting on 2 sts. over those cast off on previous row.

Rib 12 (14) (16) rows.

Repeat last 14 (16) (18) rows 4 times, then the 2 buttonhole rows again.

Continue in rib until band fits up first front, round neck and down second front to lower edge, casting off when correct length is assured.

TO MAKE UP THE CARDIGAN: Press with a warm iron over a damp cloth. Join sleeve seams. Sew front band into position setting last buttonhole level with first front dec. Add buttons.

Jacket, Hat and Mitts

Illustrated on page 39

MEASUREMENTS	*in centimetres (and inches, in brackets)*					
Chest size	56	(22)	61	(24)	66	(26)
All round at underarms, fastened	60.5	($23\frac{3}{4}$)	66.5	($26\frac{1}{4}$)	72.5	($28\frac{1}{2}$)
Side seam	23	(9)	24	($9\frac{1}{2}$)	25	($9\frac{3}{4}$)
Length	32.5	($12\frac{3}{4}$)	34.5	($13\frac{1}{2}$)	36.5	($14\frac{1}{4}$)
Sleeve seam, with cuff turned back	18.5	($7\frac{1}{4}$)	20.5	(8)	23	(9)
HAT						
Will fit an average head size						
MITTS						
Length	15.5	(6)	15.5	(6)	15.5	(6)

MATERIALS: *Allow the following quantities in 50 g balls of Pingouin Iceberg: 8 for 56 cm size; 9 for 61 cm size; 10 for 66 cm size. For any one size: a pair each of No. 4 (6 mm) and No. 5 ($5\frac{1}{2}$ mm) knitting needles; 4 buttons.*

TENSION: *Work at a tension of 13 stitches and 19 rows to measure 10 × 10 cm, over the stocking stitch, using No. 4 (6 mm) needles, to obtain the measurements given.*

ABBREVIATIONS: To be read before working: K., *knit plain; p., purl; st., stitch; tog., together; inc., increase (by working twice into same st.); dec., decrease (by working 2 sts. tog.); s.s., stocking st. (k. on the right side and p. on the wrong side); nil, meaning nothing is worked here for this size; double rib is k. 2 and p. 2 alternately.*

NOTE: *The instructions are given for the 56 cm (22 inch) size. Where they vary, work the figures within first brackets for the 61 cm (24 inch) size; work the figures within second brackets for the 66 cm (26 inch) size.*

SPECIAL NOTE: *On the hat and mitts, instructions in brackets are worked the number of times stated after the last bracket.*

CARDIGAN

THE BACK: With No. 5 ($5\frac{1}{2}$ mm) needles cast on 40 (44) (48) sts.

1st row: K. 3, * p. 2, k. 2; repeat from * until 5 sts. remain, p. 2, k. 3.

2nd row: P. 3, * k. 2, p. 2; repeat from * until 5 sts. remain, k. 2, p. 3.

Repeat last 2 rows, 3 times more.

Change to No. 4 (6 mm) needles and s.s. 36 (38) (40) rows.

Continued on page 38

Next row: Cast on 24 (27) (30) sts. for 1st sleeve, k. to end, turn and cast on 24 (27) (30) sts. for 2nd sleeve—88 (98) (108) sts.

S.s. 13 (15) (17) rows.

Divide sts. for neck: Next row: K. 37 (42) (47), turn and work on these sts. only for right front, leaving remaining sts. on a spare needle.

The right front: S.s. 15 rows.

Next row: K. to end, turn, cast on 4 sts. for neck—41 (46) (51) sts.

S.s. 5 rows.

Next row: Cast off 24 (27) (30) sts. for sleeve, k. to end—17 (19) (21) sts.

S.s. 35 (37) (39) rows.

Change to No. 5 (5½ mm) needles.

1st row: P. 2 (nil) (2), * k. 2, p. 2; repeat from * until 3 sts. remain, k. 3.

2nd row: P. 3, * k. 2, p. 2; repeat from * until 2 (nil) (2) remain, k. 2 (nil) (2).

Repeat last 2 rows, 3 times more. Cast off in rib.

The left front: With right side of work facing, rejoin yarn to inner end of sts. on spare needle, cast off 14 sts., then k. to end—37 (42) (47) sts.

S.s. 15 rows.

Next row: Cast on 4 sts. for neck, k. to end.

S.s. 4 rows.

Next row: Cast off 24 (27) (30) sts. for sleeves, p. to end—17 (19) (21) sts.

S.s. 36 (38) (40) rows.

Change to No. 5 (5½ mm) needles.

1st row: K. 3, * p. 2, k. 2; repeat from * until 2 (nil) (2) remain, p. 2 (nil) (2).

2nd row: K. 2 (nil) (2), * p. 2, k. 2; repeat from * until 3 sts. remain, p. 3.

Repeat last 2 rows, 3 times. Cast off in rib.

THE CUFFS (2 alike): With right side of work facing and using No. 5 (5½ mm) needles, pick up and k. 26 (30) (34) sts. around lower edge of sleeve.

1st row: K. 2, * p. 2, k. 2; repeat from * to end.

2nd row: P. 2, * k. 2, p. 2; repeat from * to end.

Repeat the last 2 rows, twice more, then the 1st row again. Cast off in rib.

THE COLLAR: With No. 5 (5½ mm) needles cast on 60 (64) (68) sts. and work 13 rows in rib as given on back. Cast off in rib.

THE BUTTON BAND: With No. 5 (5½ mm) needles cast on 32 (36) (40) sts. and work 6 rows in rib as given on back. Cast off in rib.

THE BUTTONHOLE BAND: With No. 5 (5½ mm) needles cast on 32 (36) (40) sts. and work 2 rows in rib as given on back.

1st buttonhole row: Rib 1 (2) (2), * cast off 2, rib 7 (8) (9); repeat from * twice, cast off 2, rib 2 (2) (3).

2nd row: Work in rib, casting on 2 sts. over those cast off on previous row.

Rib a further 2 rows. Cast off in rib.

TO MAKE UP THE CARDIGAN: Press work lightly on the wrong side, using a warm iron over a dry cloth. Join side seams. Sew on cuffs. Join sleeve seams. Sew front bands to their respective fronts. Sew on collar beginning and ending in centre of front bands. Turn back cuffs. Sew on buttons.

THE HAT

TO MAKE: With No. 5 (5½ mm) needles cast on 60 sts. and work 31 rows in double rib.

Change to No. 4 (6 mm) needles and k. 1 row.

Next (dec.) row: P. 3, (p. 2 tog., p. 4) 4 times, p. 2 tog., p. 2, (p. 2 tog., p. 4) 4 times, p. 2 tog., p. 3—50 sts.

S.s. 4 rows.

Next (dec.) row: K. 2, (k. 2 tog., k. 3) 4 times, k. 2 tog., k. 2, (k. 2 tog., k. 3) 4 times, k. 2 tog., k. 2—40 sts.

Next (dec.) row: P. 1 (p. 2 tog., p. 2) 9 times, p. 2 tog., p. 1—30 sts.

Next (dec.) row: (K. 2 tog.) 15 times.

Break yarn, leaving a long end, thread this through remaining 15 sts., draw up tightly and fasten off securely.

TO MAKE UP THE HAT: Press as for cardigan.

Join seam, reversing seam for brim. Turn brim over to right side.

THE MITTS

THE LEFT MITT: With No. 5 (5½ mm) needles cast on 21 sts.

1st row: K. 3, * p. 2, k. 2; repeat from * until 2 sts. remain, p. 2.

2nd row: K. 2, * p. 2, k. 2; repeat from * until 3 sts. remain, p. 3.

Repeat these last 2 rows, 5 times.

Change to No. 4 (6 mm) needles and k. 1 row. **

To shape for thumb: 2nd row: P. 7, inc., p. 2, inc., p. to end.

3rd row: All k.

4th row: P. 8, inc., p. 2, inc., p. to end.

5th and every alternate row: All k.

6th row: P. 9, inc., p. 2, inc., p. to end.

8th row: P. 10, inc., p. 2, inc., p. to end—29 sts.

Divide sts. for thumb: Break off yarn, slip the first 8 sts. on to a safety-pin, rejoin yarn to next st., k. 9, turn and work on these sts. only for thumb, leaving remaining 12 sts. on a spare needle.

*** **The thumb:** S.s. 5 rows.

Next row: * K. 2, k. 2 tog.; repeat from * once, k. 1.

Break off yarn, leaving a long end, thread this through remaining 7 sts., draw up tightly and fasten off securely. Join thumb seam. ***

With right side of work facing, rejoin yarn to 8 sts. on safety-pin, k. these 8 sts., pick up and k. 2 sts. from base of thumb, then k. across 12 sts. on spare needle—22 sts.

**** S.s. 4 rows.

To shape the top: 1st row: P. 2, p. 2 tog., p. 3, p. 2 tog., p. 4, p. 2 tog., p. 3, p. 2 tog., p. 2—18 sts.

2nd row: All k.

3rd row: (P. 2, p. 2 tog.) 4 times, p. 2—14 sts.

4th row: All k.

5th row: P. 1, p. 2 tog., p. 1, p. 2 tog., p. 2, p. 2 tog., p. 1, p. 2 tog., p. 1—10 sts.

6th row: (K. 2 tog.) 5 times.

Break off yarn, leaving a long end, thread this through remaining 5 sts., draw up tightly and fasten off.

THE RIGHT MITT: Work as given for left mitt to **.

To shape for thumb: 2nd row: P. 10, inc., p. 2, inc., p. to end.

3rd and every alternate row: All k.
4th row: P. 11, inc., p. 2, inc., p. to end.
6th row: P. 12, inc., p. 2, inc., p. to end.
8th row: P. 13, inc., p. 2, inc., p. to end—29 sts.
 Divide sts. for thumb: Break off yarn, slip the first 12 sts. on to a spare needle, rejoin yarn to next st., k. 9, turn and leave remaining 8 sts. on a safety-pin.
 Work as given for left mitt from *** to ***.
 With right side of work facing, rejoin yarn to 12 sts. on spare needle, k. these 12 sts., pick up and k. 2 sts. from base of thumb, then k. across 8 sts. on safety-pin—22 sts.
 Work as given for left mitt from **** to end.

TO MAKE UP THE MITTS: Press as for cardigan. Join seam.

Below *Jacket, Hat and Mitts (page 37)*

Chunky Polo-necked Sweater

Illustrated on page 42

MEASUREMENTS						
To fit chest sizes	*in centimetres (and inches, in brackets)*					
	56	(22)	61	(24)	66	(26)
All round underarms	58	$(22\frac{3}{4})$	65.5	$(25\frac{3}{4})$	69	$(27\frac{1}{4})$
Side seam	18	(7)	20.5	(8)	23	(29)
Length	31.5	$(12\frac{1}{4})$	35.5	(14)	40	$(15\frac{3}{4})$
Sleeve seam	24.5	$(9\frac{3}{4})$	27.5	$(10\frac{3}{4})$	31	$(12\frac{1}{4})$

MATERIALS: *Allow the following quantities in 40 g balls of Wendy Aran:* 6 *for* 56 *cm size;* 7 *for* 61 *cm and* 66 *cm sizes. For any one size: a pair each of No.* 6 (5 *mm*) *and No.* 8 (4 *mm*) *knitting needles.*

TENSION: *Work at a tension of* 22 *stitches and* 24 *rows to measure* 10 × 10 *cm, over the pattern, using No.* 6 (5 *mm*) *needles, to obtain measurements.*

ABBREVIATIONS: To be read before working: *K., knit plain; p., purl; st., stitch; tog., together; inc., increase (by working twice into next st.); dec., decrease (by working* 2 *sts. tog.); single rib is k.* 1, *p.* 1 *alternately; sl., slip.*

NOTE: *The instructions are given for the* 56 *cm (*22 *inch) size. Where they vary, work figures within first brackets for* 61 *cm (*24 *inch) size; work figures within second brackets for* 66 *cm (*26 *inch) size.*

THE BACK: With No. 8 (4 mm) needles cast on 64 (72) (76) sts. and work 12 rows in single rib.

Change to No. 6 (5 mm) needles and work the 4-row pattern as follows:

1st row (wrong side): All p.

2nd row: (right side): All k.

3rd row: All p. winding yarn twice round needle for each st.

4th row: * Sl. next 4 sts. on to right-hand needle dropping extra loops, sl. these 4 sts. back on to left hand needle, then k. 4 tog., p. 4 tog., k. 4 tog., p. 4 tog. into front of all these 4 sts. together; repeat from * to end.

Pattern a further 29 (35) (41) rows.

Mark each end of last row to denote end of side seams. **

Pattern 28 (32) (36) rows.

To slope the shoulders: Keeping continuity of pattern where possible, cast off 8 (9) (9) sts. at beginning of next 2 rows, then 8 (9) (10) sts. on the following 2 rows—32 (36) (38) sts.

Leave sts. on a spare needle.

THE FRONT: Work as back to **.

Pattern 15 (19) (23) rows.

To divide for neck: Next row: Pattern 20 (23) (24) and leave these sts. on a spare needle for right half neck, pattern 24 (26) (28) and leave these sts. on a stitch-holder, pattern to end and work on these 20 (23) (24) sts. for left half neck.

The left half neck: Dec. 1 st. at neck edge on next 4 (5) (5) rows—16 (18) (19) sts.

Pattern 8 (7) (7) rows—pattern 9 (8) (8) rows here when working right half neck.

To slope the shoulder: Cast off 8 (9) (9) sts. at beginning of next row—8 (9) (10) sts.

Pattern 1 row, then cast off.

The right half neck: With right side of work facing, rejoin yarn to sts. on the stitch-holder and work as left half neck, noting variation.

THE SLEEVES (both alike): With No. 8 (4 mm) needles cast on 40 (44) (44) sts. and work 14 rows in single rib.

Change to No. 6 (5 mm) needles.

Work 4 rows in pattern as given for back, then working extra sts. in pattern when possible, inc. 1 st. each end of next row, then on the 6 (7) (9) following 6th rows—54 (60) (64) sts.

Pattern 4 (6) (2) rows. Cast off.

THE POLO COLLAR: First join right shoulder seam. With right side of work facing and using No. 8 (4 mm) needles, rejoin yarn and pick up and k. 17 sts. down left half neck, k. 24 (26) (28) sts. across front, pick up and k. 17 sts. up right half neck, then k. 32 (36) (38) sts. across back—90 (96) (100) sts.

Work 24 rows in single rib. Cast off.

TO MAKE UP THE SWEATER: Press with a warm iron over a dry cloth. Join left shoulder seam, continuing seam across polo collar. Set in sleeves between markers on back and front, then join sleeve and side seams.

Fair-Isle Sweater

Illustrated on page 43

MEASUREMENTS	*in centimetres (and inches, in brackets)*			
Chest size	56 (22)	61 (24)	66 (26)	71 (28)
All round at underarms	58.5 (23)	63.5 (25)	68 (26¾)	73 (28¾)
Side seam	24.5 (9½)	26.5 (10½)	28.5 (11¼)	30.5 (12)
Length	35 (13¾)	37.5 (14¾)	41.5 (16¼)	44 (17¼)
Sleeve seam	32 (12½)	34 (13½)	36 (14¼)	38 (15)

MATERIALS: *Allow the following quantities in 50 g balls of Sirdar Country Style Double Knitting: 3 main, 1 each in cream, brown and rust for the 56 cm and 61 cm sizes; 4 main, 1 each in cream, brown and rust for the 66 cm and 71 cm sizes. For any one size: a pair each of No. 8 (4 mm) and No. 10 (3¼ mm) knitting needles.*

TENSION: *Work at a tension of 25 stitches and 29 rows, to measure 10 × 10 cm, over the plain stocking stitch, using No. 8 (4 mm) needles, to obtain the measurements given.*

ABBREVIATIONS: To be read before working: *K., knit plain; p., purl; st., stitch; tog., together; inc., increase (by working twice into next st.); dec., decrease (by taking 2 sts. tog.); single rib is k. 1 and p. 1 alternately; s.s., stocking st. (k. on the right side and p. on the wrong side); m., main; c., cream; br., brown; r., rust.*

NOTE: *The instructions are given for the 56 cm (22 inch) chest size. Where they vary, work the figures within the first brackets for the 61 cm (24 inch) chest; work the figures within the second brackets for the 66 cm (26 inch) chest, and so on.*

THE SWEATER

BACK AND FRONT (both alike): With No. 10 (3¼ mm) needles and m. cast on 72 (78) (84) (90) sts. and work 16 rows in single rib, increasing 1 st. at the end of the last row—73 (79) (85) (91) sts.

Change to No. 8 (4 mm) needles and beginning with a k. row, s.s. 58 (64) (70) (76) rows.

Mark each end of the last row, to denote the end of side seams.

S.s. a further 4 rows.

Work the 4-colour pattern, which is worked entirely in s.s., beginning with a k. row so only the colour details are given.

1st row: 1 c., * 2 m., 1 c.; repeat from * to end.

2nd row: 2 m., * 3 c., 3 m.; repeat from * ending last repeat with 2 m. instead of 3 m.

3rd row: 1 m., * 2 c., 1 m.; repeat from * to end.

4th row: All c.

5th row: 1 c., * 1 r., 1 c.; repeat from * to end.

6th row: 1 r., * 1 c., 1 r.; repeat from * to end.

7th row: All c.

8th row: 1 br., * 2 c., 1 br.; repeat from * to end.

9th row: 2 br., * 3 c., 3 br.; repeat from * ending last repeat with 2 br. instead of 3 br.

10th and 11th rows: 1 r., * 2 br., 1 r.; repeat from * to end.

12th to 20th rows: As 9th row back to 1st row in that reverse order.

Break off c., r., and br.

Change back to No. 10 (3¼ mm) needles.

Next row: With m., p. 1, * k. 1, p. 1; repeat from * to end.

Next row: K. 1, * p. 1, k. 1; repeat from * to end.

Rib a further 6 (8) (12) (14) rows. Cast off in rib.

THE SLEEVES (both alike): With No. 10 (3¼ mm) needles and m. cast on 32 (36) (40) (44) sts. and work 25 rows in single rib, increasing 1 st. at the end of the last row—33 (37) (41) (45) sts.

Next (inc.) row: Rib 1, * inc., rib 1; repeat from * to end—49 (55) (61) (67) sts.

Change to No. 8 (4 mm) needles and s.s. 2 rows. Continue as follows:

1st row: 1 c., *1 r., 1 c.; repeat from * to end.

2nd row: 1 r., * 1 c., 1 r.; repeat from * to end. Break off r.

3rd and 4th rows: All c.

5th and 6th rows: 1 m., * 2 c., 1 m.; repeat from * to end.

7th and 8th rows: 2 m., * 3 c., 3 m.; repeat from * ending last repeat with 2 m. instead of 3 m.

9th and 10th rows: 1 c., * 2 m., 1 c.; repeat from * to end. Break off c.

S.s. 2 rows.

Continuing in s.s., inc. 1 st. at each end of the next row and 5 following 6th (6th) (8th) (8th) rows—61 (67) (73) (79) sts.

S.s. 9 (15) (11) (17) rows.

Work 1st to 13th rows of 4-colour pattern given for back and front. Break off c., r. and br.

With m., s.s. 3 rows. Cast off.

TO MAKE UP THE SWEATER: Press work lightly on the wrong side, using a warm iron over a dry cloth. Join 14 (16) (18) (20) sts. of rib at shoulder edges. Set in sleeves between markers on back and front. Join sleeve and side seams.

Above *Chunky Polo-necked Sweater (page 40)*.   Opposite *Fair-Isle Sweater (page 41)*

V-neck Slipover

Illustrated below

MEASUREMENTS	*in centimetres (and inches, in brackets)*									
To fit chest sizes	56	(22)	61	(24)	66	(26)	71	(28)	76	(30)
All round at underarms	57.5	$(22\frac{3}{4})$	62.5	$(24\frac{3}{4})$	68	$(26\frac{3}{4})$	73.5	(29)	78.5	(31)
Side seam, including armhole ribbing	23.5	$(9\frac{1}{4})$	26	$(10\frac{1}{4})$	28.5	$(11\frac{1}{4})$	31	$(12\frac{1}{4})$	33.5	$(13\frac{1}{4})$
Length	34.5	$(13\frac{1}{2})$	38.5	$(15\frac{1}{4})$	42.5	$(16\frac{3}{4})$	46.5	$(18\frac{1}{4})$	50.5	$(19\frac{3}{4})$

MATERIALS: *Allow the following quantities in 50 g balls of Emu Superwash Double Knitting: 3 for 56 cm size; 4 for 61 cm and 66 cm sizes; 5 for 71 cm and 76 cm sizes. For any one size: a pair each of No. 9 ($3\frac{3}{4}$ mm) and No. 11 (3 mm) knitting needles.*

TENSION: *Work at a tension of 30 stitches and 41 rows to measure 10 × 10 cm, over the pattern, using No. 9 ($3\frac{3}{4}$ mm) needles, to obtain measurements given.*

ABBREVIATIONS: To be read before working: *K., knit plain; p., purl; st., stitch; tog., together; dec., decrease (by taking 2 sts. tog.); sl., slip; y.t.f., yarn to front; y.t.b., yarn to back; single rib is k. 1 and p. 1 alternately; k. or p. 2 tog.b., k. or p. 2 tog. through back of sts.*

NOTE: *The instructions are given for the 56 cm (22 inch) size. Where they vary, work figures within first brackets for 61 cm (24 inch) size; work figures within second brackets for 66 cm (26 inch) size, and so on.*

THE BACK: With No. 11 (3 mm) needles cast on 86 (94) (102) (110) (118) sts. and work 14 rows in single rib.

Change to No. 9 ($3\frac{3}{4}$ mm) needles and work the 4-row pattern as follows:

1st row (right side): All p.

2nd row: * K. 1, y.t.f., sl. 1 p.wise, y.t.b.; repeat from * to end.

3rd row: All p.

4th row: K. 1, * k. 1, y.t.f., sl. 1 p.wise, y.t.b.; repeat from * until 1 st. remains, k. 1.

Pattern a further 70 (80) (90) (100) (110) rows. **

To shape armholes: Cast off 4 (5) (6) (7) (8) sts. at beginning of next 2 rows, then dec. 1 st. each end of the following 8 rows—62 (68) (74) (80) (86) sts.

Pattern a further 40 (46) (52) (58) (64) rows.

To slope shoulders: Cast off 14 (16) (18) (20) (22) sts. at beginning of next 2 rows—34 (36) (38) (40) (42) sts.

Leave sts. on a spare needle.

THE FRONT: Work as back to **.

To shape armholes and divide for neck: Next row: Cast off 4 (5) (6) (7) (8) sts., p. to end.

Next (dividing) row: Cast off 4 (5) (6) (7) (8), pattern 38 (41) (44) (47) (50) and leave these 39 (42) (45) (48) (51) sts. on a spare needle for right half neck, pattern to end and work on these 39 (42) (45) (48) (51) sts. for left half neck.

The left half neck: Dec. 1 st. at armhole edge on next 8 rows, *at the same time,* dec. 1 st. at neck edge on the first of these rows and then on the 3 following alternate rows—27 (30) (33) (36) (39) sts.

Work 1 row, then dec. 1 st. at neck edge on next row, then on the 12 (13) (14) (15) (16) following 3rd rows—14 (16) (18) (20) (22) sts.

Pattern 2 (5) (8) (11) (14) rows—pattern 3 (6) (9) (12) (15) rows here for right half neck—then cast off for shoulder.

The right half neck: With right side of work facing, rejoin yarn to sts. on spare needle and work as left half neck, noting variation.

THE NECK RIBBING: First join right shoulder seam. With right side of work facing and using No. 11 (3 mm) needles rejoin yarn and pick up and k. 49 (53) (57) (61) (65) sts. down left half neck, pick up and k. into back of loop at centre front neck, pick up and k. 49 (53) (57) (61) (65) sts. up right half neck, then k. across 32 (36) (40) (44) (48) sts. at back neck—131 (143) (155) (167) (179) sts.

1st rib row: K. 1, * p. 1, k. 1; repeat from * to within 2 sts. of centre front st., p. 2 tog., p. centre front st., p. 2 tog.b., k. 1, * p. 1, k. 1; repeat from * to end.

2nd rib row: * P. 1, k. 1; repeat from * to within 2 sts. of centre front st., p. 2 tog., k. centre front st., p. 2 tog.b., k. 1, * p. 1, k. 1; repeat from * to end.

Repeat last 2 rows once.

Cast off in rib, decreasing as before.

THE ARMHOLE BANDS (2 alike): Join left shoulder seam, continuing across neck ribbing.

With right side facing, rejoin yarn and using No. 11 (3 mm) needles, pick up and k. 90 (100) (110) (120) (130) sts. all around armhole edge.

Work 4 rows in single rib.

Cast off in rib.

TO MAKE UP THE SLIPOVER: Press with a warm iron over a damp cloth. Join side seams, continuing across armhole bands.

Crew-neck, Patterned Jersey

Illustrated on page 46

MEASUREMENTS	in centimetres *(and inches, in brackets)*					
Chest size	56	(22)	61	(24)	66	(26)
All round at underarms	57.5	(22¾)	62.5	(24¾)	67.5	(26½)
Side seam	20.5	(8)	23.5	(9¼)	26.5	(10½)
Length	33	(13)	36.5	(14½)	40	(15¾)
Sleeve seam	22	(8¾)	25	(9¾)	28	(11)

MATERIALS: *Allow the following quantities in 25 g balls of Lister/Lee Target Motoravia Double Knitting: 4 navy, 4 white and 1 light blue for the 56 cm size; 4 navy, 4 white and 2 light blue for the 61 cm size; 5 navy, 5 white and 2 light blue for the 66 cm size. For any one size: 1 ball of the same wool in red; a pair each of No. 8 (4 mm) and No. 10 (3¼ mm) knitting needles.*

TENSION: *Work at a tension of 24 stitches and 28 rows to measure 10 × 10 cm, over the pattern, using No. 8 (4 mm) needles, to obtain the measurements given.*

ABBREVIATIONS: To be read before working: *K., knit plain; p., purl; st., stitch; tog., together; inc., increase (by working twice into same st.); dec., decrease (by working 2 sts. tog.); n., navy; w., white; r., red; lt.b., light blue; single rib is k. 1 and p. 1 alternately; s.s., stocking stitch (k. on the right side and p. on the wrong side).*

NOTE: *The instructions are given for the 56 cm (22 inch) size. Where they vary, work the figures within the first brackets for the 61 cm (24 inch) size; work the figures within the second brackets for the 66 cm (26 inch) size.*

THE BACK: With No. 10 (3¼ mm) needles and n. cast on 68 (74) (80) sts. and work 12 rows in single rib, increasing 1 st. at the end of the last row—69 (75) (81) sts.

Change to No. 8 (4 mm) needles. Joining and breaking colours as required, work in s.s. beginning with a k. row, so only the colour details are given.

1st row: 1 n., * 1 w., 1 n.; repeat from * to end.

2nd row: All w.

3rd row: 3 w., * 3 r., 3 w.; repeat from * to end.

4th row: All w.

5th row: 4 w., * 1 lt.b., 5 w.; repeat from * ending last repeat with 4 w.

6th row: 3 w., * 3 lt.b., 3 w.; repeat from * to end.

7th row: 1 lt.b., * 1 w., 5 lt.b.; repeat from * until 2 sts. remain, 1 w., 1 lt.b.

8th to 13th rows: As 6th back to 1st row in that reverse order.

14th to 18th rows: All n.

These 18 rows form the pattern and are repeated throughout.

Pattern a further 30 (38) (46) rows.

To shape armholes: Cast off 4 sts. at beginning of next 2 rows, then dec. 1 st. each end of the next 3 (4) (5) rows and then on the following alternate row—53 (57) (61) sts. **★★**

Pattern 23 (24) (25) rows.

Continued on page 46

To slope shoulders: Cast off 7 sts. at beginning of next 2 rows, then 6 (7) (8) sts. on the following 2 rows—27 (29) (31) sts.

Leave sts. on a stitch-holder.

THE FRONT: Work as back to ******.

Pattern 14 (15) (16) rows.

To divide for neck: Next row: Pattern 17 (18) (19) and leave these sts. on a spare needle for right half neck, pattern 19 (21) (23) and leave these sts. on a stitch-holder, pattern to end and work on these 17 (18) (19) sts. for left half neck.

The left half neck: Dec. 1 st. at neck edge on the next row and the 3 following alternate rows—13 (14) (15) sts.

Pattern 1 row—pattern 2 rows here when working right half neck.

To slope shoulder: Cast off 7 sts. at beginning of next row—6 (7) (8) sts.

Pattern 1 row, then cast off.

The right half neck: With right side of work facing, rejoin yarns to inner end of sts. on spare needle, then work as given for left half neck, noting variation.

THE SLEEVES: With No. 10 (3¼ mm) needles and n. cast on 30 (34) (38) sts. and work 15 rows in single rib, increasing 1 st. at the end of last row—31 (35) (39) sts.

Inc. row: Rib 3, * inc., rib 1; repeat from * to end—45 (51) (57) sts.

Change to No. 8 (4 mm) needles.

Working in pattern as given for back, pattern 48 (56) (64) rows.

To shape sleeve top: Cast off 4 sts. at beginning of next 2 rows, 1 st. at beginning of following 6 rows, then 2 sts. on the following 8 (10) (12) rows—15 (17) (19) sts.

Cast off.

THE NECK BAND: First join right shoulder seam. With right side of work facing and using No. 10 (3¼ mm) needles, rejoin n. and pick up and k. 11 sts. down left front neck, 19 (21) (23) sts. across front, pick up and k. 11 sts. up right front neck, then k. across 27 (29) (31) sts. at back neck—68 (72) (76) sts.

Single rib 8 rows. Cast off in rib.

TO MAKE UP THE SWEATER: Press with a warm iron over a dry cloth. Join left shoulder, continuing seam across neck band. Set in sleeves, then join sleeve and side seams.

Opposite *Sweater with Figured Yoke (page 48)*
Below *Crew-neck, Patterned Jersey (page 45)*

Sweater with Figured Yoke

Illustrated on page 47

MEASUREMENTS	in centimetres (and inches, in brackets)					
To fit chest sizes	66	(26)	71	(28)	76	(30)
All round at underarms	70	(27½)	75	(29½)	80	(31½)
Side seam	24	(9½)	26	(10¼)	28	(11)
Length	39	(15¼)	43.5	(17)	49	(19¼)
Sleeve seam	28.5	(11¼)	31	(12¼)	33	(13)

MATERIALS: *Allow the following quantities in 50 g balls of Wendy Double Knit: 5 main for the 66 cm size; 6 for the 71 cm and 76 cm sizes. For any one size: a small ball each of the same yarn in pink, blue and green; a pair each of No. 8 (4 mm) and No. 9 (3¾ mm) knitting needles; a set of No. 8 (4 mm) and No. 9 (3¾ mm) double pointed needles.*

TENSION: *Work at a tension of 24 stitches and 30 rows, to measure 10 × 10 cm, over the stocking stitch, using No. 8 (4 mm) needles, to obtain the measurements given below.*

ABBREVIATIONS: To be read before working: *K., knit plain; p., purl; st., stitch; tog., together; inc., increase (by working twice into the next st.); dec., decrease (by taking 2 sts. tog.); s.s., stocking st. (k. on the right side and p. on the wrong side); single rib is k. 1 and p. 1 alternately; m., main; pk., pink; gr., green; bl., blue.*

NOTE: *The instructions are given for the 66 cm (26 inch) chest size. Where they vary, work figures within first brackets for the 71 cm (28 inch) size, and so on.*

THE BACK AND FRONT ALIKE: With No. 9 (3¾ mm) needles and m. cast on 84 (90) (96) sts. and work 14 rows in single rib.

Change to No. 8 (4 mm) needles and beginning with a k. row, s.s. 58 (64) (70) rows.

To shape the armholes: Cast off 3 sts. at the beginning of each of the next 2 rows, then dec. 1 st. at each end of the next 9 (10) (11) rows—60 (64) (68) sts.

For 66 and 76 cm sizes only: P. 1 row.

For all sizes: Leave sts. on a spare needle.

THE SLEEVES (both alike): With No. 9 (3¾ mm) needles and m. cast on 40 (42) (44) sts. and work 14 rows in single rib.

Change to No. 8 (4 mm) needles and s.s. 4 rows.

Continuing in s.s., inc. 1 st. at each end of next row and 11 (10) (12) following 5th (6th) (6th) rows—64 (64) (70) sts.

S.s. 14 (15) (9) rows.

To shape the sleeve top: Cast off 3 sts. at the beginning of each of the next 2 rows, then dec. 1 st. at the beginning of each of the next 10 (10) (12) rows—48 (48) (52) sts.

THE YOKE: With right side of work facing and using 3 of the No. 8 (4 mm) double pointed needles and m., k. across the sts. of first sleeve, back, second sleeve and front—216 (224) (240) sts.

Using 4th needle, working in rounds instead of rows, with right side always facing, k. 1 (3) (5) round(s).

Work the 4-colour pattern which is worked every round k., so only the colour details are given.

It is not necessary in this design to weave in the yarns, but when changing from one colour to another, wind yarn round the one just used to avoid a gap.

1st round: 1 m., * 2 pk., 1 m., 2 pk., 3 m.; repeat from * ending last repeat with 2 m. instead of 3 m.

2nd, 3rd and 4th rounds: 2 m., * 1 pk., 1 m., 1 pk., 5 m.; repeat from * ending last repeat with 3 m. instead of 5 m.

5th and 6th rounds: * 7 bl., 1 m.; repeat from * to end.

7th and 8th rounds: 1 m., * 5 bl., 3 m.; repeat from * ending last repeat with 2 m.

9th and 10th rounds: * 2 m., 3 bl., 2 m., 1 pk.; repeat from * to end.

11th and 12th rounds: * 1 gr., 2 m, 1 gr., 2 m., 1 gr., 1 m.; repeat from * to end.

13th round: 1 m., * 5 gr., 3 m.; repeat from * ending last repeat with 2 m.

14th (dec.) round: * 1 m., 5 gr., 2 tog.m.; repeat from * to end—189 (196) (210) sts.

15th round: 2 m., * 3 gr., 4 m.; repeat from * ending last repeat with 2 m.

16th round: 3 m., * 1 pk., 6 m.; repeat from * ending last repeat with 3 m.

17th round: 2 m., * 3 pk., 4 m.; repeat from * ending last repeat with 2 m.

18th (dec.) round: * 3 m., 1 pk., 1 m., 2 tog.m.; repeat from * to end—162 (168) (180) sts.

Break off gr., pk. and bl.

With m., work 3 (5) (7) rounds.

Next (dec.) round: * K. 4, k. 2 tog.; repeat from * to end—135 (140) (150) sts.

Work 3 (5) (7) rounds.

Next (dec.) round: K. 3, k. 2 tog.; repeat from * to end—108 (112) (120) sts.

Work 3 (5) (7) rounds.

Next round: * K. 2, k. 2 tog.; repeat from * to end—81 (84) (90) sts.

Work 1 round, decreasing 1 st. at the end of this round on the 66 cm size only—80 (84) (90) sts.

Change to No. 9 (3¾ mm) double pointed needles and work 10 rounds in single rib.

P. 1 round for fold line.

Work a further 10 rounds in single rib. Cast off in rib.

TO MAKE UP THE SWEATER: Press work lightly on the wrong side, using a warm iron over a dry cloth. Join tiny underarm seams, then join sleeve and side seams. Fold neckband in half at fold line and slip st. in place on the inside.

Cardigan with Fancy Yoke

Illustrated on page 50

MEASUREMENTS	*in centimetres (and inches, in brackets)*					
To fit chest sizes	61	(24)	66–71	(26-28)	76	(30)
All round at underarms, fastened	65.5	$(25\frac{3}{4})$	73	$(28\frac{3}{4})$	80	$(31\frac{1}{2})$
Side seam	22.5	$(8\frac{3}{4})$	26.5	$(10\frac{1}{2})$	30	$(11\frac{3}{4})$
Length from centre back neck	37.5	$(14\frac{3}{4})$	42.5	$(16\frac{3}{4})$	47.5	$(18\frac{3}{4})$
Sleeve seam	27.5	$(10\frac{3}{4})$	30.5	(12)	33.5	$(13\frac{1}{4})$

MATERIALS: *Allow the following quantities in 20 g balls of Robin Reward Double Knitting: 9 red, 1 white for 61 cm size; 10 red, 1 white for 66–71 cm size; 12 red, 2 white for 76 cm size. For any one size: A pair each of No. 8 (4 mm) and No. 10 ($3\frac{1}{4}$ mm) knitting needles; 7 buttons.*

TENSION: *Work at a tension of 22 stitches and 28 rows to measure 10 × 10 cm, over the stocking stitch, using No. 8 (4 mm) needles, to obtain measurements given.*

ABBREVIATIONS: To be read before working: *K., knit plain; p., purl; st., stitch; tog., together; inc., increase (by working twice into same st.); dec., decrease (by working 2 sts. tog.); s.s., stocking stitch (k. on right side, p. on wrong side); single rib is k. 1, p. 1 alternately; r., red; w., white.*

NOTE: *The instructions are given for the 61 cm (24 inch) size. Where they vary, work figures within first brackets for 66–71 cm (26–28 inch) size; work figures within second brackets for 76 cm (30 inch) size.*

THE BACK: With No. 10 ($3\frac{1}{4}$ mm) needles and r. cast on 72 (80) (88) sts. and work 16 rows in single rib, increasing 1 st. at the end of the last of these rows—73 (81) (89) sts.

** Change to No. 8 (4 mm) needles and, beginning with a k. row, s.s. 2 rows.

Joining and breaking colours as required throughout pattern, work the 8-row pattern as follows, which is worked in s.s., beginning with a k. row, so only the colour details are given.

1st row: 1 w., * 3 r., 1 w.; repeat from * to end.

2nd row: 1 r., * 1 w., 1 r.; repeat from * to end.

3rd row: 2 r., * 1 w., 3 r.; repeat from * until 3 sts. remain, 1 w., 2 r.

4th and 5th rows: All r.

6th to 8th rows: As 3rd back to 1st rows, in that reverse order. **

S.s. 40 (50) (60) rows.

To shape the armholes: Cast off 3 (4) (5) sts. at beginning of next 2 rows, then dec. 1 st. each end of next row, then on the 5 (7) (9) following alternate rows—55 (57) (59) sts.

Break yarn and leave sts. on a spare needle.

THE LEFT FRONT: With No. 10 ($3\frac{1}{4}$ mm) needles and r., cast on 42 (46) (50) sts. and, beginning each row with p. 1, work 15 rows in single rib.

Next row: Rib 9 and leave these sts. on a safety-pin for button band, rib to end—33 (37) (41) sts.

Work as back from ** to **.

S.s. 40 (50) (60) rows.

*** **To shape the armhole:** Cast off 3 (4) (5) sts. at beginning of next row, work 1 row—omit this row when working right front—then dec. 1 st. at armhole edge on next row, then on the 5 (7) (9) following alternate rows—24 (25) (26) sts.

Leave sts. on a spare needle.

THE RIGHT FRONT: With No. 10 ($3\frac{1}{4}$ mm) needles and r., cast on 42 (46) (50) sts. and, beginning each row with k. 1, work 4 rows in single rib.

1st (buttonhole) row: Rib 3, cast off 3, rib to end.

2nd (buttonhole) row: Rib to end, casting on 3 sts. over those cast off on previous row.

Rib 9 rows.

Next row: Rib 33 (37) (41) sts., turn and leave remaining 9 sts. on a safety-pin for buttonhole band.

Work as back from ** to **.

S.s. 41 (51) (61) rows.

Work as left front from ***, noting variation.

THE SLEEVES (both alike): With No. 10 ($3\frac{1}{4}$ mm) needles and r., cast on 36 (38) (40) sts. and work 15 rows in single rib.

Inc. row: Rib 6 (4) (4), inc., * rib 5 (4) (3), inc.; repeat from * 3 (5) (7) times, rib 5 (3) (3)—41 (45) (49) sts.

Work as back from ** to **.

Inc. 1 st. each end of next row, then on the 6 (7) (8) following 8th rows—55 (61) (67) sts.

S.s. 5 rows.

To shape the sleeve top: Work as armhole shaping on back when 37 sts. will remain.

Leave sts. on a spare needle.

THE YOKE: With wrong side of work facing and using No. 8 (4 mm) needles, rejoin r. and p. across left front, first sleeve, back, second sleeve, then right front—177 (181) (185) sts.

Work the 28-row pattern as follows:

1st (dec.) row: With r., k. 10 (7) (9), * k. 2 tog., k. 20 (13) (9); repeat from * until 13 (9) (11) sts. remain, k. 2 tog., k. 11 (7) (9)—169 sts.

2nd to 4th rows: As 6th to 8th rows of back.

5th row: All r.

6th (dec.) row: With r., p. 3, * p. 2 tog., p. 5; repeat from * until 5 sts. remain, p. 2 tog., p. 3—145 sts.

7th row: 1 r., * 1 w., 4 r., 1 w., 4 r., 1 w., 1 r.; repeat from * to end.

8th row: 1 w., * 5 r., 1 w.; repeat from * to end.

9th row: 3 r., * 1 w., 2 r., 1 w., 2 r., 1 w., 5 r.; repeat from * until 10 sts. remain, 1 w., 2 r., 1 w., 2 r., 1 w., 3 r.

10th row: 4 r., * 1 w., 1 r., 1 w., 1 r., 1 w., 7 r.; repeat from * ending last repeat with 4 r.

Continued on page 52

Above *Cardigan with Fancy Yoke (page 49).*   Opposite *Smocked Dress (page 52)*

11th row: 5 r., * 1 w., 1 r., 1 w., 9 r.; repeat from * ending last repeat with 5 r.

12th row: 2 r., * 4 w., 1 r., 4 w., 3 r.; repeat from * ending last repeat with 2 r.

13th to 17th rows: As 11th back to 7th rows in that reverse order.

18th row: With r., all p.

19th (dec.) row: With r., k. 4, * k. 2 tog., k. 3; repeat from * until 1 st. remains, k. 1—117 sts.

20th to 23rd rows: As 1st to 4th rows on back.

24th (dec.) row: With r., p. 2, * p. 2 tog., p. 3; repeat from * to end—94 sts.

25th to 27th rows: With r., s.s. 3 rows.

28th (dec.) row. * With r., p. 3 (4) (6), p. 2 tog.; repeat from * until 4 (4) (6) sts. remain, p. 2, p. 2 tog. (p. 4) (p. 6)—75 (79) (83) sts.

Break yarn and leave sts. on a spare needle.

THE BUTTONHOLE BAND: With wrong side of work facing, and using No. 10 ($3\frac{1}{4}$ mm) needles, rejoin r. to sts. on safety-pin and rib 9 (11) (13) rows.

Next row: Rib 3, cast off 3, rib to end.

Next row: Rib to end, casting on 3 sts. over those cast off on previous row.

Rib 18 (20) (22) rows.

Repeat the last 20 (22) (24) rows, 3 times more, then the 2 buttonhole rows again.

Rib 16 (18) (20) rows.

Break yarn and leave sts. on a safety-pin.

THE BUTTON BAND: With right side of work facing and using No. 10 ($3\frac{1}{4}$ mm) needles, rejoin r. to sts. on safety-pin and rib 106 (118) (130) rows.

Break yarn and leave sts. on a safety-pin.

THE NECK RIBBING: With right side of work facing and using No. 10 ($3\frac{1}{4}$ mm) needles, rejoin r. and rib across 9 sts. of buttonhole band, 75 (79) (83) sts. across yoke, then 9 sts. of button band—93 (97) (101) sts.

Rib 1 (1) (3) row(s), make a buttonhole on the next 2 rows, then rib a further 4 (4) (2) rows.

Cast off in rib.

TO MAKE UP THE CARDIGAN: Press with a warm iron over a dry cloth. Join underarm seams, then join sleeve and side seams. Sew front bands into position. Add buttons.

Smocked Dress

Illustrated on page 51

MEASUREMENTS						
To fit chest sizes	in centimetres (and inches, in brackets)					
	56	(22)	61	(24)	66	(26)
Length from picot edge to waist (slot row)	35	($13\frac{3}{4}$)	37	($14\frac{1}{2}$)	40	($15\frac{3}{4}$)
Length to back neck	57.5	($22\frac{1}{2}$)	60	($23\frac{1}{2}$)	64	($25\frac{1}{4}$)
Sleeve seam (excluding cuff)	24.5	($9\frac{3}{4}$)	28.5	($11\frac{1}{4}$)	32.5	($12\frac{3}{4}$)

MATERIALS: *Allow the following quantities in 40 g balls of Sirdar Wash 'n' Wear Double Crepe: 6 balls main for the 56 cm size; 7 balls main for the 61 cm size; 8 balls main for the 66 cm size. For any one size: one 20 g ball of Sirdar Wash 'n' Wear 4-ply in contrasting colour, small amounts in each of 2 contrasting colours for smocking; a pair each of No. 8 (4 mm) and No. 9 ($3\frac{3}{4}$ mm) knitting needles; a 3.00 crochet hook; 3 buttons; $1\frac{1}{2}$ metres of 1 cm ($\frac{1}{2}$ inch) wide velvet ribbon.*

TENSION: *Work at a tension of 23 stitches and 31 rows to measure 10 × 10 cm, over the stocking stitch, to obtain the measurements given.*

ABBREVIATIONS: To be read before working: *K., knit plain; p., purl; st., stitch; tog., together; dec., decrease (by working 2 sts. tog.); y.fwd., yarn forward to make a st.; s.s., stocking st. (k. on the right side and p. on the wrong side); k. or p. 1b., k. or p. 1 through back of sts.; inc., increase (by working twice into next st.); nil, meaning nothing is worked here for this size; m., main; ch., chain; d.c., double crochet; lp(s)., loop(s); sl., slip.*

NOTE: *The instructions are given for the 56 cm (22 inch) size. Where they vary, work the figures within the first brackets for the 61 cm (24 inch) size; work the figures within the second brackets for the 66 cm (26 inch) size.*

THE BACK: With No. 9 ($3\frac{3}{4}$ mm) needles and m., cast on 119 (129) (139) sts. and, beginning with a k. row, s.s. 4 rows.

Picot row: K. 1, * y.fwd., k. 2 tog.; repeat from * to end.

Beginning with a p. row, s.s. 50 rows.

Change to No. 8 (4 mm) needles and s.s. 16 rows.

Keeping continuity of s.s., dec. 1 st. at each end of the next and 8 (9) (10) following 10th rows—101 (109) (117) sts.

S.s. 4 (nil) (nil) rows.

Dec. row: P. nil (3) (nil), * p. 5 (5) (6), p. 2 tog.; repeat from * until 3 (8) (5) sts. remain, p. to end—87 (95) (103) sts.

Next row (slot row): K. to end, winding yarn 3 times round needle for each st.

Next row: P. each st., allowing extra loops to fall.

Change to No. 9 ($3\frac{3}{4}$ mm) needles and work the 6-row pattern as follows:

1st row: P. 1, * k. 1b., p. 3; repeat from * until 2 sts. remain, k. 1b., p. 1.

2nd row: K. 1, * p. 1b., k. 3; repeat from * until 2 sts. remain, p. 1b, k. 1.

3rd and 4th rows: As 1st and 2nd rows.

5th row: All p.

6th row: As 2nd row.

Pattern a further 12 (16) (20) rows.

To shape the armholes: Next row: Keeping continuity of the pattern, cast off 4 sts. at the beginning of the next 2 rows, then dec. 1 st. at each end of the following 4 rows—71 (79) (87) sts.

Pattern 3 (5) (7) rows. ***

To divide for back opening: Next row: Pattern 35 (39) (43), leave these sts. on a spare needle for left half back, work 2 tog., pattern to end and work on these 35 (39) (43) sts. for right half back.

The right half back: Pattern 28 rows – pattern 29 rows here when working left half back.

To slope the shoulder: Cast off 6 (7) (8) sts. at the beginning of the next and following alternate row, then 7 (8) (9) sts. on the next alternate row— 16 (17) (18) sts.

Work 1 row.

Cast off.

The left half back: With right side of work facing, rejoin yarn to the 35 (39) (43) sts. left on spare needle and work as given for right half back, noting variation.

THE FRONT: Work as given for back to ***.

Pattern 18 rows.

To divide for neck: Next row: Pattern 28 (31) (34), leave these sts. on a spare needle for right half front, cast off the next 15 (17) (19) sts., pattern to end and work on the last set of 28 (31) (34) sts. for left half front.

The left half front: Dec. 1 st. at neck edge on the next 9 rows— 19 (22) (25) sts.

Pattern 1 row—pattern 2 rows here when working right half front.

To slope the shoulder: Cast off 6 (7) (8) sts. at the beginning of the next and following alternate row— 7 (8) (9) sts.

Work 1 row.

Cast off.

The right half front: With right side of work facing, rejoin yarn to the 28 (31) (34) sts. left on spare needle and work as given for left half front, noting variation.

THE SLEEVES (both alike): With No. 8 (4 mm) needles and m., cast on 37 (39) (41) sts. and, beginning with a k. row, s.s. 6 rows.

Keeping continuity of s.s., inc. 1 st. at each end of the next and 7 (8) (9) following 8th rows—53 (57) (61) sts.

S.s. 13 (17) (21) rows.

To shape the sleeve top: Cast off 4 sts. at the beginning of the next 2 rows, dec. 1 st. at the beginning of the following 11 (13) (15) rows—34 (36) (38) sts.

Work 1 row.

Dec. 1 st. at each end of the next 10 rows—14 (16) (18) sts.

Cast off.

THE CUFFS (2 alike): With No. 3.00 crochet hook and contrasting 4-ply yarn, make 52 (56) (60) ch.

1st row: 1 d.c. into 8th ch. from hook, * 4 ch., miss 3 ch., 1 d.c. into next ch. *; repeat from * to * 10 (11) (12) times more, turn—12 (13) (14) lps.

2nd row: * 4 ch., 1 d.c. into centre of next lp. *; repeat from * to * 11 (12) (13) times more, turn.

Repeat the 2nd row 5 (6) (7) times more.

Next row: * 2 d.c., 3 ch., 2 d.c. into next lp. *; repeat from * to * 11 (12) (13) times more and fasten off.

THE COLLAR (2 alike): With No. 3.00 crochet hook and contrasting 4-ply yarn, make 56 (60) (64) ch.

First mark 4th ch. from hook with a coloured thread to indicate commencement of collar edging.

1st row: 1 d.c. into 8th ch. from hook, * 4 ch., miss 3 ch., 1 d.c. into next ch. *; repeat from * to * 11 (12) (13) times more, turn—13 (14) (15) lps.

2nd row: * 4 ch., 1 d.c. into centre of next lp. *; repeat from * to * 12 (13) (14) times more, turn.

Repeat the 2nd row, twice more.

5th row: Sl. st. into centre of first lp., * 4 ch., 1 d.c. into next lp. *; repeat from * to * 11 (12) (13) times more, turn.

6th row: Sl. st. into centre of first lp., * 4 ch., 1 d.c. into next lp. *; repeat from * to * 10 (11) (12) times more, turn.

7th row: Sl. st. into centre of first lp., * 4 ch., 1 d.c. into next lp. *; repeat from * to * 9 (10) (11) times more, turn.

Break off yarn and rejoin yarn to side edge of collar to ch. marked with a coloured thread, working around shaped edge, across last row to second shaped edge for collar edging, continue as follows:

Collar edging: Next row: * 4 ch., miss first lp., 1 d.c. into next lp., *; repeat from * to * twice more, ** 4 ch., 1 d.c. into centre of next lp.; repeat from ** 8 (9) (10) times more; repeat from * to * twice, turn.

Next row: * 2 d.c., 3 ch., 2 d.c. all into next lp. *; repeat from * to * 13 (14) (15) times more, fasten off.

THE BACK OPENING: With No. 3.00 crochet hook and m., work 18 d.c. evenly down left side back, then 1 d.c. into centre and finally 18 d.c. evenly up right side back— 37 d.c.

Next row: * 1 d.c. into each of the next 3 d.c., 3 ch., miss 2 d.c., 1 d.c. into next d.c. *; repeat from * to * twice, 1 d.c. into each d.c. to end and fasten off.

TO MAKE UP THE DRESS: Press on the wrong side with a cool iron over a dry cloth. Beginning at waist and using contrasting yarns, oversew the k. sts. tog. at alternate positions marked by the p. sts. on the 5th pattern row, for smocking effect. Join shoulder seams, set in sleeves. Join side and sleeve seams. Turn up hem at picot edge and sew to wrong side. Join side edges of cuffs, then sew cuffs to cast on edge of sleeves. Sew collar halves around neck edge. Thread ribbon through slot at waist to tie at centre front, working over and under 4 strands of slot row.

Family Knitting

Fancy Rib Sweater

Illustrated opposite

MEASUREMENTS	*in centimetres (and inches, in brackets)*									
To fit sizes	61	(24)	66	(26)	71	(28)	76	(30)	81	(32)
All round at underarms	66	(26)	71	(28)	76	(30)	81	(32)	86	(34)
Side seam	21.5	(8½)	24	(9½)	26.5	(10½)	29	(11½)	32.5	(12¾)
Length	37.5	(14¾)	41.5	(16¼)	45	(17¾)	49	(19¼)	54	(21¼)
Sleeve seam	22	(8¾)	26	(10¼)	30.5	(12)	35	(13¾)	41	(16)
To fit sizes	86	(34)	91	(36)	97	(38)	102	(40)	107	(42)
All round at underarms	91	(36)	96	(37¾)	101	(39¾)	106	(41¾)	111	(43¾)
Side seam	32.5	(12¾)	32.5	(12¾)	34	(13½)	34	(13½)	34	(13½)
Length	55	(21½)	56.5	(22¼)	59	(23¼)	60	(23½)	61.5	(24¼)
Sleeve seam	41	(16)	41	(16)	44.5	(17½)	44.5	(17½)	44.5	(17½)

MATERIALS: *Allow the following quantities in 50 g balls of Emu Mix 'n' Match Double Knitting: Crew neck version: 4 for 61 cm and 66 cm sizes; 5 for 71 cm size; 6 for 76 cm size; 7 for 81 cm size; 8 for 86 cm size; 9 for 91 cm and 97 cm sizes; 10 for 102 cm and 107 cm sizes. Polo neck version: One extra ball of yarn; for all sizes: a pair each of No. 8 (4 mm) and No. 10 (3¼ mm) knitting needles.*

TENSION: *Work at a tension of 24 stitches and 32 rows to measure 10 × 10 cm, over the pattern with ribs slightly stretched, using No. 8 (4 mm) needles, to obtain measurements given.*

ABBREVIATIONS: To be read before working: *K., knit plain; p., purl; st., stitch; tog., together; sl., slip; p.s.s.o., pass sl. st. over; s.k.p.o., (sl. 1, k. 1, p.s.s.o.); inc., increase (by working twice into next st.); dec., decrease (by taking 2 sts. tog.); single rib is k. 1 and p. 1 alternately.*

NOTE: *The instructions are given for the 61 cm (24 inch) size. Where they vary, work figures within first brackets for the 66 cm (26 inch) size; work figures within second brackets for the 71 cm (28 inch) size, and so on.*

THE BACK: With No. 10 (3¼ mm) needles cast on 78 (84) (90) (96) (102) (108) (114) (120) (126) (132) sts. and work 12 rows in single rib, increasing 1 st. at end of the last row—79 (85) (91) (97) (103) (109) (115) (121) (127) (133) sts.

Change to No. 8 (4 mm) needles.

1st pattern row (right side): K. 1, * p. 1, k. 1; repeat from * to end.

2nd row: P. 2, k. 3, * p. 3, k. 3; repeat from * until 2 sts. remain, p. 2.

These 2 rows form the pattern. Pattern a further 54 (62) (70) (78) (90) (90) (90) (94) (94) (94) rows.

To shape raglan armholes: 1st and 2nd rows: Cast off 1 st., pattern to end.

3rd row: K. 2, s.k.p.o., pattern until 4 sts. remain, k. 2 tog., k. 2.

4th row: K. 1, p. 2, pattern until 3 sts. remain, p. 2, k. 1.

Repeat 3rd and 4th rows, 23 (25) (27) (29) (31) (33) (35) (37) (39) (41) times more—29 (31) (33) (35) (37) (39) (41) (43) (45) (47) sts.

Next row: K. 2, sl. l, k. 2 tog., p.s.s.o., pattern until 5 sts. remain, k. 3 tog., k. 2.

Next row: K. 1, p. 2, pattern until 3 sts. remain, p. 2, k. 1.

Break yarn and leave remaining 25 (27) (29) (31) (33) (35) (37) (39) (41) (43) sts. on a spare needle.

THE FRONT: Work as given for back until the 4th armhole shaping row has been completed.

Repeat the 3rd and 4th rows, 17 (19) (20) (22) (23) (25) (26) (28) (29) (31) times more, then 3rd row once again—39 (41) (45) (47) (51) (53) (57) (59) (63) (65) sts.

To divide for neck: Next row: Pattern 13 (14) (16) (16) (18) (18) (20) (21) (23) (24) and leave these sts. on a spare needle for right front neck, pattern 13 (13) (13) (15) (15) (17) (17) (17) (17) (17) and leave these sts. on a stitch-holder, pattern to end and work on these last 13 (14) (16) (16) (18) (18) (20) (21) (23) (24) sts. for left front neck.

The left front neck: Dec. 1 st. at armhole edge as before on next row and the 4 (4) (5) (5) (6) (6) (7) (7) (8) (8) following alternate rows, *at the same time*, dec. 1 st. at neck edge on the first 4 (5) (6) (6) (7) (7) (8) (9) (10) (11) of these rows, then the following alternate row.

Work 1 row, then take remaining 3 sts. tog. and fasten off.

The right front neck: With right side of work facing, rejoin yarn to inner end of sts. on spare needle and work as given for left front neck to end.

THE SLEEVES (2 alike): With No. 10 (3¼ mm) needles cast on 42 (42) (42) (48) (48) (48) (54) (54) (54) (60) sts. and work 16 (16) (16) (16) (20) (20) (20) (24) (24) (24) rows in single rib increasing 1 st. at end of last row—43 (43) (43) (49) (49) (49) (55) (55) (55) (61) sts.

Change to No. 8 (4 mm) needles and work 4 rows in pattern as given on back.

Keeping continuity of the pattern, and working extra sts. into pattern as they occur, inc. 1 st. at each end of next row and the 3 (5) (7) (6) (9) (11) (10) (12) (14) (13)

following 10th (8th) (8th) (12th) (10th) (8th) (8th)
(6th) (6th) rows—51 (55) (59) (63) (69) (73) (77) (81) (85)
(89) sts.

Pattern 19 (23) (21) (19) (15) (17) (25) (17) (29) (35)
rows.

To shape the raglan sleeve top: 1st and 2nd rows:
Cast off 1 st., pattern to end.

3rd row: K. 3, pattern until 3 sts. remain, k. 3.

4th row: K. 1, p. 2, pattern until 3 sts. remain, p. 2, k. 1.

5th row: K. 2, s.k.p.o., pattern until 4 sts. remain, k. 2
tog., k. 2.

6th row: As 4th row.

Repeat 3rd to 6th rows, twice (twice) (twice) (twice)
(twice) (twice) (twice) (3 times) (3 times) (3 times), then
the 5th and 6th rows a further 18 (20) (22) (24) (27) (29)
(31) (31) (33) (35) times.

For the 61 cm, 66 cm, 71 cm, and 76 cm sizes only:
Next row: K. 2, sl. 1, k. 2 tog., p.s.s.o., k. 2.

Next row: K. 1, p. 3, k. 1.

For all sizes: Break yarn and leave remaining 5 (5) (5)
(5) (7) (7) (7) (9) (9) (9) sts. on a safety pin.

THE NECK RIBBING: First join right raglan seams,
then left sleeve to front only.

With right side facing, rejoin yarn and using No. 10 (3¼
mm) needles, k. across sts. at top of left sleeve, pick up and
k. 11 (12) (13) (14) (15) (16) (17) (18) (19) (20) sts. from

row ends of left front neck, k. across front neck sts., pick
up and k. 11 (12) (13) (14) (15) (16) (17) (18) (19) (20) sts.
from row ends of right front neck, k. across sts. at top of
right sleeve, and finally k. across sts. at back neck—70 (74)
(78) (84) (92) (98) (102) (110) (114) (118) sts.

For crew-neck only: Work 5 (5) (5) (5) (7) (7) (7) (9)
(9) (9) rows in single rib.

P. 1 row for fold line, then rib a further 5 (5) (5) (5) (7)
(7) (7) (9) (9) (9) rows.

Cast off loosely in rib.

For polo collar only: Work 10 (10) (10) (10) (14) (14)
(14) (18) (18) (18) rows in single rib.

Change to No. 8 (4 mm) needles and rib a further 13 (13)
(13) (13) (17) (17) (17) (23) (23) (23) rows.

Cast off loosely in rib.

TO MAKE UP THE SWEATER: Do not press. Join
remaining raglan seam continuing across neck ribbing
with a flat seam. Join side and sleeve seams. Fold crew-
neck in half at fold line and catch to inside, or fold polo in
half to right side.

Below *Fancy Rib Sweaters for all the family*

Short-sleeve Summer Top

Illustrated on page 58

MEASUREMENTS	*in centimetres (and inches, in brackets)*				
To fit sizes	61–66 (24–26)	71 (28)	76 (30)	81 (32)	86 (34)
All round at underarms	70 (27½)	75 (29½)	80 (31½)	85 (33½)	91 (36)
Side seam	31 (12¼)	32 (12½)	33 (13)	33.5 (13¼)	40 (15¾)
Length	43.5 (17)	46 (18)	48 (19)	49.5 (19½)	58 (22¾)
Sleeve seam	4.5 (1¾)	6 (2¼)	6 (2¼)	7.5 (3)	9.5 (3¾)
To fit sizes	91 (36)	97 (38)	102 (40)	107 (42)	112 (44)
All round at underarms	97 (38)	101.5 (39¾)	106.5 (41¾)	113.5 (44¾)	118.5 (46½)
Side seam	40 (15¾)	40 (15¾)	42.5 (16¾)	42.5 (16¾)	42.5 (16¾)
Length	59 (23¼)	60 (24)	64 (25¼)	65 (25½)	66.5 (26¼)
Sleeve seam	9.5 (3¾)	9.5 (3¾)	11.5 (4½)	11.5 (4½)	11.5 (4½)

MATERIALS: *Allow the following quantities in 50 g balls of Sirdar The Terry Look in main shade: For plain version: 3 for the 61–66 cm and 71 cm sizes; 4 for the 76 cm, 81 cm and 86 cm sizes; 5 for the 91 cm and 97 cm sizes; 6 for the 102 cm size; 7 for the 107 and 112 cm sizes. For the striped version: 2 main shade, 1 first contrast, 1 second contrast for the 61–66 cm and 71 cm sizes; 3 main shade, 1 first contrast, 1 second contrast for the 76 cm and 81 cm sizes; 3 main shade, 1 first contrast, 2 second contrast for the 86 cm size; 4 main shade, 1 first contrast, 2 second contrast for the 91 cm, 97 cm and 102 cm sizes; 5 main shade, 1 first contrast, 2 second contrast for the 107 cm and 112 cm sizes. For any one size: a pair each of No. 10 (3¼ mm) and No. 12 (2¾ mm) knitting needles; a medium-sized crochet hook, and 2 (3) (3) (4) buttons for the 61–66 cm, 71 cm, 76 cm and 81 cm crew neck sizes only; 4 buttons for open neck version.*

TENSION: *Work at a tension of 24 stitches and 36 rows to measure 10 × 10 cm over the stocking stitch, using No. 10 (3¼ mm) needles to obtain the measurements given.*

ABBREVIATIONS: To be read before working: *K., knit plain; p., purl; st., stitch; tog., together; inc., increase (by working twice into same st.); dec., decrease (by working 2 sts. tog.); a., main shade; b., first contrast; c., second contrast; s.s., stocking st. (k. on right side and p. on wrong side).*

NOTE: *The instructions are given for the 61–66 cm (24–26 inch) size. Where they vary, work figures within the first brackets for 71 cm (28 inch) size; work figures within the second brackets for 76 cm (30 inch) size, and so on.*

STRIPED VERSION: BACK: With No. 12 (2¾ mm) needles and a., cast on 84 (90) (96) (102) (110) (116) (122) (128) (136) (142) sts. and k. 11 (11) (11) (13) (13) (13) (13) (15) (15) (15) rows.
Change to No. 10 (3¼ mm) needles and work as follows:
1st row: All k.
2nd row: K. 5 (5) (5) (6) (6) (6) (7) (7) (7) (7), p. until 5 (5) (5) (6) (6) (6) (7) (7) (7) (7) sts. remain, k. to end.
Repeat these 2 rows 6 (6) (6) (4) (4) (4) (4) (8) (8) (8) times more.
Continue in s.s. across all sts.
For the 86 cm, 91 cm and 97 cm sizes only: Beginning with a k. row, s.s. 8 rows.

For all sizes: Continue in s.s. and, beginning with a k. row, work 4 rows b., 6 rows c., 2 rows a., 6 rows c. K. 4 rows b., 18 rows a. These 40 rows form the strip pattern.
Pattern a further 50 (54) (58) (62) (78) (78) (78) (84) (84) (84) rows. ★★
To shape the armholes: Keeping continuity of the pattern, cast off 4 (4) (4) (4) (5) (5) (5) (5) (6) (6) sts. at the beginning of the next 2 rows, then dec. 1 st. at each end of the next row and the 5 (6) (7) (8) (9) (10) (11) (11) (12) (13) following alternate rows—64 (68) (72) (76) (80) (84) (88) (94) (98) (102) sts. ★★★
Pattern 27 (29) (31) (33) (37) (39) (41) (47) (49) (51) rows.
To slope the shoulders: Cast off 6 (7) (7) (8) (8) (8) (9) (10) (10) (11) sts. at the beginning of each of the next 4 rows, then 7 (6) (7) (7) (8) (9) (8) (9) (10) (9) sts. at the beginning of the next 2 rows—26 (28) (30) (30) (32) (34) (36) (36) (38) (40) sts.
Leave these sts. on a spare needle.

THE FRONT (crew neck): Work as given for back to ★★★.
Pattern a further 8 (10) (12) (14) (16) (14) (16) (20) (22) (24) rows.
To divide for neck: Next row: Pattern 26 (27) (29) (30) (32) (33) (35) (37) (39) (41) and leave these sts. on a spare needle for right half neck, pattern 12 (14) (14) (16) (16) (18) (18) (20) (20) (20) and leave these sts. on a stitch-holder for neckband, pattern to end and work on these 26 (27) (29) (30) (32) (33) (35) (37) (39) (41) sts. for left half neck.
The left half neck: Dec. 1 st. at neck edge on the next row and the 6 (6) (7) (6) (7) (7) (8) (7) (8) (9) following alternate rows—19 (20) (21) (23) (24) (25) (26) (29) (30) (31) sts.
Pattern 5 (5) (3) (5) (5) (9) (7) (11) (9) (7) rows—pattern 6 (6) (4) (6) (6) (10) (8) (12) (10) (8) rows here when working right half neck.
To slope the shoulder: Cast off 6 (7) (7) (8) (8) (8) (9) (10) (10) (11) sts. at the beginning of the next row and the following alternate row—7 (6) (7) (7) (8) (9) (8) (9) (10) (9) sts.
Work 1 row.
Cast off.
The right half neck: With right side of work facing,

rejoin yarn to the 26 (27) (29) (30) (32) (33) (35) (37) (39) (41) sts. left on spare needle and work as given for left half neck, noting variations.

THE FRONT (open neck version): Work exactly as given for back until ****** has been reached.

To shape the armholes and divide for front opening: Next row: Cast off 4 (4) (4) (4) (5) (5) (5) (5) (6) (6) sts., pattern to end.

Next row: Cast off 4 (4) (4) (4) (5) (5) (5) (5) (6) (6) sts., pattern 35 (38) (41) (44) (46) (49) (52) (55) (57) (60) and leave these 36 (39) (42) (45) (47) (50) (53) (56) (58) (61) sts. on a spare needle for right half front, cast off 4 (4) (4) (4) (6) (6) (6) (6) (8) (8) sts., pattern to end and work on these 36 (39) (42) (45) (47) (50) (53) (56) (58) (61) sts. for left half front.

The left half front: Dec. 1 st. at armhole edge on the next row and the 5 (6) (7) (8) (9) (10) (11) (11) (12) (13) following alternate rows—30 (32) (34) (36) (37) (39) (41) (44) (45) (47) sts.

To work neck: Pattern 4 (6) (4) (6) (8) (6) (8) (12) (14) (16) rows—pattern 3 (5) (3) (5) (7) (5) (7) (11) (13) (15) rows here when working right half front.

Next row: Cast off 4 (5) (5) (6) (6) (6) (6) (6) (6) (6) sts., pattern to end.

Work 1 row here when working right half front.

Dec. 1 st. at neck edge on the next row and the 6 (6) (7) (6) (6) (7) (8) (8) (8) (9) following alternate rows—19 (20) (21) (23) (24) (25) (26) (29) (30) (31) sts.

Pattern 9 (9) (11) (13) (15) (17) (15) (17) (17) (15) rows—pattern 10 (10) (12) (14) (16) (18) (16) (18) (18) (16) rows here when working right half front.

To slope the shoulder: Cast off 6 (7) (7) (8) (8) (8) (9) (10) (10) (11) sts. at the beginning of the next row and the following alternate row—7 (6) (7) (7) (8) (9) (8) (9) (10) (9) sts.

Work 1 row. Cast off.

The right half front: With right side of work facing, rejoin yarn to the 36 (39) (42) (45) (47) (50) (53) (56) (58) (61) sts. left on spare needle and work as given for left half front, noting variations.

THE SLEEVES (both alike): With No. 12 (2¾ mm) needles and a., cast on 52 (56) (58) (62) (64) (68) (70) (74) (78) (82) sts. and k. 10 (10) (10) (12) (12) (12) (12) (14) (14) (14) rows.

Next (inc.) row: K. 7 (9) (10) (5) (6) (8) (3) (5) (7) (5), ***** inc., K. 11 (11) (11) (9) (9) (9) (8) (8) (8) (9); repeat from ***** 2 (2) (2) (4) (4) (4) (6) (6) (6) (6) times, inc., k. to end—56 (60) (62) (68) (70) (74) (78) (82) (86) (90) sts.

Change to No. 10 (3¼ mm) needles and working in s.s. beginning with a k. row, taking extra sts. into s.s. as they occur, inc. 1 st. at each end of the next row and the 1 (1) (2) (1) (2) (3) (3) (4) (5) (6) following 4th row(s)—60 (64) (68) (72) (76) (82) (86) (92) (98) (104) sts.

S.s. a further 5 (9) (5) (13) (17) (13) (13) (13) (9) (5) rows.

To shape the sleeve top: Cast off 4 (4) (4) (4) (5) (5) (5) (5) (6) (6) sts. at the beginning of the next 2 rows, then dec. 1 st. at each end of the next row and the 10 (12) (12) (14) (14) (16) (18) (20) (21) (23) following alternate rows—30 (30) (34) (34) (36) (38) (38) (40) (42) (44) sts.

Work 1 row.

Cast off 3 sts. at the beginning of each of the next 4 (4) (6) (6) (8) (8) (8) (8) (8) (8) rows—18 (18) (16) (16) (12) (14) (14) (16) (18) (20) sts. Cast off.

THE NECKBAND (crew neck): First join right shoulder seam. With right side of work facing, using No. 12 (2¾

mm) needles and a., pick up and k. 19 (19) (19) (19) (21) (24) (24) (26) (26) (26) sts. down left side of neck, k. across the 12 (14) (14) (16) (18) (18) (20) (20) (20) (20) sts. at centre front, pick up and k. 19 (19) (19) (19) (21) (24) (24) (26) (26) (26) sts. up right side of neck and finally k. across the 26 (28) (30) (30) (32) (34) (36) (36) (38) (40) sts. at back neck—76 (80) (82) (84) (90) (100) (102) (108) (110) (112) sts.

K. 10 (10) (10) (12) (12) (12) (14) (14) (14) (14) rows. Cast off k.wise.

THE NECKBAND (open neck): First join shoulder seams.

With right side facing, rejoin a. and using No. 12 (2¾ mm) needles and a., pick up and k. 22 (23) (27) (28) (33) (34) (34) (36) (36) (36) sts. from row ends of right front neck shaping, k. across back neck sts., then pick up and k. 22 (23) (27) (28) (33) (34) (34) (36) (36) (36) sts. from row ends of left front neck shaping—70 (74) (84) (86) (94) (102) (104) (108) (110) (112) sts.

K. 10 (10) (10) (12) (12) (12) (14) (14) (14) (14) rows. Cast off k.wise.

THE BUTTONHOLE BORDER: With No. 12 (2¾ mm) needles and a, cast on 5 (5) (5) (5) (6) (6) (6) (6) (8) (8) sts. and k. 4 (2) (2) (10) (10) (10) (12) (12) (14) (16) rows.

1st buttonhole row: K. 2 (2) (2) (2) (3) (3) (3) (3) (3) (3), cast off 1 (1) (1) (1) (1) (1) (1) (1) (2) (2), k. to end.

2nd buttonhole row: K. to end, casting on 1 (1) (1) (1) (1) (1) (1) (1) (2) (2) st(s). over those cast off in previous row.

K. 10 (12) (12) (12) (14) (14) (14) (16) (16) (16) rows. Repeat the last 12 (14) (14) (14) (16) (16) (16) (18) (18) (18) rows, twice, then the 2 buttonhole rows again.

K. 3 (3) (3) (3) (3) (3) (5) (5) (5) (5) rows. Cast off k. wise.

THE BUTTON BORDER: Work as given for buttonhole border omitting buttonholes.

TO MAKE UP THE T-SHIRT (crew neck): Do not press. Join left shoulder seam leaving the last 7 (8) (9) (10) cm—2¾ (3¼) (3½) (4) inches including neckband open on the 61-66 cm, 71 cm, 76 and 81 cm sizes only. Set in sleeves. Join sleeve and side seams leaving the garter st. section of side seams free. For the 61-66 cm, 71 cm, 76 cm and 81 cm sizes only, using a medium size crochet hook, work a row of double crochet evenly along shoulder opening, making 2 (3) (3) (4) button loops at front edge. Sew on buttons.

Open neck: Do not press. Sew on front borders, placing buttonhole section on the right side for lady and the left side for man. Catch down row ends of borders at base of neck opening. Complete as for crew neck. Add buttons.

TO MAKE THE PLAIN VERSION: Work as given for striped version but using a. throughout.

Above and left *This Short-sleeve Summer top comes in a wide range of sizes and with alternative necklines (page 56)*
Opposite *Pocketed Cardigan in Slipstitch (page 60)*

Pocketed Cardigan in Slipstitch

Illustrated on page 59

MEASUREMENTS	in centimetres (and inches, in brackets)			
To fit chest or bust sizes	66 (26)	71 (28)	76 (30)	81 (32)
All round at widest part	69.5 (27¼)	74.5 (29¼)	80 (31½)	86 (34)
Side seam	26.5 (10½)	29.5 (11½)	33 (13)	35.5 (14)
Length	44.5 (17½)	48.5 (19)	53 (21)	57.5 (22¾)
Sleeve seam	35 (13¾)	38.5 (15¼)	40.5 (16)	43.5 (17)
To fit chest or bust sizes	86 (34)	91 (36)	97 (38)	102 (40)
All round at widest part	91 (36)	96.5 (37¾)	103 (40½)	107.5 (42¼)
Side seam	38.5 (15¼)	38.5 (15¼)	38.5 (15¼)	38.5 (15¼)
Length	60 (23½)	62 (24½)	62 (24½)	63 (24¾)
Sleeve seam	43.5 (17)	43.5 (17)	43.5 (17)	43.5 (17)

MATERIALS: *Allow the following quantities in 40 g balls of Emu Mistique: 5 for 66 cm size; 6 for 71 cm size; 7 for 76 cm size; 8 for 81 cm size; 9 for 86 cm size; 9 for 91 cm size; 10 for 97 cm size; 10 for 102 cm size. For any one size: a pair each of No. 6 (5 mm) and No. 8 (4 mm) knitting needles; 4 buttons.*

TENSION: *Work at a tension of 21 stitches and 22 rows to measure 10 × 10 cm, over the pattern, using No. 6 (5 mm) needles, to obtain measurements given.*

ABBREVIATIONS: To be read before working: *K., knit plain; p., purl; st., stitch; tog., together; inc., increase (by working twice into next st.); dec., decrease (by taking 2 sts. tog.); s.s., stocking stitch (k. on the right side and p. on the wrong side); sl., slip; y.fwd., yarn forward to make a st.; p.s.s.o., pass slipped st. over; sl. 1d., slip 1 down (sl. next loop off left hand needle); single rib is k. 1 and p. 1 alternately.*

NOTE: *The instructions are given for the 66 cm (26 inch) size. Where they vary, work figures within first brackets for the 71 cm (28 inch) size; work figures within second brackets for the 76 cm (30 inch) size, and so on.*

THE BACK: With No. 6 (5 mm) needles cast on 71 (77) (81) (89) (93) (99) (105) (111) sts. and, beginning odd-numbered rows with k. 1 and even-numbered rows with p. 1, work 7 rows in single rib.

1st pattern row (wrong side): K. 1, * y.fwd., sl. 1, k. 1, y.fwd., p.s.s.o.; repeat from * to end.

2nd row: * K. 2, sl. 1d.; repeat from * until 1 st. remains, k. 1.

3rd row: K. 2, * y.fwd., sl. 1, k. 1, y.fwd., p.s.s.o.; repeat from * until 1 st. remains, k. 1.

4th row: K. 3, * sl. 1d., k. 2; repeat from * to end. These 4 rows form the pattern.

Pattern a further 49 (55) (63) (69) (75) (75) (75) (75) rows.

To shape the armholes: Not counting the sl. 1d. as sts. as these are lost on alternate rows, cast off 4 (6) (6) (8) (8) (8) (10) (10) sts. at beginning of next 2 rows.

Work 1 row—63 (65) (69) (73) (77) (83) (85) (91) sts.

Note that during pattern, when shaping of any kind is worked, the sl. 1d. worked on 2nd and 4th rows are not counted as sts., and are not included in any st. counts quoted throughout this pattern.

Pattern a further 31 (33) (35) (39) (39) (43) (43) (45) rows.

To slope the shoulders: Cast off 6 (6) (6) (6) (7) (6) (8) (8) (8) sts. at beginning of next 2 rows, and 6 (6) (7) (7) (8) (8) (8) (9) sts. on the following 4 rows.

Cast off remaining 27 (29) (29) (31) (33) (35) (37) (39) sts.

THE POCKET BACKS (2 alike): With No. 6 (5 mm) needles cast on 19 (21) (21) (22) (22) (22) (22) (22) sts. and s.s. 23 (23) (23) (27) (27) (27) (27) (27) rows, increasing 2 (2) (2) (3) (3) (3) (3) (3) sts. across last row. Break yarn and leave 21 (23) (23) (25) (25) (25) (25) (25) sts. on stitch-holder.

THE LEFT FRONT: With No. 6 (5 mm) needles cast on 35 (37) (41) (43) (47) (49) (53) (55) sts. and work 7 rows in single rib as on back.

Work 22 (22) (22) (26) (26) (26) (26) (26) rows in pattern as given on back.

Pocket row: Pattern across 7 (7) (9) (9) (11) (12) (14) (15) sts., sl. next 21 (23) (23) (25) (25) (25) (25) (25) sts. onto a stitch-holder and leave at right side of work; in their place, pattern across sts. of one pocket back, then pattern to end of row—35 (37) (41) (43) (47) (49) (53) (55) sts.

Pattern a further 20 (26) (34) (36) (42) (42) (42) (42) rows.

To shape front edge: Dec. 1 st. at end—read beginning here when working right front—of next row and same edge on the 3 following 3rd rows.

Work 1 row here when working right front only.

To shape armhole: Cast off 4 (6) (6) (8) (8) (8) (10) (10) sts. at beginning of next row—27 (27) (31) (31) (35) (37) (39) (41) sts.

Work 1 row – omit this row when working right front.

Dec. 1 st. at front edge on next row and the 8 (8) (10) (9) (12) (12) (14) (14) following 3rd rows—18 (18) (20) (21) (22) (24) (24) (26) sts.

Pattern 7 (9) (5) (12) (3) (7) (1) (3) row(s)—pattern 8 (10) (6) (13) (4) (8) (2) (4) rows here when working right front.

To slope the shoulder: Cast off 6 (6) (6) (7) (6) (8) (8) (8) sts. at beginning of next row, then 6 (6) (7) (7) (8) (8) (8) (9) sts. on following alternate row.

Work 1 row, then cast off 6 (6) (7) (7) (8) (8) (8) (9) sts.

THE RIGHT FRONT: Work as left front, noting variations where indicated.

THE SLEEVES (both alike): With No. 8 (4 mm) needles cast on 37 (39) (43) (47) (47) (49) (49) (51) sts. and work (11) (11) (11) (15) (15) (15) (15) (15) rows in single rib as on back.

Change to No. 6 (5 mm) needles and work 5 rows in pattern as given on back.

Keeping continuity of the pattern, and working extra sts. into pattern as they occur, inc. 1 st. each end of next row and the 11 (12) (12) (14) (14) (17) (17) (18) following 5th (5th) (5th) (5th) (5th) (4th) (4th) (4th) rows—61 (65) (69) (77) (77) (85) (85) (89) sts.

Pattern 8 (11) (15) (9) (9) (11) (11) (7) rows—mark each end of last row to denote end of sleeve seam.

Pattern a further 4 (6) (6) (8) (8) (8) (10) (10) rows. Cast off.

THE POCKET TOPS (both alike): With wrong side facing, rejoin yarn to sts. on stitch-holder and using No. 6 (5 mm) needles, beginning with p. 1, work 5 (5) (5) (7) (7)

(7) (7) (7) rows in single rib.
Cast off in rib.

THE FRONT BAND: First join shoulder seams. With No. 8 (4 mm) needles cast on 8 sts. and work 4 rows in single rib.

1st buttonhole row: Rib 3, cast off 2, rib to end.

2nd buttonhole row: Rib 3, turn, cast on 2, turn, rib 3.
Rib 16 (18) (21) (24) (26) (26) (26) (26) rows, then repeat the 2 buttonhole rows again.

Repeat the last 18 (20) (23) (26) (28) (28) (28) (28) rows, twice more.

Continue in rib until band fits up right front, round neck, and down left front, casting off in rib when the correct length is assured.

TO MAKE UP THE CARDIGAN: Do not press. Set in sleeves, sewing row ends above markers on sleeves to cast-off groups at underarms on back and fronts. Join side and sleeve seams. Sew down row ends of pocket tops on right side and pocket backs to wrong side. Placing top buttonhole level with first front decrease on right front, sew front band in position. Add buttons.

Cricket Sweater

Illustrated on page 63

Illustrated on page 63

| **MEASUREMENTS** | *in centimetres (and inches, in brackets)* | | | | | |
To fit chest sizes	86 (34)	91 (36)	97 (38)	102 (40)	107 (42)	112 (44)
Side seam	40 (15¾)	40 (15¾)	40 (15¾)	41.5 (16¼)	41.5 (16¼)	41.5 (16¼)
Length	63 (24¾)	63.5 (25)	64 (25¼)	66 (26)	67 (26¼)	67.5 (26½)
Sleeve seam	43.5 (17)	43.5 (17)	43.5 (17)	43.5 (17)	43.5 (17)	43.5 (17)

MATERIALS: *Allow the following quantities in 50 g balls of Lister/Lee Lady Love Double Knitting: 9 main for 86 cm size; 10 for 91 cm size; 11 for 97 cm size; 12 for 102 cm size; 13 for 107 cm size; 14 for 112 cm size. For any one size: a ball of the same yarn in each of 2 contrasting colours; a pair each of No. 8 (4 mm) and No. 10 (3¼ mm) knitting needles; a cable needle.*

TENSION: *Work at a tension of 30 stitches and 29 rows to measure 10 × 10 cm, over the pattern slightly stretched, using No. 8 (4 mm) needles, to obtain measurements given.*

ABBREVIATIONS: To be read before working: *K., knit plain; p., purl; st., stitch; tog., together; inc., increase (by working twice into next st.); dec., decrease (by taking 2 sts. tog.); c. 6, cable 6 (slip next 3 sts. on to cable needle and leave at back of work, k. 3, then k. 3 from cable needle); nil, meaning nothing is worked here for this size; m., main colour; single rib is k. 1 and p. 1 alternately; k. or p. 2 tog.b., k. or p. 2 tog. through back of sts.*

NOTE: *The instructions are given for the 86 cm (34 inch) size. Where they vary, work figures within first brackets for the 91 cm (36 inch) size; work figures within second brackets for the 97 cm (38 inch) size, and so on.*

THE BACK: With No. 10 (3¼ mm) needles and m. cast on

131 (139) (145) (153) (159) (167) sts. and beginning odd-numbered rows with k. 1 and even-numbered rows with p. 1, work in single rib for 12 rows m., 2 rows 1st contrast, 2 rows m., 2 rows 2nd contrast, then 12 rows m. Break off 1st and 2nd contrasts and continue with m. only.

Change to No. 8 (4 mm) needles.

1st pattern row: P. 4 (p. 8) (p. 2, k. 6, p. 3) (nil) (p. 3) (p. 7), *k. 1, p. 1, k. 1, p. 3, k. 6, p. 3; repeat from * until 7 (11) (14) (3) (6) (10) sts. remain, k. 1, p. 1, k. 1, then p. 4 (p. 8) (p. 3, k. 6, p. 2) (nil) (p. 3) (p. 7).

2nd row: K. 4 (k. 8) (k. 2, p. 6, k. 3) (nil) (k. 3) (k. 7), *p. 3, k. 3, p. 6, k. 3; repeat from * until 7 (11) (14) (3) (6) (10) sts. remain, p. 3, then k. 4 (k. 8) (k. 3, p. 6, k. 2) (nil) (k. 3) (k. 7).

3rd to 6th rows: Repeat 1st and 2nd rows, twice.

7th row: P. 4 (p. 8) (p. 2, c. 6, p. 3) (nil) (p. 3) (p. 7), *k. 1, p. 1, k. 1, p. 3, c. 6, p. 3; repeat from * until 7 (11) (14) (3) (6) (10) sts. remain, k. 1, p. 1, k. 1, then p. 4 (p. 8) (p. 3, c. 6, p. 2) (nil) (p. 3) (p. 7).

8th row: As 2nd row.

These 8 rows form the pattern, pattern a further 82 (82) (82) (86) (86) (86) rows—pattern 81 (81) (81) (85) (85) (85) rows here when working front. ★★

Continued on page 62

To shape the armholes: Keeping continuity of the pattern where possible, cast off 6 (6) (6) (7) (7) (7) sts. at beginning of next 2 rows, then dec. 1 st. each end of the following 5 (5) (7) (7) (7) (9) rows.

Work 1 row, then dec. 1 st. each end of next row and the 3 (4) (3) (3) (4) (3) following alternate rows—101 (107) (111) (117) (121) (127) sts.

Pattern 43 (43) (45) (47) (47) (49) rows.

To slope the shoulders: Cast off 7 (7) (7) (8) (8) (8) sts. at beginning of next 6 rows, then 5 (7) (8) (7) (8) (10) sts. on the following 2 rows.

Break yarn and leave 49 (51) (53) (55) (57) (59) sts. on a spare needle.

THE FRONT: Work as back to **, noting variation.

To divide for neck: Next row: Pattern 65 (69) (72) (76) (79) (83) and leave these sts. on a spare needle for right half front, cast off 1 st., pattern to end and work on these last 65 (69) (72) (76) (79) (83) sts. for left half front.

The left half front: To shape armhole and shape front edge: 1st row: Cast off 6 (6) (6) (7) (7) (7) sts., pattern until 2 sts. remain, dec.

2nd row: Pattern to end.

***Dec. 1 st. at armhole edge on next 5 (5) (7) (7) (7) (9) rows, then the 4 (5) (4) (4) (5) (4) following alternate rows, *at the same time*, dec. 1 st. at neck edge on 1st of these rows and every following alternate row—42 (44) (46) (49) (50) (53) sts.

Pattern 1 row, then dec. 1 st. at neck edge only on next row and the 11 (10) (11) (13) (13) (13) following alternate rows, then the 4 (5) (5) (4) (4) (5) following 4th rows—26 (28) (29) (31) (32) (34) sts.

Pattern 3 (1) (1) (3) (3) (1) row(s)—pattern 4 (2) (2) (4) (4) (2) rows here when working right half front.

To slope shoulder: Cast off 7 (7) (7) (8) (8) (8) sts. at beginning of next row and the 2 following alternate rows.

Work 1 row, then cast off remaining 5 (7) (8) (7) (8) (10) sts.

The right half front: With right side facing, rejoin m. to inner end of sts. on spare needle.

1st row: Dec., pattern to end.

2nd row: Cast off 6 (6) (6) (7) (7) (7) sts., pattern to end.

Work as given for left half front from *** to end, noting variation.

THE SLEEVES (2 alike): With No. 10 (3¼ mm) needles and m. cast on 63 (65) (67) (71) (73) (75) sts. and working in rib as given on back, work 12 rows m., 2 rows 1st contrast, 2 rows m., 2 rows 2nd contrast and 11 rows m.

Inc. row: Rib 3 (4) (5) (2) (3) (4), inc., * rib 4 (4) (4) (5) (5) (5), inc. in next st.; repeat from * until 4 (5) (6) (2) (3) (4) sts. remain, rib to end—75 (77) (79) (83) (85) (87) sts.

Break off 1st and 2nd contrast colours and continue with m. only.

Change to No. 8 (4 mm) needles.

1st pattern row: K. 3 (k. 4) (k. 5) (p. 1, k. 6) (p. 2, k. 6) (p. 3, k. 6), p. 3, k. 1, p. 1, k. 1, p. 3, * k. 6, p. 3, k. 1, p. 1, k. 1, p. 3; repeat from * until 3 (4) (5) (7) (8) (9) sts. remain, k. 3 (k. 4) (k. 5) (k. 6, p. 1) (k. 6, p. 2) (k. 6, p. 3).

2nd row: P. 3 (p. 4) (p. 5) (k. 1, p. 6) (k. 2, p. 6) (k. 3, p. 6), k. 3, p. 3, k. 3, * p. 6, k. 3, p. 3, k. 3; repeat from * until 3 (4) (5) (7) (8) (9) sts. remain, p. 3 (p. 4) (p. 5) (p. 6, k. 1) (p. 6, k. 2) (p. 6, k. 3).

These 2 rows set the position of the pattern. Keeping continuity of the pattern to match back, and working extra sts. into pattern as they occur, work 4 rows, then inc. 1 st.

each end of next row and the 14 following 6th rows—105 (107) (109) (113) (115) (117) sts.

Pattern 9 rows.

To shape sleeve top: Cast off 6 (6) (6) (7) (7) (7) sts. at beginning of next 2 rows, then dec. 1 st. each end of the following 7 rows, then the 10 (11) (12) (13) (14) (15) following alternate rows—59 sts.

Work 1 row, then dec. 1 st. each end of next 12 rows.

Cast off remaining 35 sts.

THE NECK RIBBING: Join right shoulder seam.

With right side facing, rejoin m. and using No. 10 (3¼ mm) needles, pick up and k. 55 (57) (59) (61) (63) (65) sts. from row ends of left front neck, 2 sts. from centre front, 55 (57) (59) (61) (63) (65) sts. from row ends of right front neck, and finally, k. across 49 (51) (53) (55) (57) (59) sts. at back neck—161 (167) (173) (179) (185) (191) sts.

1st rib row: P. 1, * k. 1, p. 1 *; repeat from * to * to centre front sts., p. 2 centre front sts., p. 1, repeat from * to * to end.

2nd rib row: Rib to within 2 sts. of 2 centre front sts., k. 2 tog. b., k. 2 centre front sts., k. 2 tog., rib to end.

3rd row: Rib to within 2 sts. of 2 centre front sts., p. 2 tog., p. 2 centre front sts., p. 2 tog. b., rib to end.

Continuing to decrease each side of 2 centre front sts. as before, rib a further 1 row in m., 2 rows 1st contrast, 2 rows m., 2 rows 2nd contrast and 4 rows m.

Cast off in rib decreasing as before.

TO MAKE UP THE SWEATER: Do not press. Join remaining shoulder seam, continuing across neck ribbing. Set in sleeves, then join side and sleeve seams.

Opposite Cricket Sweater (page 61)

V-neck Fisherman's Rib Sweater

Illustrated on page 66

MEASUREMENTS To fit sizes	*in centimetres (and inches, in brackets)*					
	81 (32)	86 (34)	91 (36)	97 (38)	102 (40)	107 (42)
All round at underarms	86.5 ($34\frac{1}{4}$)	92 ($36\frac{1}{4}$)	97.5 ($38\frac{1}{4}$)	102.5 ($40\frac{1}{4}$)	108 ($42\frac{1}{2}$)	113.5 ($44\frac{1}{2}$)
Side seam	45.5 ($17\frac{3}{4}$)	45.5 ($17\frac{3}{4}$)	45.5 ($17\frac{3}{4}$)	47.5 ($18\frac{3}{4}$)	47.5 ($18\frac{3}{4}$)	47.5 ($18\frac{3}{4}$)
Length, to shoulder	61.5 ($24\frac{1}{4}$)	62 ($24\frac{1}{2}$)	62.5 ($24\frac{3}{4}$)	68.5 (27)	69.5 ($27\frac{1}{4}$)	70.5 ($27\frac{3}{4}$)
Sleeve seam	40.5 (16)	40.5 (16)	40.5 (16)	45.5 ($17\frac{3}{4}$)	45.5 ($17\frac{3}{4}$)	45.5 ($17\frac{3}{4}$)

MATERIALS: *Allow the following quantities in 50 g balls of Hayfield Beaulon DK: 9 for 81 cm size; 10 for 86 cm size; 11 for 91 cm size; 12 for 97 cm size; 13 for 102 cm size; 14 for 107 cm size. For any one size: a pair each of No. 8 (4 mm) and No. 10 ($3\frac{1}{4}$ mm) knitting needles.*

TENSION: *Work at a tension of 22 stitches and 38 rows to measure 10 × 10 cm, over the pattern, using No. 8 (4 mm) needles, to obtain measurements given.*

ABBREVIATIONS: To be read before working: *K., knit plain; p., purl; st., stitch; tog., together; inc., increase (by working twice into next st.); dec., decrease (by taking 2 sts. tog.); sl., slip; y.t.f., yarn to front of work; y.o.n., yarn over needle to make a st.; single rib is k. 1 and p. 1 alternately; nil, meaning nothing is worked here for this size; s.k.p.o., sl. 1, k. 1, pass sl.st. over.*

NOTE: *The instructions are given for the 81 cm (32 inch) size. Where they vary, work the figures within the first brackets for the 86 cm (34 inch) size; work the figures within the second brackets for the 91 cm (36 inch) size, and so on.*

THE BACK: With No. 10 ($3\frac{1}{4}$ mm) needles cast on 95 (101) (107) (113) (119) (125) sts. and, beginning odd-numbered rows with k. 1 and even-numbered rows with p. 1, work 14 rows in single rib.

Change to No. 8 (4 mm) needles and work in pattern as follows:

1st row: Sl. 1, * y.t.f., sl. 1 p.wise, y.o.n., k. 1; repeat from * to end.

2nd row: Sl. 1, * k. 2 tog. the y.o.n. and sl.st. of previous row, p. 1; repeat from * to end. **

Repeat the last two rows, 76 (76) (76) (81) (81) (81) times. Mark each end of the last row with a coloured thread to denote end of side seams. Pattern a further 62 (64) (66) (80) (84) (86) rows.

To slope the shoulders: Cast off 6 (6) (7) (7) (8) (8) sts. at the beginning of each of the next 8 rows, then 7 (9) (7) (9) (7) (9) sts. at the beginning of each of the next 2 rows. Leave remaining 33 (35) (37) (39) (41) (43) sts. on a stitch-holder.

THE FRONT: Work as for back to **.

Pattern a further 133 (133) (133) (149) (149) (149) rows.

Divide sts. for "v" neck: Next row: Pattern 47 (50) (53) (56) (59) (62) and leave these sts. on a spare needle for right half front, pattern next st. and leave on a safety pin for centre front, pattern to end and work on these 47 (50) (53) (56) (59) (62) sts. for left half front.

The left half front: To shape the neck: Dec. 1 st. at neck edge on the next row and 4 (4) (4) (2) (2) (2) following 4th rows.

Pattern 1 (1) (1) (3) (3) (3) row(s). Mark end—read

beginning here when working right half front—of the last row.

For the 81 (86) (91) cm sizes only: Pattern 2 rows.

For all sizes: Dec. 1 st. at neck edge on the next row and the 10 (11) (12) (15) (16) (17) following 4th rows—31 (33) (35) (37) (39) (41) sts.

Pattern 19 (17) (15) (19) (19) (17) rows—pattern 20 (18) (16) (20) (20) (18) rows here when working right half neck.

To slope the shoulder: Cast off 6 (6) (7) (7) (8) (8) sts. at the beginning of the next row and the 3 following alternate rows—7 (9) (7) (9) (7) (9) sts.

Pattern 1 row. Cast off.

The right half front: With right side of work facing, rejoin yarn to inner end of sts. on spare needle and work as given for left half front to end, noting variations.

THE SLEEVES (both alike): With No. 10 ($3\frac{1}{4}$ mm) needles cast on 41 (43) (45) (47) (49) (51) sts. and work 13 rows in rib as given for back.

Next (inc.) row: Rib 2 (3) (nil) (1) (4) (6), * inc., rib 3 (3) (3) (3) (2) (2); repeat from * until 3 (4) (1) (2) (6) (6) sts. remain, inc., rib 2 (3) (nil) (1) (5) (5)—51 (53) (57) (59) (63) (65) sts.

Change to No. 8 (4 mm) needles and work 6 rows in pattern as given for back.

Maintaining continuity of the pattern and taking extra sts. into the pattern as they occur, inc. 1 st. at each end of the next row and the 12 (13) (13) (14) (14) (15) following 10th (8th) (8th) (10th) (10th) (8th) rows—71 (81) (85) (89) (93) (97) sts.

Pattern 9 (25) (25) (9) (9) (29) rows. Cast off.

THE NECK BAND: First join right shoulder seam. With right side of work facing and using No. 10 ($3\frac{1}{4}$ mm) needles, pick up and k. 57 (61) (65) (69) (73) (77) sts. down left front neck edge, k. the st. from safety-pin at centre front, pick up and k. 57 (61) (65) (69) (73) (77) sts. up right front neck edge, then k. across the 33 (35) (37) (39) (41) (43) sts. at back neck—148 (158) (168) (178) (188) (198) sts.

1st row: * K. 1, p. 1; repeat from * to within 2 sts. of centre front st., k. 2 tog., p. 1, k. 2 tog., * p. 1, k. 1; repeat from this * until 1 st. remains, p.1.

2nd row: Rib to within 2 sts. of the centre front st., s.k.p.o., k. 1, k. 2 tog., rib to the end.

Repeat the last 2 rows, 3 (3) (3) (4) (4) (4) times.

Cast off in rib, decreasing as before.

TO MAKE UP THE SWEATER: Do not press. Join left shoulder seam, continuing seam across neck band. Set in sleeves between markers on back and front. Join sleeve and side seams.

Aran-style Slipover

Illustrated on page 10

MEASUREMENTS

in centimetres (and inches, in brackets)

To fit bust or chest sizes	81 (32)	86 (34)	91 (36)	97 (38)	102 (40)	107 (42)	112 (44)
Side seams, including armhole ribbing	41.5 (16¼)	41.5 (16¼)	41.5 (16¼)	43.5 (17)	43.5 (17)	43.5 (17)	43.5 (17)
Length	64 (25¼)	65 (25½)	67 (26¼)	70.5 (27¾)	71.5 (28¼)	72.5 (28½)	74 (29)

MATERIALS: *Allow the following quantities in 50 g balls of Emu Aran:* 8 *for* 81 *cm size;* 9 *for* 86 *cm size;* 10 *for* 91 *cm and* 97 *cm sizes;* 11 *for* 102 *cm and* 107 *cm sizes;* 12 *for* 112 *cm size. For any one size: a pair each of No. 8 (4 mm) and No. 6 (5 mm) knitting needles; a cable needle.*

TENSION: *Work at a tension of* 21 *stitches to measure* 11 *cm in width over the* 21-*stitch centre panel and* 23 *rows to measure* 10 *cm in depth, using No. 6 (5 mm) needles for measurements given.*

ABBREVIATIONS: To be read before working: *K., knit plain; p., purl; st., stitch; tog., together; inc., increase (by working twice into next st.); dec., decrease (by working 2 sts. tog.); cr. 3, cross 3 (slip next 2 sts. on to cable needle and leave at back of work, k. 1, then p. 1, k. 1 from cable needle); tw. 2 rt., twist 2 right (slip next st. on to cable needle and leave at back, k. 1, then k. st. from cable needle); tw. 2 lt., twist 2 left (slip next st. on to cable needle and leave at front, k. 1, then k. st. from cable needle); 3 from 1, k. 1, p. 1, k. 1 all into next st.; cr. 2 rt., cross 2 right (slip next st. on to cable needle and leave at back, k. 1, then p. 1 from cable needle); cr. 2 lt., cross 2 left (slip next st. on to cable needle and leave at front, p. 1, then k. 1 from cable needle); single rib is k. 1, p. 1 alternately; nil, meaning nothing is worked for this size.*

NOTE: *The instructions are given for the* 81 *cm (32 inch) size. Where they vary, work figures within first brackets for* 86 *cm (34 inch) size; work figures within second brackets for* 91 *cm (36 inch) size, and so on.*

THE BACK: With No. 8 (4 mm) needles cast on 78 (82) (86) (90) (94) (98) (102) sts. and work 7 (7) (7) (11) (11) (11) (11) rows in single rib.

Inc. row: Rib 4 (6) (7) (9) (5) (7) (3), inc., * rib 6 (6) (5) (5) (5) (5), inc.; repeat from * 9 (9) (11) (11) (13) (13) (15) times, rib 3 (5) (6) (8) (4) (6) (2)—89 (93) (99) (103) (109) (113) (119) sts.

Change to No. 6 (5 mm) needles and work in pattern as follows:

1st row: P. nil (nil) (1) (1) (nil) (nil) (1), * k. 1, p. 1; repeat from * 4 (5) (6) (5) (7) (6) (7) times, ** tw. 2 rt., tw. 2 lt., p. 16 (16) (16) (20) (20) (24) (24), tw. 2 rt., tw. 2 lt., **, for panel p. 9, cr. 3, p. 9, then repeat from ** to ** once, * p. 1, k. 1; repeat from this * 4 (5) (6) (5) (7) (6) (7) times, p. nil (nil) (1) (1) (nil) (nil) (1).

2nd row: K. nil (nil) (1) (1) (nil) (nil) (1), * p. 1., k. 1; repeat from * 4 (5) (6) (5) (7) (6) (7) times, *** p. 4, ** 3 from 1, p. 3 tog.; repeat from ** 3 (3) (3) (4) (4) (5) (5) times, p. 4 ***, for panel k. 9, p. 3, k. 9, then repeat from *** to *** once, * k. 1, p. 1; repeat from this * 4 (5) (6) (5) (7) (6) (7) times, k. nil (nil) (1) (1) (nil) (nil) (1).

3rd row: K. nil (nil) (1) (1) (nil) (nil) (1), * p. 1, k. 1; repeat from * 4 (5) (6) (5) (7) (6) (7) times, ** tw. 2 lt., tw. 2 rt., p. 16 (16) (16) (20) (20) (24) (24), tw. 2 lt., tw. 2 rt. **, for panel p. 8, tw. 2 rt., p. 1, tw. 2 lt., p. 8, then repeat from ** to ** once, * k. 1, p. 1; repeat from this * 4 (5) (6) (5) (7) (6) (7) times, k. nil (nil) (1) (1) (nil) (nil) (1).

4th row: P. nil (nil) (1) (1) (nil) (nil) (1), * k. 1, p. 1; repeat from * 4 (5) (6) (5) (7) (6) (7) times, *** p. 4, ** p. 3 tog., 3 from 1; repeat from ** 3 (3) (3) (4) (4) (5) (5) times, p. 4 ***, for panel k. 8, p. 1, k. 1, p. 1, k. 1, p. 1, k. 8, then repeat from *** to *** once, * p. 1, k. 1; repeat from this * 4 (5) (6) (5) (7) (6) (7) times, p. nil (nil) (1) (1) (nil) (nil) (1).

These 4 rows form the 4-row pattern at either side of panel and are repeated throughout work.

5th row: Pattern 34 (36) (39) (41) (44) (46) (49), for panel p. 7, cr. 2 rt., k. 1, p. 1, k. 1, cr. 2 lt., p. 7, pattern to end.

6th row: Pattern to panel, k. 7, p. 2, k. 1, p. 1, k. 1, p. 2, k. 7, pattern to end.

7th row: Pattern to panel, p. 6, tw. 2 rt., p. 1, k. 1, p. 1, k. 1, p. 1, tw. 2 lt., p. 6, pattern to end.

8th row: Pattern to panel, k. 6, p. 1, k. 1, p. 1, k. 1, p. 1, k. 1, p. 1, k. 6, pattern to end.

9th row: Pattern to panel, p. 5, cr. 2 rt., k. 1, p. 1, k. 1, p. 1, k. 1, p. 1, k. 1, cr. 2 lt., p. 5, pattern to end.

10th row: Pattern to panel, k. 5, p. 2, k. 1, p. 1, k. 1, p. 1, k. 1, p. 1, k. 1, p. 2, k. 5, pattern to end.

11th row: Pattern to panel, p. 4, tw. 2 rt., p. 1, k. 1, p. 1, k. 1, p. 1, k. 1, p. 1, k. 1, p. 1, tw. 2 lt., p. 4, pattern to end.

12th row: Pattern to panel, k. 4, p. 1, * k. 1, p. 1; repeat from * 5 times, k. 4, pattern to end.

13th row: Pattern to panel, p. 4, cr. 2 lt., k. 1, p. 1, k. 1, p. 1, k. 1, p. 1, k. 1, p. 1, cr 2 rt., p. 4, pattern to end.

14th row: Pattern to panel, k. 5, p. 2, k. 1, p. 1, k. 1, p. 1, k. 1, p. 1, k. 1, p. 2, k. 5, pattern to end.

15th row: Pattern to panel, p. 5, cr. 2 lt., k. 1, p. 1, k. 1, p. 1, k. 1, p. 1, k. 1, cr. 2 rt., p. 5, pattern to end.

16th row: Pattern to panel, k. 6, p. 1, k. 1, p. 1, k. 1, p. 1, k. 1, p. 1, k. 6, pattern to end.

17th row: Pattern to panel, p. 6, cr. 2 lt., k. 1, p. 1, k. 1, cr. 2 rt., p. 6, pattern to end.

18th row: Pattern to panel, k. 7, p. 2, k. 1, p. 1, k. 1, p. 2, k. 7, pattern to end.

19th row: Pattern to panel, p. 7, cr. 2 lt., k. 1, p. 1, k. 1, cr. 2 rt., p. 7, pattern to end.

20th row: Pattern to panel, k. 8, p. 1, k. 1, p. 1, k. 1, p. 1, k. 8 pattern to end.

21st row: Pattern to panel, p. 8, cr. 2 lt., p. 1, cr. 2 rt., p. 8, pattern to end.

Continued on page 68

Opposite *V-neck Fisherman's Rib Sweater (page 64)*.   Above *Chunky His and Hers Sweater (page 68)*

22nd row: Pattern to panel, k. 9, p. 3, k. 9, pattern to end.

These 22 rows form the pattern for the centre panel, keeping continuity of side panels and centre panel, work a further 68 rows.**★★**

To shape the armholes: Keeping continuity of pattern, cast off 4 (4) (5) (5) (6) (6) (7) sts. at beginning of next 2 rows, then dec. 1 st. at each end of next row, then on the 4 (5) (5) (5) (6) (6) (6) following alternate rows—71 (73) (77) (81) (83) (87) (91) sts.

Work 35 (35) (39) (43) (43) (45) (49) rows.

To slope the shoulders: Cast off 7 (7) (8) (8) (8) (8) (9) sts. at beginning of next 4 (4) (2) (2) (4) (4) (2) rows, then 6 (7) (7) (7) (7) (7) (8) sts. on the following 2 (2) (4) (4) (2) (2) (4) rows—31 (31) (33) (37) (37) (41) (41) sts. Leave sts. on a spare needle.

THE FRONT: Work as back to **★★**.

To shape the armholes and divide for neck: Next row: Cast off 4 (4) (5) (5) (6) (6) (7) sts., work to end.

Next (dividing) row: Cast off 4 (4) (5) (5) (6) (6) (7), pattern 39 (41) (43) (45) (47) (49) (51) and leave these 40 (42) (44) (46) (48) (50) (52) sts. on a spare needle for right half neck, pattern 1 and leave this st. on a safety pin, pattern to end and work on these 40 (42) (44) (46) (48) (50) (52) sts. for left half neck.

The left half neck: Dec. 1 st. at armhole edge on next row, then on the 4 (5) (5) (5) (6) (6) (6) following alternate rows, *at the same time*, dec. 1 st. at neck edge on the first of these rows, then on the 2 (3) (3) (3) (4) (4) (4) following 3rd rows—32 (32) (34) (36) (36) (38) (40) sts.

Pattern nil (1) (1) (1) (2) (2) (2) row(s), then dec. 1 st. at neck edge on next row, then on the 11 (10) (11) (13) (12) (14) (14) following 3rd row(s)—20 (21) (22) (22) (23) (23) (25) sts.

Pattern 1 (3) (4) (2) (4) (nil) (4) row(s)—pattern 2 (4) (5)

(3) (5) (1) (5) row(s) here when working right half neck.

To slope the shoulder: Cast off 7 (7) (8) (8) (8) (8) (9) sts. at beginning of next row, then 7 (7) (7) (7) (8) (8) (8) sts. on the following alternate row—6 (7) (7) (7) (7) (7) (8) sts.

Pattern 1 row, then cast off.

The right half neck: With right side of work facing, rejoin yarn to the 40 (42) (44) (46) (48) (50) (52) sts. left on spare needle and work as left half neck, noting variation.

THE NECK RIBBING: First join right shoulder seam. With right side of work facing and using No. 8 (4 mm) needles, rejoin yarn and pick up and k. 54 (56) (60) (62) (66) (68) (72) sts. down left half neck, k. 1 st. from safety pin, pick up and k. 54 (56) (60) (62) (66) (68) (72) sts. up right half neck, then k. 31 (31) (33) (37) (37) (41) (41) sts. across back neck—140 (144) (154) (162) (170) (178) (186) sts.

1st rib row: P. 1, * k. 1, p. 1; repeat from * to within 2 sts. of centre front st., k. 2 tog., p. 1, k. 2 tog., rib to end.

2nd rib row: Rib to within 2 sts. of centre front st., p. 2 tog., k. 1, p. 2 tog., rib to end.

Repeat the last 2 rows 3 times more.

Cast off in rib, decreasing as before.

THE ARMHOLE BANDS (both alike): First join left shoulder seam, continuing seam across neck ribbing. With right side of work facing and using No. 8 (4 mm) needles, rejoin yarn and pick up and k. 95 (101) (107) (113) (119) (125) (131) sts. evenly around armhole edge.

Beginning odd-numbered rows with k. 1 and even-numbered rows with p. 1, work 8 rows in single rib.

Cast off in rib.

TO COMPLETE THE SLIPOVER: Press with a warm iron over a dry cloth. Join side seams.

Chunky His and Her Sweaters

Illustrated on page 67

MEASUREMENTS	*in centimetres (and inches, in brackets)*						
To fit bust or chest sizes	81 (32)	86 (34)	91 (36)	97 (38)	102 (40)	107 (42)
All round at underarms	85.5 (33¾)	90 (35½)	97 (38)	101 (39¾)	105.5 (41½)	112 (44)
Side seam	44.5 (17½)	44.5 (17½)	44.5 (17½)	49 (19¼)	49 (19¼)	49 (19¼)
Length	64 (25¼)	64.5 (25½)	65.5 (25¾)	70.5 (27¾)	71.5 (28¼)	72.5 (28½)
Sleeve seam	43.5 (17¼)	43.5 (17¼)	43.5 (17¼)	49.5 (19½)	49.5 (19½)	49.5 (19½)

MATERIALS: *Allow the following quantities in 40 g balls of Argyll Ferndale Chunky: 9 main, 4 contrast for 81 cm size; 9 main, 5 contrast for 86 cm size; 10 main, 5 contrast for 91 cm size; 11 main, 5 contrast for 97 cm size; 12 main, 5 contrast for 102 cm size; 13 main, 5 contrast for 107 cm size. For any one size: a pair each of No. 6 (5 mm), No. 7 (4½ mm) and No. 9 (3¾ mm) knitting needles; a 30 inch No. 7 (4½ mm) and 24 inch No. 8 (4 mm) circular knitting needles; a set of No. 9 (3¾ mm) double pointed knitting needles.*

TENSION: *Work at a tension of 18 stitches and 23 rows to measure 10 × 10 cm, over the stocking stitch, using No. 7 (4½ mm) needles and main, to obtain measurements given below.*

ABBREVIATIONS: To be read before working: *K., knit plain; p., purl; st., stitch; tog., together; inc., increase (by working twice into same st.); dec., decrease (by working 2 sts. tog.); s.s., stocking st. (k. on right side, p. on wrong side); s.k.p.o., slip 1, k. 1, pass slipped st. over; m., main colour; c., contrast colour; single rib is k. 1, p. 1 alternately.*

NOTE: *The instructions are given for the 81 cm (32 inch) size. Where they vary, work figures within first brackets for 86 cm (34 inch) size; work figures within second brackets for 91 cm (36 inch) size, and so on up the scale of sizes.*

THE BACK AND FRONT (alike): With No. 9 (3¾ mm) needles and c. cast on 77 (81) (87) (91) (95) (101) sts. and, beginning odd-numbered rows with k. 1 and even-numbered rows with p. 1, work 14 (14) (14) (16) (16) (16) rows in single rib.

Change to No. 6 (5 mm) needles, join in m. and work the 22-row border pattern, which is worked entirely in s.s., beginning with a k. row, so only the colour details are given:

1st to 3rd rows: 5 (4) (4) (nil) (5) (5) c., * 1 m., 5 c.; repeat from * until 6 (5) (5) (1) (6) (6) st(s). remain(s), 1 m., 5 (4) (4) (nil) (5) (5) c.

4th row: 1 m., 3 c. (3 c.) (3 c.) (2m.) (3 c.) (3 c.) (1m., 3 c.), * 3 m., 3 c.; repeat from * until 1 (6) (6) (2) (1) (1) st(s). remain(s), 1 m. (3 m., 3 c.) (3 m., 3 c.) (2 m.) (1 m.) (1m.).

5th row: 2 (1) (1) (nil) (2) (2) m., * 1 c., 2 m.; repeat from * until nil (2) (2) (1) (nil) (nil) st(s). remain(s), nil (1) (1) (1) (nil) (nil) c., nil (1) (1) (nil) (nil) (nil) m.

6th row: As 4th row, but working m. for c., and c. for m.

7th to 9th rows: 2 (1) (1) (3) (2) (2) c., * 1 m., 5 c.; repeat from * until 3 (2) (2) (4) (3) (3) sts. remain, 1 m., 2 c. (1 m., 1 c.) (1 m., 1 c.) (1 m., 3 c.) (1 m., 2 c.) (1 m., 2 c.).

10th to 15th rows: As 6th row back to 1st row, in that reverse order.

16th row: As 4th row.

17th and 18th rows: As 7th row then 1st row, but working m. for c., and c. for m.

19th row: As 10th row.

20th row: As 18th row.

21st row: All m.

22nd row: As 17th row.

Change to No. 7 (4½ mm) needles.

Continuing in m. only, s.s. 62 (62) (62) (72) (72) (72) rows.

To shape the armholes: Cast off 3 (4) (6) (3) (4) (6) sts. at beginning of next 2 rows, then dec. 1 st. each end of next row, then on 3 (4) (5) (6) (7) (8) following alternate rows—63 (63) (63) (71) (71) (71) sts.

P. 1 row; leave sts. on a spare needle.

THE SLEEVES (both alike): With No. 9 (3¾ mm) needles and c. cast on 43 (43) (43) (49) (49) (49) sts. and work 14 (14) (14) (16) (16) (16) rows in rib as given for back.

Change to No. 6 (5 mm) needles, join in m. and work 8 rows in pattern as given for back, working instructions for 4th size of back for all sizes.

Keeping continuity of border pattern to match back and taking extra sts. into the pattern as they occur, inc. 1 st. each end of next row, then on the following 8th row—47 (47) (47) (53) (53) (53) sts.

Pattern 5 rows.

Change to No. 7 (4½ mm) needles.

Continuing in m. only, work 2 rows, then inc. 1 st. each end of next row, then on the 8 (10) (13) (10) (12) (15) following 6th (5th) (4th) (6th) (5th) (4th) rows—65 (69) (75) (75) (79) (85) sts.

S.s. 9 (7) (5) (11) (11) (11) rows.

To shape sleeve top: Work exactly as given for armhole shaping on back and front to end—51 (51) (51) (55) (55) (55) sts.

Break yarn and leave sts. on a spare needle.

THE YOKE: Using No. 7 (4½ mm) circular needle, rejoin m. and work across sts. of one sleeve, front, other sleeve, then back as follows: k. 2 (2) (2) (10) (10) (10), * k. 2 tog., k. 11 (11) (11) (8) (8) (8); repeat from * until 5 (5) (5) (12) (12) (12) sts. remain, k. 2 tog., then k. 3 (3) (3) (10) (10) (10)—210 (210) (210) (228) (228) (228) sts.

Working in rounds, so that every round is k., work yoke pattern as follows, marking first st. with a coloured thread to denote beginning of rounds:

1st round: * 1 c., 5 m.; repeat from * to end.

2nd round: All k. with m.

3rd round: 3 m., * 1 c., 5 m.; repeat from * until 3 sts. remain, 1 c., 2 m.

4th round: 2 m., * 3 c., 3 m.; repeat from * until 4 sts. remain, 3 c., 1 m.

5th round: As 3rd round.

6th round: As 1st round.

7th round: 2 c., * 3 m., 3 c.; repeat from * until 4 sts. remain, 3 m., 1 c.

8th to 10th rounds: 3 c., * 1 m., 5 c.; repeat from * until 3 sts. remain, 1 m., 2 c.

11th round: As 7th round.

12th round: * 1 c., 2 m.; repeat from * to end.

Change to No. 8 (4 mm) circular needle.

13th round: As 4th round.

14th round: * 1 m., 5 c.; repeat from * to end.

15th round: * 1 m., 2 c., k. 2 tog. c., 1 c.; repeat from * to end—175 (175) (175) (190) (190) (190) sts.

16th round: * 1 m., 4 c.; repeat from * to end.

17th round: 2 m., * 2 c., 3 m.; repeat from * until 3 sts. remain, 2 c., 1 m.

18th round: * 1 c., 1 m., k. 2 tog. c., 1 m.; repeat from * to end—140 (140) (140) (152) (152) (152) sts.

19th round: * 1 c., 3 m.; repeat from * to end.

20th to 22nd rounds: 2 c., * 1 m., 3 c.; repeat from * until 2 sts. remain, 1 m., 1 c.

Break off m. and continue in c. only.

1st dec. round: K. 5 (5) (5) (6) (6) (6), s.k.p.o.; repeat from * to end—120 (120) (120) (133) (133) (133) sts.

K. 3 rounds.

2nd dec. round: K. 4 (4) (4) (5) (5) (5), s.k.p.o.; repeat from * to end—100 (100) (100) (114) (114) (114) sts.

K. 3 rounds.

3rd dec. round: * K. 3 (3) (3) (4) (4) (4), k. 2 tog.; repeat from * to end—80 (80) (80) (95) (95) (95) sts.

K. 3 rounds.

4th dec. round: * K. 6 (6) (6) (3) (3) (3), s.k.p.o.; repeat from * end—70 (70) (70) (76) (76) (76) sts.

K. 1 round.

Change to the set of No. 9 (3¾ mm) double-pointed needles and work 7 rounds in single rib.

P. 1 round for fold line, then rib a further 7 rounds.

Cast off fairly loosely in rib.

TO MAKE UP THE SWEATER: Do not press. Join underarm seams, then join sleeve and side seams. Fold neck ribbing in half to wrong side and catch into place.

Knitting for Men

Cable Pattern Waistcoat

Illustrated opposite

MEASUREMENTS	*in centimetres (and inches, in brackets)*		
To fit chest sizes	97 (38)	102 (40)	107 (42)
Side seam, including armhole band	42.5 (16¾)	42.5 (16¾)	42.5 (16¾)
Length	65 (25½)	65.5 (25¾)	66 (26)

MATERIALS: *Allow the following quantities in 50 g balls of Wendy Double Knit: 9 for 97 cm size; 10 for 102 cm size; 10 for 107 cm size. For any one size: a pair each of No. 8 (4 mm) and No. 10 (3¼ mm) knitting needles; a cable needle; 5 buttons.*

TENSION: *Work at a tension of 1 repeat of the 24-stitch pattern to measure 7 cm in width, with pattern unstretched, and 29 rows to measure 10 cm in depth, using No. 8 (4 mm) needles, to obtain measurements given.*

ABBREVIATIONS: To be read before working: *K., knit plain, p., purl; st., stitch; tog., together; sl., slip; inc., increase (by working twice into next st.); dec., decrease (by taking 2 sts. tog.); tw. 2 rt., twist 2 right (sl. next st. on to cable needle and leave at back of work, k. 1, then p. 1 from cable needle); tw. 2 lt., twist 2 left (sl. next st. on to cable needle and leave at front of work, p. 1, then k. 1 from cable needle); c. 4, cable 4 (sl. next 2 sts. on to cable needle and leave at back of work, k. 2, then k. 2 from cable needle); c. 10, cable 10 (sl. next 5 sts. on to cable needle and leave at back of work, k. 5, then k. 5 from cable needle); single rib is k. 1 and p. 1 alternately.*

NOTE: *The instructions are given for the 97 cm (38 inch) chest size. Where they vary, work figures within first brackets for the 102 cm (40 inch) chest size; work figures within second brackets for the 107 cm (42 inch) chest size.*

THE BACK: With No. 10 (3¼ mm) needles cast on 138 (144) (150) sts. and work 17 rows in single rib.

Inc. row: Rib 16 (19) (22), inc., * rib 20, inc.; repeat from * 4 times, rib 16 (19) (22)—144 (150) (156) sts.

Change to No. 8 (4 mm) needles.

1st pattern row: P. 7 (10) (13), k. 10, * p. 2 tw.2 lt., tw.2 lt., tw.2 lt., p. 6, k. 10 *; repeat from * to * until 7 (10) (13) sts. remain, p. to end.

2nd row: K. 7 (10) (13), p. 10, * k. 6, p. 1, k. 1, p. 1, k. 1, p. 1, k. 3, p. 10 *; repeat from * to * until 7 (10) (13) sts. remain, k. to end.

3rd row: P. 7 (10) (13), c. 10, * p. 3, tw.2 lt., tw.2 lt., tw.2 lt., p. 5, c. 10 *; repeat from * to * until 7 (10) (13) sts. remain, p. to end.

4th row: K. 7 (10) (13), p. 10, * k. 5, p. 1, k. 1, p. 1, k. 1, p. 1, k. 4, p. 10 *; repeat from * to * until 7 (10) (13) sts. remain, k. to end.

5th row: P. 7 (10) (13), k. 2, p. 1, k. 4, p. 1, k. 2, * p. 4, tw.2 lt., tw.2 lt., tw.2 lt., p. 4, k. 2, p. 1, k. 4, p. 1, k. 2 *; repeat from * to * until 7 (10) (13) sts. remain, p. to end.

6th row: K. 7 (10) (13), p. 2, k. 1, p. 4, k. 1, p. 2, * k. 4, p. 1, k. 1, p. 1, k. 1, p. 1, k. 5, p. 2, k. 1, p. 4, k. 1, p. 2 *; repeat from * to * until 7 (10) (13) sts. remain, k. to end.

7th row: P. 7 (10) (13), k. 2, p. 1, c. 4, p. 1, k. 2, * p. 5, tw.2 lt., tw.2 lt., tw.2 lt., p. 3, k. 2, p. 1, c. 4, p. 1, k. 2 *; repeat from * to * until 7 (10) (13) sts. remain, p. to end.

8th row: K. 7 (10) (13), p. 2, k. 1, p. 4, k. 1, p. 2, * k. 3, p. 1, k. 1, p. 1, k. 1, p. 1, k. 6, p. 2, k. 1, p. 4, k. 1, p. 2 *; repeat from * to * until 7 (10) (13) sts. remain, k. to end.

9th row: P. 7 (10) (13), k. 2, p. 1, k. 4, p. 1, k. 2, * p. 6, tw.2 lt., tw.2 lt., tw.2 lt., p. 2, k. 2, p. 1, k. 4, p. 1, k. 2 *; repeat from * to * until 7 (10) (13) sts. remain, p. to end.

10th row: K. 7 (10) (13), p. 2, k. 1, p. 4, k. 1, p. 2, * k. 2, p. 1, k. 1, p. 1, k. 1, p. 1, k. 7, p. 2, k. 1, p. 4, k. 1, p. 2 *; repeat from * to * until 7 (10) (13) sts. remain, k. to end.

11th row: P. 7 (10) (13), k. 2, p. 1, c. 4, p. 1, k. 2, * p. 6, tw.2 rt., tw.2 rt., tw.2 rt., p. 2, k. 2, p. 1, c. 4, p. 1, k. 2 *; repeat from * to * until 7 (10) (13) sts. remain, p. to end.

12th row: As 8th row.

13th row: P. 7 (10) (13), k. 2, p. 1, k. 4, p. 1, k. 2, * p. 5, tw.2 rt., tw.2 rt., tw.2 rt., p. 3, k. 2, p. 1, k. 4, p. 1, k. 2 *; repeat from * to * until 7 (10) (13) sts. remain, p. to end.

14th row: As 6th row.

15th row: P. 7 (10) (13), k. 2, p. 1, c. 4, p. 1, k. 2, * p. 4, tw.2 rt., tw.2 rt., tw.2 rt., p. 4, k. 2, p. 1, c. 4, p. 1, k. 2 *; repeat from * to * until 7 (10) (13) sts. remain, p. to end.

16th row: K. 7 (10) (13), p. 2, k. 1, p. 4, k. 1, p. 2, * k. 5, p. 1, k. 1, p. 1, k. 1, p. 1, k. 4, p. 2, k. 1, p. 4, k. 1, p. 2 *; repeat from * to * until 7 (10) (13) sts. remain, k. to end.

17th row: P. 7 (10) (13), k. 2, p. 1, k. 4, p. 1, k. 2, * p. 3, tw.2 rt., tw.2 rt., tw.2 rt., p. 5, k. 2, p. 1, k. 4, p. 1, k. 2 *; repeat from * to * until 7 (10) (13) sts. remain, p. to end.

18th row: K. 7 (10) (13), p. 2, k. 1, p. 4, k. 1, p. 2, * k. 6, p. 1, k. 1, p. 1, k. 1, p. 1, k. 3, p. 2, k. 1, p. 4, k. 1, p. 2 *; repeat from * to * until 7 (10) (13) sts. remain, k. to end.

19th row: P. 7 (10) (13), k. 10, * p. 2, tw.2 rt., tw.2 rt., tw.2 rt., p. 6, k. 10 *; repeat from * to * until 7 (10) (13) sts. remain, p. to end.

20th row: K. 7 (10) (13), p. 10, * k. 7, p. 1, k. 1, p. 1, k. 1, p. 1, k. 2, p. 10 *; repeat from * to * until 7 (10) (13) sts. remain, k. to end.

These 20 rows form the pattern. Pattern a further 76 rows.

To shape the armholes: Keeping continuity of pattern, cast off 6 (7) (8) sts. at beginning of next 2 rows, then dec. 1 st. each end of next row and the 10 (11) (12) following alternate rows—110 (112) (114) sts.

Pattern 45 rows.

Above *Cable Pattern Waistcoat*

To slope shoulders: Cast off 8 sts. at beginning of next 6 rows then 8 (9) (10) sts. on the following 2 rows. Cast off.

THE LEFT FRONT: With No. 10 (3¼ mm) needles cast on 64 (66) (70) sts. and work 17 rows in single rib.

Inc. row: Rib 9 (9) (12), inc., * rib 14 (11) (14), inc.; repeat from * until 9 (8) (12) sts. remain, rib to end—68 (71) (74) sts.

Change to No. 8 (4 mm) needles.

1st pattern row: P. 7 (10) (13), k. 10, repeat from * to * twice of 1st pattern row of back, p.3.

2nd row: K. 3, p. 10, repeat from * to * twice of 2nd pattern row of back, k. 7 (10) (13).

3rd row: P. 7 (10) (13), c. 10, repeat from * to * twice of 3rd pattern row of back, p. 3.

4th row: K. 3, p. 10, repeat from * to * twice of 4th pattern row of back, k. 7 (10) (13).

These 4 rows set the position of the pattern for the left front. Keeping continuity of the pattern to match back, pattern a further 92 rows.

To shape armhole and shape front edge: 1st row: Cast off 6 (7) (8), pattern until 2 sts. remain, dec.

2nd row: Pattern to end.

★★Dec. 1 st. at armhole edge on next row and the 10 (11) (12) following alternate rows, *at the same time*, dec. 1 st. at front edge on the 2nd row and every following 3rd row until 19 decreases have been worked in all at front edge—32 (33) (34) sts.

Pattern 13 (15) (17) rows—pattern 14 (16) (18) rows here when working right front.

Continued on page 72

To slope shoulder: Cast off 8 sts. at beginning of next row and the 2 following alternate rows.

Work 1 row, then cast off remaining 8 (9) (10) sts.

THE RIGHT FRONT: Work as given for left front until the inc. row has been completed—68 (71) (74) sts.

Change to No. 8 (4 mm) needles.

1st pattern row: P. 3, k. 10, * p. 6, tw.2 rt., tw.2 rt., tw.2 rt., p. 2, k. 10 *; repeat from * to * once, p. 7 (10) (13).

2nd row: K. 7 (10) (13), p. 10, * k. 3, p. 1, k. 1, p. 1, k. 1, p. 1, k. 6, p. 10 *; repeat from * to * once, k. 3.

3rd row: P. 3, c. 10, * p. 5, tw.2 rt., tw.2 rt., tw.2 rt., p. 3, c. 10 *; repeat from * to * once, p. 7 (10) (13).

4th row: K. 7 (10) (13), p. 10, * k. 4, p. 1, k. 1, p. 1, k. 1, p. 1, k. 5, p. 10 *; repeat from * to * once, k. 3.

These 4 rows set the position of the pattern for the right front.

Keeping continuity of the pattern panels as set to match back panels, pattern a further 92 rows.

To shape front: Next row: Dec., pattern to end.

To shape armhole and continue front shaping: 1st row: Cast off 6 (7) (8) sts., pattern to end.

Work as given for left front from ** to end, noting variation where indicated.

THE FRONT BAND: First join shoulder seams. With No. 10 ($3\frac{1}{4}$ mm) needles cast on 12 sts. and work 4 rows in single rib.

1st buttonhole row: Rib 4, cast off 4, rib to end.

2nd buttonhole row: Rib to end, casting on 4 sts. over those cast off on previous row. Rib 28 rows.

Repeat last 30 rows, 3 times, then the 2 buttonhole rows again.

Continue in rib until band fits up left front, round neck and down right front, casting off when correct length is assured.

THE ARMHOLE BANDS (2 alike): With right side facing, rejoin yarn and using No. 10 ($3\frac{1}{4}$ mm) needles, pick up and k. 120 (124) (130) sts. all round armhole edge and work 12 rows in single rib.

Cast off in rib.

TO MAKE UP THE WAISTCOAT: Press lightly with a warm iron over a damp cloth. Join side seams, including armhole bands. Sew on front band, setting top buttonhole level with first front decrease on left front. Add buttons.

Waistcoat in Moss Stitch

Illustrated opposite

MEASUREMENTS	*in centimetres (and inches, in brackets)*				
To fit chest sizes	97 (38)	102 (40)	107 (42)	112 (44)	117 (46)
All round at underarms—fastened	102.5 ($40\frac{1}{2}$)	108.5 ($42\frac{3}{4}$)	113 ($44\frac{1}{2}$)	119.5 (47)	124 (49)
Side seam, including armhole border	36.5 ($14\frac{1}{2}$)	36.5 ($14\frac{1}{2}$)	36.5 ($14\frac{1}{2}$)	36.5 ($14\frac{1}{2}$)	36.5 ($14\frac{1}{2}$)
Length	56.5 ($22\frac{1}{4}$)	57.5 ($22\frac{3}{4}$)	58.5 (23)	59.5 ($23\frac{1}{2}$)	60.5 ($23\frac{3}{4}$)

MATERIALS: *Allow the following quantities in 50 g balls of Hayfield Beaulon Double Knitting: 6 for 97 cm size; 7 for 102 cm size; 8 for 107 cm size; 9 for 112 cm size; 9 for 117 cm size. For any one size: a pair each of No. 9 ($3\frac{3}{4}$ mm) and No. 11 (3 mm) knitting needles; 6 buttons.*

TENSION: *Work at a tension of 18 stitches to measure 8 cm in width and 38 rows to measure 10 cm in depth, over the moss stitch, using 9 ($3\frac{3}{4}$ mm) needles, to obtain the measurements given.*

ABBREVIATIONS: To be read before working: *K., knit plain, p., purl; st., stitch; tog., together; inc., increase (by working twice into same st.); dec., decrease (by working 2 sts. tog.); m.st., moss stitch.*

NOTE: *The instructions are given for the 97 cm (38 inch) size. Where they vary, work the figures within the first brackets for the 102 cm (40 inch) size; work the figures within the second brackets for the 107 cm (42 inch) size, and so on.*

THE BACK: With No. 11 (3 mm) needles cast on 115 (121) (127) (133) (139) sts. and work as follows:

1st rib row: K. 2, * p. 1, k. 1; repeat from * until 1 st. remains, k. 1.

2nd rib row: K. 1, * p. 1, k. 1; repeat from * to end.

Repeat these 2 rows, 14 times more.

Change to No. 9 ($3\frac{3}{4}$ mm) needles and work as follows:

Next (pattern) row: K. 1, * p. 1, k. 1; repeat from * to end.

This row forms the m.st., pattern a further 97 rows.

To shape the armholes: Cast off 4 sts. at the beginning of the next 2 rows.

Dec. 1 st. at each end of the next 12 rows, then dec. 1 st. at each end of the next row and 3 (5) (6) (8) (9) following alternate rows—75 (77) (81) (83) (87) sts.

Pattern 59 (59) (61) (61) (63) rows.

To slope the shoulders: Cast off 7 (7) (7) (8) (8) sts. at the beginning of the next 4 rows, then cast off 6 (7) (8) (7) (8) sts. at the beginning of the following 2 rows.

Cast off remaining 35 (35) (37) (37) (39) sts.

THE POCKET BACKS (both alike): With No. 9 ($3\frac{3}{4}$ mm) needles cast on 31 sts. and m.st. 30 rows. Break yarn and leave.

THE LEFT FRONT: With No. 11 (3 mm) needles cast on 63 (67) (69) (73) (75) sts. and work 6 rows in rib as given on back.

1st (buttonhole) row: Rib until 6 sts. remain, cast off 2 sts., rib 4.

2nd (buttonhole) row: Rib to end, casting on 2 sts. over those cast off on previous row.

Rib 20 rows. Work 1st buttonhole row.

Next row: Rib 4, turn, cast on 2 sts., turn, rib 1, inc. in next st., leave these 9 sts. on a safety-pin, rib to end and work on these 55 (59) (61) (65) (67) sts. as follows:

Change to No. 9 (3¾ mm) needles.

M.st. 30 rows.

Next (pocket) row: M.st. 8 (12) (14) (18) (20), slip next 31 sts. onto a stitch-holder and leave at front of work, m.st. across 31 sts. of one pocket back, m.st. to end.

** M.st. 67 rows—m.st. 68 rows here when working right front.

To shape the armhole: Cast off 4 sts. at the beginning of the next row.

Work 1 row—omit this row when working right front.

Dec. 1 st. at armhole edge on the next 12 rows, *at the same time*, dec. 1 st. at neck edge on the 1st, and 2 following 4th rows—36 (40) (42) (46) (48) sts.

Dec. 1 st. at armhole edge on the next row and 3 (5) (6) (8) (9) following alternate rows, *at the same time*, dec. 1 st. at neck edge on the 1st and 1 (2) (3) (4) (4) following 4th rows—30 (31) (31) (32) (33) sts.

Work 1 (1) (3) (3) (1) row(s).

Dec. 1 st. at neck edge on the next row and 9 (9) (8) (8) (8) following 4th rows—20 (21) (22) (23) (24) sts.

M.st. 21 (21) (25) (25) (29) rows—m.st. 22 (22) (26) (26) (30) rows here when working right front.

To slope the shoulder: Cast off 7 (7) (7) (8) (8) sts. at the beginning of the next row and the following alternate row.

Work 1 row.

Cast off remaining 6 (7) (8) (7) (8) sts.

THE RIGHT FRONT: With No. 11 (3 mm) needles cast on 63 (67) (69) (73) (75) sts. and work 30 rows in rib as given on back.

Next row: Rib 7, inc. in next st., leave these 9 sts. on a safety-pin.

Change to No. 9 (3¾ mm) needles and m.st. 30 rows on these remaining 55 (59) (61) (65) (67) sts.

Next (pocket) row: M.st. 16, slip next 31 sts. onto a stitch-holder and leave at front of work, m.st. across 31 sts. of other pocket back, m.st. to end.

Work as given for left front from ** to end, noting variations where indicated.

THE BUTTONHOLE BAND: With right side of work facing using No. 11 (3 mm) needles, rejoin yarn to 9 sts. on safety-pin and rib 20 rows.

1st (buttonhole) row: Rib 3, cast off 2 sts., rib to end.

2nd (buttonhole) row: Rib, casting on 2 sts. over those cast off on previous row.

Repeat the last 22 rows, 3 times more.

Continue in rib until band fits up front, round to centre back neck, casting off when correct length is assured and setting last buttonhole level with 1st front dec.

THE BUTTON BAND: With wrong side of work facing, rejoin yarn to sts. on safety-pin and work as given for buttonhole band to end, omitting buttonholes.

THE ARMHOLE BORDERS (both alike): First join shoulder seams. With right side of work facing, rejoin yarn and using No. 11 (3 mm) needles, pick up and k. 139 (143) (147) (151) (155) sts. round armhole edge and work 8 rows in rib as given on back, beginning with a 2nd rib row.

Cast off.

THE POCKET TOPS (both alike): With right side of work facing, using No. 11 (3 mm) needles, rejoin yarn to 31 sts. of one pocket and work 6 rows in rib as given on back.

Cast off.

TO MAKE UP THE WAISTCOAT: Press on the wrong side with a cool iron over a dry cloth.

Join the side seams, continuing the seam across the armhole borders. Sew pocket backs to wrong side and row ends of pocket tops to right side. Join front bands at centre back neck and sew on front bands. Sew on buttons.

Man's Rice Stitch Cardigan

Illustrated opposite

MEASUREMENTS	in centimetres *(and inches, in brackets)*		
To fit chest sizes	97 (38)	102 (40)	107 (42)
All round underarms fastened	101 (39¾)	105 (41¼)	110.5 (43½)
Side seam	40.5 (16)	40.5 (16)	40.5 (16)
Length	64 (25¼)	64.5 (25½)	65.5 (25¾)
Sleeve seam	46.5 (18¼)	46.5 (18¼)	46.5 (18¼)

MATERIALS: *Allow the following quantities in 50 g balls of King Cole Superspun Superwash Double Knitting:* 12 *for* 97 *cm size;* 12 *for* 102 *cm size;* 13 *for* 107 *cm size. For any one size: a pair each of No.* 8 *(4 mm) and No.* 11 *(3 mm) knitting needles;* 5 *buttons.*

TENSION: *Work at a tension of 25 stitches and 34 rows to measure* 10 × 10 *cm, over the pattern, using No.* 8 *(4 mm) needles, to obtain measurements given.*

ABBREVIATIONS: To be read before working: *K., knit plain; p., purl; st., stitch; tog., together; inc., increase (by working twice into same st.); dec., decrease (by working 2 sts. tog.); k. 2 tog.b., k. 2 tog. through back of sts.; single rib is k.* 1*, p.* 1 *alternately.*

NOTE: *The instructions are given for the 97 cm (38 inch) size. Where they vary, work figures within first brackets for 102 cm (40 inch) size; work figures within second brackets for 107 cm (42 inch) size.*

THE BACK: With No. 11 (3 mm) needles cast on 125 (131) (137) sts. and, beginning odd-numbered rows with k. 1 and even-numbered rows with p. 1, work 22 rows in single rib.

Change to No. 8 (4 mm) needles and work the 2-row pattern as follows:

1st row: K. 1, * p. 1, k. 1; repeat from * to end.

2nd row: All k.

Pattern a further 114 rows.

To shape the raglan armholes: 1st and 2nd rows: Cast off 5 (6) (7) sts., pattern to end.

3rd row: K. 1, k. 2 tog.b., pattern until 3 sts. remain, k. 2 tog., k. 1.

4th row: P. 2, k. until 2 sts. remain, p. 2.

Repeat 3rd and 4th rows 38 (39) (40) times more—37 (39) (41) sts.

Cast off.

THE POCKET LININGS (2 alike): With No. 8 (4 mm) needles cast on 35 sts. and pattern 34 rows. Break yarn and leave.

THE LEFT FRONT: With No. 11 (3 mm) needles cast on 61 (63) (67) sts. and work 22 rows in rib as given for back.

Change to No. 8 (4 mm) needles and pattern 34 rows. **

To work pocket: Next row: Pattern 16 (18) (22), leave remaining 45 sts. on a spare needle, then pattern across 35 sts. of one pocket lining—51 (53) (57) sts.

Pattern 12 rows.

Leave sts. on a stitch-holder.

With right side of work facing, rejoin yarn to inner end

of 45 sts. on spare needle and cast off 4 sts. at beginning of next row, 7 sts. on the 4 following alternate rows, then 3 sts. on the next alternate row—10 sts.

Pattern 2 rows.

Next (joining) row: K. 10, then k. across sts. on stitch-holder—61 (63) (67) sts.

Pattern 68 rows.

To shape the raglan armhole and shape front edge: 1st row: Cast off 5 (6) (7), pattern to end.

2nd row: K. until 2 sts. remain, p. 2.

3rd row: K. 1, k. 2 tog.b., pattern until 2 sts. remain, k. 2 tog.

4th row: As 2nd row.

5th row: K. 1, k. 2 tog.b., pattern to end.

*** Repeat 2nd to 5th rows 14 (14) (16) times more, then the 4th and 5th rows, 9 (10) (7) times—2 sts.

K. 2 tog. and fasten off.

THE RIGHT FRONT: Work as left front to **.

To work pocket: Next row: Pattern 45, turn and leave remaining 16 (18) (22) sts. on a spare needle.

Cast off 4 sts. at beginning of next row, 7 sts. on the 4 following alternate rows, then 3 sts. on the next alternate row—10 sts.

Pattern 1 row.

Leave sts. on a stitch-holder.

With No. 8 (4 mm) needles, rejoin yarn and pattern across 35 sts. of second pocket lining, then with same needle pattern across 16 (18) (22) sts. from spare needle—51 (53) (57) sts.

Pattern 12 rows.

Next row: K. to end, then k. across 10 sts. on stitch-holder—61 (63) (67) sts.

Pattern 69 rows.

To shape the raglan armhole and front edge: 1st row: Cast off 5 (6) (7) sts., k. to end.

2nd row: K. 2 tog., pattern until 3 sts. remain, k. 2 tog., k. 1.

3rd row: P. 2, k. to end.

4th row: Pattern until 3 sts. remain, k. 2 tog., k. 1.

5th row: As 3rd row.

Work as left front from ***.

THE SLEEVES: (both alike): With No. 11 (3 mm) needles cast on 49 (53) (57) sts. and work 22 rows in rib as given for back.

Change to No. 8 (4 mm) needles.

Taking extra sts. into the pattern as they occur, work 4 rows in pattern as given on back, then inc. 1 st. each end of next row, then on the 23 following 5th rows—97 (101) (105) sts.

Pattern 16 rows.

To shape raglan sleeve top: Work exactly as given for armhole shaping on back, when 9 sts. will remain.

Cast off.

THE FRONT BAND: First join raglan seams. With No. 11 (3 mm) needles cast on 9 sts.

1st rib row: K. 2, * p. 1, k. 1; repeat from * twice, k. 1 more.

2nd rib row: K. 1, * p. 1, k. 1; repeat from * to end. Repeat these 2 rows, once more.

1st buttonhole row: Rib 3, cast off 3, rib to end.

2nd buttonhole row: Rib to end, casting on 3 sts. over those cast off on previous row.

Rib 30 rows.

Repeat the last 32 rows 3 times more, then the 2 buttonhole rows again.

Continue in rib until band is long enough to fit up left front, across back neck and down right front, casting off in rib when correct length is assured.

THE POCKET TOPS (both alike): With right side of work facing and using No. 11 (3 mm) needles, rejoin yarn and pick up and k. 33 sts. across top of pocket.

Beginning with an even-numbered row, work 8 rows in rib as given for back.

Cast off in rib.

TO MAKE UP THE CARDIGAN: Press lightly with a warm iron over a damp cloth. Join sleeve and side seams. Sew front band into position, placing top buttonhole level with 1st front dec. Add buttons. Sew down row ends of pocket tops to right side and pocket linings to wrong side.

Below *Man's Rice Stitch Cardigan*

V-neck Aran Cardigan

Illustrated on page 78

MEASUREMENTS				
	in centimetres (and inches, in brackets)			
To fit chest sizes	86 (34)	91 (36)	97 (38)	102 (40)
All round at widest part	92 (36¼)	98 (38½)	104.5 (41¼)	110.5 (43½)
Side seam	42 (16½)	42 (16½)	42 (16½)	42 (16½)
Length	67 (26½)	67.5 (26¾)	68.5 (27)	69 (27¼)
Sleeve seam	47 (18½)	47 (18½)	47 (18½)	47 (18½)

To fit chest sizes	107 (42)	112 (44)	117-122 (46-48)
All round at widest part	116.5 (45¾)	123 (48½)	129 (50¾)
Side seam	43.5 (17)	43.5 (17)	43.5 (17)
Length	70.5 (27¾)	71.5 (28)	72 (28¼)
Sleeve seam	48.5 (19¼)	48.5 (19¼)	48.5 (19¼)

MATERIALS: *Allow the following quantities in 50 g balls of Emu Superwash Wool Double Knitting: 14 for the 86 cm size; 15 for the 91 cm size; 16 for the 97 cm size; 17 for the 102 cm size; 18 for the 107 cm size; 19 for the 112 cm size; 20 for the 117–122 cm size. For any one size: a pair each of No. 8 (4 mm) and No. 10 (3¼ mm) knitting needles; a cable needle; 5 buttons.*

TENSION: *Work at a tension of 26 sts. and 32 rows to measure 10 × 10 cm, over the rice st., 1 pattern panel measures 15 cm (5¾ inches), using No. 8 (4 mm) needles to obtain the measurements given.*

ABBREVIATIONS: To be read before working: *K., knit plain; p., purl; st., stitch; r.st., rice st.; sl., slip; dec., decrease (by taking 2 sts. together); inc., increase (by working twice into same st.); p.1b. or k.1b., p. or k. 1 through back of st.; tw.2f., twist 2 front (sl. next st. on to cable needle and leave at front of work, k. 1, then k. st. from cable needle); tw.2b., twist 2 back (sl. next st. on to cable needle and leave at back of work, k. 1, then k. st. from cable needle); cr.3r., cross 3 right (sl. next st. on to cable needle and leave at back of work, k. 2, then k. st. from cable needle); cr.3lt., cross 3 left (sl. next 2 sts. on to cable needle and leave at front of work, p. 1, then k. 2 from cable needle); c.4b., cable 4 back (sl. next 2 sts. on to cable needle and leave at back of work, k. 2, then k. 2 from cable needle); c.4f., cable 4 front (sl. next 2 sts. on to cable needle and leave at front of work, k. 2, then k. 2 from cable needle); cr.4lt., cross 4 left (sl. next 2 sts. on to cable needle and leave at front of work, p. 2, then p. 2 from cable needle); single rib is k. 1 and p. 1 alternately.*

NOTE: *The instructions are given for the 86 cm (34 inch) size. Where they vary, work the figures within the first brackets for the 91 cm (36 inch) size; work the figures within the second brackets for the 97 cm (38 inch) size, and so on.*

THE BACK: With No. 10 (3¼ mm) needles cast on 142 (150)(158)(166)(174)(182)(190) sts. and work 16 rows in single rib increasing 1 st. at the end of the last of these rows—143 (151)(159)(167)(175)(183)(191) sts.

Change to No. 8 (4 mm) needles and work the 24-row pattern as follows:

1st row: * For r.st. p. 1, k.1b., *; work from * to * 4 (5)(6)(7)(8)(9)(10) times, p. 1 **, then *** k. 8, p. 2, tw.2f., tw.2b., p. 8, cr.3r., cr.3lt., p. 8, tw.2f., tw.2b., p. 2, k. 8 ***, work from * to * 10 (12)(14)(16)(18)(20)(22) times,

p. 1, work from *** to *** once, work from first * to ** once.

2nd row: * For r.st. k. 11 (13)(15)(17)(19)(21)(23) *, then *** p. 8, k. 2, p. 4, k. 8, p. 2, k. 1, p.1b., p. 2, k. 8, p. 4, k. 2, p. 8 ***, for r.st. k. 21 (25)(29)(33)(37)(41)(45), work from *** to *** once, work from * to * once.

These 2 rows form the r.st. pattern for the back at each end and in centre, keeping continuity of r.st. continue as follows:

3rd row: R.st. 11 (13)(15)(17)(19)(21)(23), *** k. 8, p. 2, tw.2b., tw.2f., p. 7, cr.3r., k.1b., p. 1, cr.3lt., p. 7, tw.2b., tw.2f., p. 2, k. 8 ***, r.st. 21 (25)(29)(33)(37)(41)(45), work from *** to *** once, r.st. to end.

4th row: R.st. 11 (13)(15)(17)(19)(21)(23), *** p. 8, k. 2, p. 4, k. 7, p. 2, p.1b., k. 1, p.1b., k. 1, p. 2, k. 7, p. 4, k. 2, p. 8 ***, r.st. 21 (25)(29)(33)(37)(41)(45), work from *** to *** once, r.st. to end.

5th row: R.st. 11 (13)(15)(17)(19)(21)(23), *** c.4f., c.4b., p. 2, tw.2f., tw.2b., p. 6, cr.3r., p. 1, k.1b., p. 1, k.1b., cr.3lt., p. 6, tw.2f., tw.2b., p. 2, c.4f., c.4b. ***, r.st. 21 (25)(29)(33)(37)(41)(45), work from *** to *** once, r.st. to end.

6th row: R.st. 11 (13)(15)(17)(19)(21)(23), *** p. 8, k. 2, p. 4, k. 6, p. 2, k. 1, p.1b., k. 1, p.1b., k. 1, p.1b., p.2, k. 6, p. 4, k. 2, p. 8 ***, r.st. 21 (25)(29)(33)(37)(41)(45), work from *** to *** once, r.st. to end.

7th row: R.st. 11 (13)(15)(17)(19)(21)(23), *** k. 8, p. 2, tw.2b., tw.2f., p. 5, cr.3r., k.1b., p. 1, k. 1b., p. 1, k.1b., p. 1, cr.3lt., p. 5, tw.2b., tw.2f., p. 2, k. 8 ***, r.st. 21 (25)(29)(33)(37)(41)(45), work from *** to *** once, r.st. to end.

8th row: R.st. 11 (13)(15)(17)(19)(21)(23), *** p. 8, k. 2, p. 4, k. 5, p. 2, p.1b., k. 1, p.1b., k. 1, p.1b., k. 1, p.1b., k. 1, p.2, k. 5, p. 4, k. 2, p. 8 ***, r.st. 21 (25)(29)(33)(37)(41)(45), work from *** to *** once, r.st. to end.

9th row: R.st. 11 (13)(15)(17)(19)(21)(23), *** c.4f., c.4b., p. 2, tw.2f., tw.2b., p. 4, cr.3r., p. 1, k. 1b., p. 1, k. 1b., p. 1, k. 1b., cr.3lt., p. 4, tw.2f., tw.2b., p. 2, c.4f., c.4b. ***, r.st. 21 (25)(29)(33)(37)(41)(45), work from *** to *** once, r.st. to end.

10th row: R.st 11 (13)(15)(17)(19)(21)(23), *** p. 8, k. 2, p. 4, k. 4, p. 2, k. 1, p.1b., k. 1, p.1b., k. 1, p.1b., k. 1, p.1b., p. 2, k. 4, p. 4, k. 2, p. 8 ***, r.st. 21 (25)(29)(33)(37)(41)(45), work from *** to *** once, r.st. to end.

11th row: R.st. 11 (13) (15) (17) (19) (21) (23), *** k. 8, p. 2, tw.2b., tw.2f., p. 3, cr.3r., k.1b., p. 1, k.1b., p. 1, k.1b., p. 1, k.1b., p. 1, k.1b., p. 1, cr.3lt., p. 3, tw.2b., tw.2f., p. 2, k. 8 ***, r.st 21 (25) (29) (33) (37) (41) (45), work from *** to *** once, r.st. to end.

12th row: R.st 11 (13) (15) (17) (19) (21) (23), *** p. 8, k. 2, p. 4, k. 3, p. 2, p.1b., k. 1, p.1b., k. 1, p.1b., k. 1, p.1b., k. 1, p.1b., k. 1, p. 2, k. 3, p. 4, k. 2, p. 8 ***, r.st. 21 (25) (29) (33) (37) (41) (45), work from *** to *** once, r.st. to end.

13th row: R.st. 11 (13) (15) (17) (19) (21) (23), *** c.4b., c.4f., p. 2, tw.2f., tw.2b., p. 3, cr.3lt., k.1b., p. 1, k.1b., p. 1, k.1b., p. 1, k.1b., p. 1, k.1b., p. 1, cr.3r., p. 3, tw.2f., tw.2b., p. 2, c.4b., c.4f. ***, r.st. 21 (25) (29) (33) (37) (41) (45), work from *** to *** once, r.st. to end.

14th row: R.st. 11 (13) (15) (17) (19) (21) (23), *** p. 8, k. 2, p. 4, k. 4, p. 2, k. 1, p.1b., k. 1, p.1b., k. 1, p.1b., k.1, p.1b., p. 2, k. 4, p. 4, k. 2, p. 8 ***, r.st. 21 (25) (29) (33) (37) (41) (45), work from *** to *** once, r.st. to end.

15th row: R.st. 11 (13) (15) (17) (19) (21) (23), *** k. 8, p. 2, tw.2b., tw.2f., p. 4, cr.3lt., p. 1, k.1b., p. 1, k.1b., p. 1, k.1b., p. 1, k.1b., cr.3r., p. 4, tw.2b., tw.2f., p. 2, k. 8 ***, r.st. 21 (25) (29) (33) (37) (41) (45), work from *** to *** once, r.st. to end.

16th row: R.st 11 (13) (15) (17) (19) (21) (23), *** p. 8, k. 2, p. 4, k. 5, p. 2, p.1b., k. 1, p.1b., k. 1, p.1b., k. 1, p.1b., k. 1, p. 2, k. 5, p. 4, k. 2, p. 8 ***, r.st. 21 (25) (29) (33) (37) (41) (45), work from *** to *** once, r.st. to end.

17th row: R.st. 11 (13) (15) (17) (19) (21) (23), *** c.4b., c.4f., p. 2, tw.2f., tw.2b., p. 5, cr.3lt., k.1b., p. 1, k.1b., p. 1, cr.3r., p. 5, tw.2f., tw.2b., p. 2, c.4b., c.4f. ***, r.st. 21 (25) (29) (33) (37) (41) (45), work from *** to *** once, r.st. to end.

18th row: R.st. 11 (13) (15) (17) (19) (21) (23), *** p. 8, k. 2, p. 4, k. 6, p. 2, k. 1, p.1b., k. 1, p.1b., k. 1, p.1b., p. 2, k. 6, p. 4, k. 2, p. 8 ***, r.st. 21 (25) (29) (33) (37) (41) (45), work from *** to *** once, r.st. to end.

19th row: R.st. 11 (13) (15) (17) (19) (21) (23), *** k. 8, p. 2, tw.2b., tw.2f., p. 6, cr.3lt., p.l, k. 1b., p.l, k1b., cr. 3r., p. 6, tw.2b., tw.2f., p. 2, k. 8 ***, r.st. 21 (25) (29) (33) (37) (41) (45), work from *** to *** once, r.st. to end.

20th row: R.st. 11 (13) (15) (17) (19) (21) (23), *** p. 8, k. 2, p. 4, k. 7, p. 2, p.1b., k. 1, p.1b., k. 1, p. 2, k. 7, p. 4, k. 2, p. 8 ***, r.st. 21 (25) (29) (33) (37) (41) (45), work from *** to *** once, r.st. to end.

21st row: R.st. 11 (13) (15) (17) (19) (21) (23), *** k. 8, p. 2, tw.2f., tw.2b., p. 7, cr.3lt., k.1b., p. 1, cr.3r., p. 7, tw.2f., tw.2b., p. 2, k. 8 ***, r.st. 21 (25) (29) (33) (37) (41) (45), work from *** to *** once, r.st. to end.

22nd row: R.st. 11 (13) (15) (17) (19) (21) (23), *** p. 8, k. 2, p. 4, k. 8, p. 2, k. 1, p. 1b., p. 2, k. 8., p. 4, k. 2, p. 8 ***, r.st. 21 (25) (29) (33) (37) (41) (45), work from *** to *** once, r.st. to end.

23rd row: R.st. 11 (13) (15) (17) (19) (21) (23), *** k. 8, p. 2, tw.2b., tw.2f., p. 8, cr.3lt., cr.3r., p. 8, tw.2b., tw.2f., p. 2, k. 8 ***, r.st. 21 (25) (29) (33) (37) (41) (45), work from *** to *** once, r.st. to end.

24th row: R.st. 11 (13) (15) (17) (19) (21) (23), *** p. 8, k. 2, p. 4, k. 9, cr.4lt., k. 9, p. 4, k. 2, p. 8 ***, r.st. 21 (25) (29) (33) (37) (41) (45), work from *** to *** once, r.st. to end.

Pattern a further 96 (96) (96) (96) (100) (100) (100) rows.

To shape the armholes: Keeping continuity of the pattern, cast off 8 (9) (10) (11) (12) (13) (14) sts. at the beginning of each of the next 2 rows, then dec. 1 st. at each end of the next 10 (10) (12) (12) (14) (14) (16) rows—107 (113) (115) (121) (123) (129) (131) sts.

Pattern 60 (62) (62) (64) (64) (66) (66) rows.

To slope the shoulders: Cast off 5 (6) (6) (7) (7) (7) (7) sts. at the beginning of each of the next 4 rows, then cast off 6 (6) (6) (6) (6) (7) (7) sts. at the beginning of the following 4 rows—63 (65) (67) (69) (71) (73) (75) sts. Cast off.

THE LEFT FRONT: With No. 10 (3¼ mm) needles cast on 72 (76) (80) (84) (88) (92) (96) sts. and work 16 rows in single rib.

Change to No. 8 (4 mm) needles.

1st row: For r.st. * p. 1, k.1b.; repeat from * 4 (5) (6) (7) (8) (9) (10) times, p. 1, **, then work from *** to *** as given on 1st row of back once, work from * to ** once.

2nd row: For r.st. k. 11 (13) (15) (17) (19) (21) (23), work from *** to *** as given on 2nd row of back once, k. to end.

These 2 rows set the position of the pattern for the left front.

Keeping continuity of pattern to match back, work a further 100 (100) (100) (100) (102) (102) (102) rows. ****

To shape the front: Dec. 1 st. at end of next row and the 8 (8) (8) (8) (9) (9) (9) following alternate rows—63 (67) (71) (75) (78) (82) (86) sts.

Work 1 row.

To shape the armhole and continue shaping the front: Next row: Cast off 8 (9) (10) (11) (12) (13) (14) sts., pattern until 2 sts. remain, dec.

Next row: Pattern to end.

Next row: Dec., pattern until 2 sts. remain, dec.

Next row: Pattern until 2 sts. remain, dec.

Repeat the last 2 rows 4 (4) (5) (5) (6) (6) (7) times.

***** Keeping armhole edge straight, dec. 1 st. at front edge on the next row and the 16 (17) (17) (18) (17) (18) (18) following alternate rows—22 (24) (24) (26) (26) (28) (28) sts.

Pattern 27 (27) (27) (27) (29) (29) (29) rows—pattern 28 (28) (28) (28) (30) (30) (30) rows here when working right front.

To slope the shoulder: Cast off 5 (6) (6) (7) (7) (7) (7) sts. at the beginning of the next row and the following alternate row, then cast off 6 (6) (6) (6) (6) (7) (7) sts. on the next following alternate row—6 (6) (6) (6) (6) (7) (7) sts.

Work 1 row.

Cast off.

THE RIGHT FRONT: Work as given for left front to ****.

To shape the front: Dec. 1 st. at front edge on the next row and the 9 (9) (9) (9) (10) (10) (10) following alternate rows—62 (66) (70) (74) (77) (81) (85) sts.

To shape the armhole: Next row: Cast off 8 (9) (10) (11) (12) (13) (14) sts., pattern to end.

Next row: Dec., pattern until 2 sts. remain, dec.

Next row: Dec., pattern to end.

Repeat the last 2 rows 4 (4) (5) (5) (6) (6) (7) times.

Work as given for the left front from ***** to end, noting variation.

THE SLEEVES (both alike): With No. 10 (3¼ mm) needles cast on 68 (68) (72) (72) (72) (72) (72) sts. and work 16 rows in single rib.

Change to No. 8 (4 mm) needles and work as follows:

1st row: * For r.st. p. 1, k.1b.; repeat from * 3 (3) (4) (4)

Continued on page 78

(4) (4) (4) times, p. 1 **, then work from *** to *** as given on 1st row of back once, work from 1st * to ** once.

2nd row: For r.st. k. 9 (9) (11) (11) (11) (11) (11), work from *** to *** as given on 2nd row of back once, k. to end.

These 2 rows set the position of the pattern for the sleeves.

Maintaining continuity of the pattern to match back, pattern 2 rows, then, taking extra sts. into r.st. as they occur, inc. 1 st. at each end of the next row and the 14 (16) (16) (18) (20) (22) (24) following 8th (6th) (6th) (6th) (6th) (4th) (4th) rows—98 (102) (106) (110) (114) (118) (122) sts.

Pattern 19 (35) (35) (23) (15) (47) (39) rows.

To shape the sleeve top: Cast off 8 (9) (10) (11) (12) (13) (14) sts. at the beginning of each of the next 2 rows, dec. 1 st. at each end of the next row and the 4 (5) (5) (6) (7) (8) (8) following 4th rows, dec. 1 st. at each end of the 10 (8) (9) (8) (6) (4) (6) following alternate rows, then dec. 1 st. at each of the next 13 (15) (15) (15) (17) (19) (17) rows— 26 (26) (26) (28) (28) (28) (30) sts.

Cast off.

THE FRONT BORDER: With No. 10 (3¼ mm) needles cast on 11 sts., and beginning odd-numbered rows with k. 1 and even-numbered rows with p. 1, work 6 rows in single rib.

1st buttonhole row: Rib 4, cast off 3 sts., rib to end.

2nd buttonhole row: Rib, casting on 3 sts. over those cast off in previous row.

Rib 22 (22) (22) (22) (24) (24) (24) rows.

Repeat the last 24 (24) (24) (24) (26) (26) (26) rows 3 times, then the 2 buttonhole rows again.

Continue in rib until border is long enough when slightly stretched to fit up left front, across back neck and down right front. Cast off in rib.

TO MAKE UP THE CARDIGAN: Press with a warm iron over a damp cloth. Join shoulder seams. Set in sleeves. Join side and sleeve seams. Sew on front border. Sew on buttons.

Opposite *Traditional Guernsey (page 80)*
Below *V-neck Aran Cardigan (page 76)*

Traditional Guernsey

Illustrated on page 79

MEASUREMENTS	*in centimetres (and inches, in brackets)*				
To fit loosely chest sizes	91 (36)	97 (38)	102 (40)	107 (42)	112 (44)
All round at underarms	102 (40)	105.5 (41½)	112 (44)	115 (45¼)	121.5 (47¾)
Side seam	40.5 (16)	40.5 (16)	40.5 (16)	40.5 (16)	40.5 (16)
Length	63 (24¾)	63 (24¾)	64 (25¼)	64 (25¼)	65.5 (25¾)
Sleeve seam	48.5 (19)	48.5 (19)	48.5 (19)	48.5 (19)	48.5 (19)

MATERIALS: *Allow the following quantities in 50 g balls of Emu Guernsey 5-ply: 14 for 91 cm size; 15 each for 97 and 102 cm sizes; 16 for 107 cm size; 17 for 112 cm size. For any one size: a pair each of No. 11 (3 mm) and No. 12 (2¾ mm) knitting needles; a set of 4 double-pointed No. 12 (2¾ mm) needles.*

TENSION: *Work at a tension of 25 stitches and 33 rows to measure 10 × 10 cm, over the stocking st., using No. 11 (3 mm) needles, to obtain measurements given.*

ABBREVIATIONS: To be read before working: *K., knit plain; p., purl; st., stitch; inc., increase (by working twice into next st.); s.s., stocking st. (k. on right side and p. on wrong side); sl., slip.*

NOTE: *The instructions are given for the 91 cm (36 inch) chest size. Where they vary, work figures within first brackets for the 97 cm (38 inch) size; work figures within second brackets for the 102 cm (40 inch) size, and so on.*

THE BACK AND FRONT ALIKE: With No. 12 (2¾ mm) needles cast on 120 (124) (130) (134) (140) sts. and k. 26 rows.

Inc. row: K. 7 (9) (6) (8) (9), inc., ⋆ k. 14 (14) (12) (12) (10), inc.; repeat from ⋆ until 7 (9) (6) (8) (9) sts. remain, k. to end—128 (132) (140) (144) (152) sts.

1st rib row: K. 1, ⋆ p. 2, k. 2; repeat from ⋆ ending last repeat with k. 1 instead of k. 2.

2nd rib row: P. 1, ⋆ k. 2, p. 2; repeat from ⋆ ending last repeat with p. 1 instead of p. 2.

Repeat last 2 rows, twice more.

Change to No. 11 (3 mm) needles.

Beginning with a k. row, s.s. 110 rows—mark each end of last row to denote end of side seams.

S.s. a further 8 rows.

Next row: K. 4, p. 6, k. until 10 sts. remain, p. 6, k. 4.

Next row: P. to end.

Repeat last 2 rows, 33 (33) (35) (35) (37) times more.

Break yarn and leave sts. on a spare double-pointed needle.

THE NECK BAND AND SHOULDERS: With wrong sides of shoulder sts. of back and front together, using No. 11 (3 mm) needles, rejoin yarn to sleeve edge and, working through back and front sts. together, cast off 31 (33) (36) (38) (41) sts.—1 st. left on needle.

1st row: K. 1 from front needle, turn—2 sts.

2nd row: Sl. 1, p. 1, p. 1 from back needle, turn.

3rd row: Sl. 1, k. 2, k. 1 from front needle, turn.

4th row: Sl. 1, p. 3, p. 1 from back needle, turn.

Continue in this way for a further 14 rows, working 1 st. extra from front and back needle at end of row alternately—19 sts.

P. 46 (46) (48) (48) (50) sts. from back needle.

Break yarn and leave 65 (65) (67) (67) (69) sts. on a spare needle.

Turn work and work second shoulder in the same way.

Arrange the 130 (130) (134) (134) (138) sts. on to 3 double-pointed No. 12 (2¾ mm) needles.

Using 4th double-pointed needle, rejoin yarn and k. 1 round decreasing 1 st. in centre of each shoulder gusset— 128 (128) (132) (132) (136) sts.

Work 19 rounds in k. 2, p. 2 rib.

Cast off in rib.

THE SLEEVES (2 alike): With No. 12 (2¾ mm) needles cast on 76 (76) (80) (80) (84) sts. and work 36 rows in rib as given on back and front.

Change to No. 11 (3 mm) needles and beginning with a k. row, s.s. 2 rows, then inc. 1 st. each end of next row and the 10 (10) (13) (13) (13) following 8th (8th) (6th) (6th) (6th) rows—100 (100) (108) (108) (112) sts.

S.s. 23 (23) (25) (25) (25) rows.

To shape gusset: Inc. 1 st. each end of next row and the 5 following alternate rows.

P. 1 row—112 (112) (120) (120) (124) sts.

Next row: K. 7, ⋆ p. 2, k. 2; repeat from ⋆ until 9 sts. remain, p. 2, k. 7.

Next row: P. 7, ⋆ k. 2, p. 2; repeat from ⋆ until 9 sts. remain, k. 2, p. 7.

Repeat last 2 rows, twice. Cast off.

TO MAKE UP THE SWEATER: Press lightly with a warm iron over a damp cloth. Sew cast off sts. at top of sleeves to row ends between markers on back and front. Join side and sleeve seams, leaving row ends of garter st. at lower edges free.

Fashions for Women

Lacy-Panelled Waistcoat

Illustrated on page 82

MEASUREMENTS	*in centimetres (and inches, in brackets)*								
To fit bust sizes	81	(32)	86	(34)	91	(36)	97	(38)	102	(40)
Side seam	32	(12½)	32	(12½)	32	(12½)	33	(13)	33	(13)
Length at centre back	50.5	(19¾)	51	(20)	51.5	(20¼)	53	(20¾)	53.5	(21)
To fit bust sizes	107	(42)	112	(44)	117	(46)	122	(48)	127	(50)
Side seam	33	(13)	34	(13½)	34	(13½)	34	(13½)	34	(13½)
Length at centre back	54	(21¼)	55	(21½)	55.5	(21¾)	56	(22)	56.5	(22¼)

MATERIALS: *Allow the following quantities in 25 g balls of Jaeger 3-ply Wool Pure Botany: 6 for 81 cm and 86 cm sizes; 7 for 91 cm, 97 cm, 102 cm and 107 cm sizes; 8 for 112 cm, 117 cm, 122 cm and 127 cm sizes. For any one size: a pair each of No. 11 (3 mm) and No. 13 (2¼ mm) knitting needles; 4 buttons.*

TENSION: *Work at a tension of 32 stitches and 42 rows over the pattern and 34 stitches and 44 rows over stocking st., to measure 10 × 10 cm, using No. 11 (3 mm) needles, to obtain measurements given.*

ABBREVIATIONS: To be read before working: *K., knit plain; p., purl; st., stitch; tog., together; inc., increase (by working twice into same st.); dec., decrease (by taking 2 sts. tog.); s.s., stocking st. (k. on the right side and p. on the wrong side); double rib is k. 2 and p. 2 alternately; sl., slip; y.fwd., yarn forward to make a st.; s.k.p.o., sl. 1, k. 1, pass sl. st. over.*

NOTE: *The instructions are given for the 81 cm (32 inch) size. Where they vary, work the figures within the first brackets for the 86 cm (34 inch) size, and so on.*

THE BACK: With No. 13 (2¼ mm) needles cast on 138 (146) (154) (162) (170) (178) (186) (194) (202) (210) sts. and beginning odd-numbered rows with k. 2 and even-numbered rows with p. 2, work 44 rows in double rib, increasing 1 st. at each end of the last row— 140 (148) (156) (164) (172) (180) (188) (196) (204) (212) sts.

Change to No. 11 (3 mm) needles and beginning with a k. row, s.s. 90 (90) (90) (94) (94) (94) (98) (98) (98) (98) rows.

To shape the armholes: Cast off 5 sts. at the beginning of each of the next 2 rows, then dec. 1 st. at each end of the next row and the 9 (10) (11) (12) (13) (14) (15) (16) (17) (18) following alternate rows—110 (116) (122) (128) (134) (140) (146) (152) (158) (164) sts.

S.s. 61 rows.

To slope the shoulders: Cast off 5 (4) (5) (6) (5) (5) (7) (7) (6) (7) sts. at the beginning of each of the next 2 rows, 5 (4) (5) (6) (5) (6) (6) (7) (6) (7) sts. at the beginning of each of the next 2 rows, 5 (5) (5) (5) (5) (6) (6) (7) (7) (7) sts. at the beginning of each of the next 2 rows and finally 4 (5) (5) (5) (6) (6) (6) (6) (7) (7) sts. at the beginning of each of the

following 8 rows. Cast off remaining sts.

THE LEFT FRONT: With No. 13 (2¼ mm) needles cast on 58 (62) (66) (70) (74) (78) (82) (86) (90) (94) sts. and work 44 rows in double rib as given for back, increasing 2 (2) (3) (2) (2) (2) (2) (2) (3) (2) sts. on the last row—60 (64) (69) (72) (76) (80) (84) (88) (93) (96) sts.

Change to No. 11 (3 mm) needles. **

1st row: K. 3 (3) (2) (1) (3) (2) (1) (3) (3) (1), *k. 2 tog., k. 5, y.fwd., k. 1, y.fwd., s.k.p.o., k. 1 (2) (1) (2) (2) (1) (2) (2) (1) (2); repeat from * until 13 (13) (12) (11) (13) (12) (11) (13) (13) (11) sts. remain, k. 2 tog., k. 5, y.fwd., k. 1, y.fwd., s.k.p.o., k. to end.

2nd and alternate rows: All p.

3rd row: K. 3 (3) (2) (1) (3) (2) (1) (3) (3) (1), *k. 2 tog., k. 4, y.fwd., k. 1, y.fwd., k. 1, s.k.p.o., k. 1 (2) (1) (2) (2) (1) (2) (2) (1) (2); repeat from * until 13 (13) (12) (11) (13) (12) (11) (13) (13) (11) sts. remain, k. 2 tog., k. 4, y.fwd., k. 1, y.fwd., k. 1, s.k.p.o., k. to end.

5th row: K. 3 (3) (2) (1) (3) (2) (1) (3) (3) (1), *k. 2 tog., k. 3, y.fwd., k. 1, y.fwd., k. 2, s.k.p.o., k. 1 (2) (1) (2) (2) (1) (2) (2) (1) (2); repeat from * until 13 (13) (12) (11) (13) (12) (11) (13) (13) (11) sts. remain, k. 2 tog., k. 3, y.fwd., k. 1, y.fwd., k. 2, s.k.p.o., k. to end.

7th row: K. 3 (3) (2) (1) (3) (2) (1) (3) (3) (1), *k. 2 tog., k. 2, y.fwd., k. 1, y.fwd., k. 3, s.k.p.o., k. 1 (2) (1) (2) (2) (1) (2) (2) (1) (2); repeat from * until 13 (13) (12) (11) (13) (12) (11) (13) (13) (11) sts. remain, k. 2 tog., k. 2, y.fwd., k. 1, y.fwd., k. 3, s.k.p.o., k. to end.

9th row: K. 3 (3) (2) (1) (3) (2) (1) (3) (3) (1), *k. 2 tog., k. 1, y.fwd., k. 1, y.fwd., k. 4, s.k.p.o., k. 1 (2) (1) (2) (2) (1) (2) (2) (1) (2); repeat from * until 13 (13) (12) (11) (13) (12) (11) (13) (13) (11) sts. remain, k. 2 tog., k. 1, y.fwd., k. 1, y.fwd., k. 4, s.k.p.o., k. to end.

11th row: K. 3 (3) (2) (1) (3) (2) (1) (3) (3) (1), *k. 2 tog., y.fwd., k. 1, y.fwd., k. 5, s.k.p.o., k. 1 (2) (1) (2) (2) (1) (2) (2) (1) (2); repeat from * until 13 (13) (12) (11) (13) (12) (11) (13) (13) (11) sts. remain, k. 2 tog., y.fwd., k. 1, y.fwd., k. 5, s.k.p.o., k. to end.

12th row: All p.

These 12 rows form the pattern.

Continued on page 82

Pattern a further 54 (54) (54) (58) (58) (58) (62) (62) (62) (62) rows.

To slope the front edge: Maintaining continuity of the pattern, dec. 1 st. at the end of the next row and the 4 following 4th rows— 55 (59) (64) (67) (71) (75) (79) (83) (88) (91) sts.

Pattern 3 rows.

To shape the armhole and continue to slope front edge: Cast off 5 sts. at the beginning and dec. 1 st. at end of the next row, pattern 1 row.

***Dec. 1 st. at armhole edge on the next row and the 7 (8) (9) (10) (11) (12) (13) (14) (15) (16) following alternate rows and *at the same time*, dec. 1 st. at front edge on the 4th row from previous dec., then on every following 4th row— 37 (40) (43) (45) (47) (50) (52) (55) (58) (60) sts.

Continue to dec. at front edge only on the 3 (3) (3) (6) (7) (7) (8) (9) (12) (11) following 4th rows from previous front dec.—34 (37) (40) (39) (40) (43) (44) (46) (46) (49) sts.

Pattern 5 rows, then dec. 1 st. at front edge on the next row and the 5 (6) (7) (4) (3) (4) (3) (3) (1) (2) following 6th rows—28 (30) (32) (34) (36) (38) (40) (42) (44) (46) sts.

Pattern 13 (9) (1) (9) (9) (5) (5) (1) (1) (1) row(s)—work 14 (10) (2) (10) (10) (6) (6) (4) (2) (2) rows here for right front.

To slope the shoulder: Cast off 4 (5) (4) (4) (6) (6) (5) (6) (7) (6) sts. at the beginning of the next row and 4 (5) (4) (5) (5) (6) (5) (6) (7) (6) sts. on the next alternate row, 4 (4) (4) (5) (5) (6) (6) (6) (6) (6) sts. on the next alternate row and finally 4 (4) (5) (5) (5) (5) (6) (6) (6) (7) on the following 3 alternate rows.

Pattern 1 row, then cast off.

THE RIGHT FRONT: Work as given for left front to **.

1st row: As 11th row on left front.

2nd and every alternate row: All p.

3rd row: As 9th row on left front.

5th row: As 7th row on left front.

7th row: As 5th row on left front.

9th row: As 3rd row on left front.

11th row: As 1st row on left front.

12th row: All p.

These 12 rows form the pattern. Pattern a further 54 (54) (54) (58) (58) (58) (62) (62) (62) (62) rows.

To slope the front edge: Maintaining continuity of the pattern, dec. 1 st. at the beginning of the next row and the 5 following 4th rows—54 (58) (63) (66) (70) (74) (78) (82) (87) (90) sts.

To shape the armhole and continue to slope front edge: Cast off 5 sts. at the beginning of the next row.

Work as given for left front from *** to end, noting variation.

THE ARMHOLE BORDERS (both alike): First join shoulder seams. With right side of work facing and using No. 13 ($2\frac{1}{4}$ mm) needles, pick up and k. 142 (146) (150) (154) (158) (162) (166) (170) (174) (178) sts. around armhole edge and work 14 rows in rib as given for back.

Cast off in rib.

THE FRONT BORDER: With No. 13 ($2\frac{1}{4}$ mm) needles cast on 19 sts.

1st row: K. 2, * p. 1, k. 1; repeat from * until 1 st. remains, k. 1.

2nd row: K. 1, * p. 1, k. 1; repeat from * to end.

Repeat last 2 rows, 4 times.

1st buttonhole row: Rib 8, cast off 3, rib to end.

2nd buttonhole row: Rib to end, casting on 3 sts. over those cast off on previous row.

Rib 26 (26) (26) (28) (28) (28) (30) (30) (30) (30) rows.

Repeat the last 28 (28) (28) (30) (30) (30) (32) (32) (32) (32) rows, twice more, then the 2 buttonhole rows again.

Continue in rib until border is long enough when slightly stretched to fit up right front, across back neck and down left front, cast off.

TO MAKE UP THE WAISTCOAT: Press work lightly on the wrong side, using a warm iron over a dry cloth. Join side seams. Sew on front border.

Add buttons.

Above *Lacy-panelled Waistcoat (page 81)*
Opposite *Waistcoat with Drawstring Waist (page 84)*

Waistcoat with Drawstring Waist

Illustrated on page 83

MEASUREMENTS To fit bust sizes	in centimetres (and inches, in brackets)			
	81 (32)	86 (34)	91 (36)	97 (38)
Side seam, including armhole border	39 ($15\frac{1}{2}$)	39 ($15\frac{1}{2}$)	39 ($15\frac{1}{2}$)	39 ($15\frac{1}{2}$)
Length	58 ($22\frac{3}{4}$)	59 ($23\frac{1}{4}$)	59.5 ($23\frac{1}{2}$)	61 (24)

MATERIALS: *Allow the following quantities in 50 g balls of Patons Kismet; 4 balls for the 81 cm, 86 cm and 91 cm sizes; 5 balls for the 97 cm size. For any one size: a pair each of No. 9 ($3\frac{3}{4}$ mm) and No. 11 (3 mm) knitting needles; a medium size crochet hook; 7 buttons.*

TENSION: *Work at a tension of 25 stitches and 31 rows to measure 10 × 10 cm over the pattern, using No. 9 ($3\frac{3}{4}$ mm) needles, to obtain the measurements given.*

ABBREVIATIONS: To be read before working: *K., knit plain; p., purl; st., stitch; tog., together; dec., decrease (by taking 2 sts. tog.); sl., slip; p.s.s.o., pass sl. st. over; s.k.p.o., sl. 1, k. 1, p.s.s.o.; y.fwd., yarn forward to make a st.; m. 1, make 1 (by taking yarn to front of work and over needle before knitting a st. and taking yarn round needle before purling a st.); single rib is k. 1 and p. 1 alternately.*

NOTE: *The instructions are given for the 81 cm (32 inch) size. Where they vary, work the figures within the first brackets for the 86 cm (34 inch) size; figures within second brackets for the 91 cm (36 inch) size, and so on.*

THE BACK: With No. 11 (3 mm) needles cast on 103 (109) (115) (121) sts. and beginning odd-numbered rows with k. 1 and even-numbered rows with p. 1, work 60 rows in single rib.

Next (slot) row: Rib 5 (8) (8) (14), * m. 1, k. 3 tog., m. 1, rib 15 (12) (13) (15); repeat from * 4 (5) (5) (4) times, m. 1, k. 3 tog., m. 1, rib to end.

Rib 3 rows.

Change to No. 9 ($3\frac{3}{4}$ mm) needles and work the 6-row pattern as follows:

1st row: K. 10 (12) (15) (18), * k. 2 tog., y.fwd., k. 1, y.fwd., s.k.p.o., k. 2, ** k. 2 tog., y.fwd., k. 5 **; repeat from ** to ** twice, k. 2 tog., y.fwd., k. 3, k. 2 **; y.fwd., k. 1, y.fwd., s.k.p.o. ***, k. 7 (9) (9) (9); repeat from * to *** once, k. to end.

2nd and every alternate row: All p.

3rd row: K. 10 (12) (15) (18), * k. 2 tog., y.fwd., k. 1, y.fwd., s.k.p.o., k. 1, ** k. 2 tog., y.fwd., k. 1, y.fwd., s.k.p.o., k. 2; repeat from ** twice, k. 2 tog., y.fwd., k. 1, y.fwd., s.k.p.o., k. 1, k. 2 tog., y.fwd., k. 1, y.fwd., s.k.p.o. ***, k. 7 (9) (9) (9); repeat from * to *** once, k. to end.

5th row: K. 10 (12) (15) (18),* k. 2 tog., y.fwd., k. 1, y.fwd., s.k.p.o., ** k. 2 tog., y.fwd., k. 3, y.fwd., s.k.p.o.; repeat from ** 3 times, k. 2 tog., y.fwd., k. 1, y.fwd., s.k.p.o. ***, k. 7 (9) (9) (9); repeat from * to *** once, k. to end.

6th row: All p.

Pattern a further 54 rows.

To shape the armholes: Maintaining continuity of the pattern, cast off 6 (7) (7) (8) sts. at the beginning of each of the next 2 rows, then dec. 1 st. at each end of the next row and the 2 (3) (3) (4) following alternate rows—85 (87) (93) (95) sts.

P. 1 row.

Continue shaping armholes as follows:

Next row: K. 1 (1) (4) (5), k. 2 tog., y.fwd., k. 1, y.fwd., sl. 1, k. 2 tog., p.s.s.o., pattern until 7 (7) (10) (11) sts. remain, k. 3 tog., y.fwd., k. 1, y.fwd., s.k.p.o., k. 1 (1) (4) (5).

Next row: All p.

Repeat the last 2 rows, 6 times—71 (73) (79) (81) sts.

Pattern 40 (40) (42) (44) rows.

To slope the shoulders: Cast off 6 (6) (7) (7) sts. at the beginning of each of the next 4 rows, then 7 sts. at the beginning of each of the following 2 rows.

Cast off remaining 33 (35) (37) (39) sts.

THE LEFT FRONT: With No. 11 (3 mm) needles cast on 63 (65) (69) (73) sts. and work 60 rows in rib as given for back.

Next (slot) row: Rib 11 (5) (5) (1), * m. 1, k. 3 tog., m. 1, rib 15 (12) (13) (15); repeat from * once (twice) (twice) (twice), m. 1, k. 3 tog., m. 1, rib to end.

Rib 2 rows.

Next row: Rib 12 and leave these sts. on a safety-pin, rib to end—51 (53) (57) (61) sts.

Change to No. 9 ($3\frac{3}{4}$ mm) needles and work in pattern as follows:

1st row: K. 10 (12) (15) (18), work as 1st row of back from * to ***, k. to end.

2nd and every alternate row: All p.

3rd row: K. 10 (12) (15) (18), work as 3rd row of back from * to ***, k. to end.

5th row: K. 10 (12) (15) (18), work as 5th row of back from * to ***, k. to end.

6th row: All p.

Pattern a further 46 rows.

To slope front edge: Next row: Pattern until 9 (9) (10) (11) sts. remain, k. 3 tog., y.fwd., k. 1, y.fwd., s.k.p.o., k. to end.

Pattern 3 rows.

Repeat the last 4 rows once—49 (51) (55) (59) sts.

To shape the armhole and continue to slope front edge: Cast off 6 (7) (7) (8) sts. at the beginning of the next row, then dec. 1 st. at armhole edge on the 3 (4) (4) (5) following alternate rows, *at the same time*, dec. 1 st. at front edge as before on the 1st row and the 1 (2) (2) (2) following 4th row(s)—38 (37) (41) (43) sts.

**** Dec. 1 st. at armhole edge as on back on the 7 following alternate rows, *at the same time*, dec. 1 st. at front edge on the 4th row from previous dec. and then on every following 4th row—27 (27) (31) (32) sts.

Maintaining continuity of the pattern, dec. 1 st. at front edge only on every 4th row from previous dec. until a further 8 (8) (10) (11) front decreases have been worked—19 (19) (21) (21) sts.

Pattern 9 (11) (5) (1) row(s) – pattern 10 (12) (6) (2) rows here when working right front.

To slope the shoulder: Cast off 6 (6) (7) (7) sts. at the beginning of the next row and the following alternate row—7 sts.

P. 1 row. Cast off.

THE RIGHT FRONT: With No. 11 (3 mm) needles cast on 63 (65) (69) (73) sts. and work 4 rows in single rib as given on back.

1st buttonhole row: Rib 5, cast off 2, rib to end.

2nd buttonhole row: Rib to end, casting on 2 sts. over those cast off on previous row.

Rib 18 rows.

Repeat the last 20 rows, once, then repeat the 2 buttonhole rows again.

Rib a further 14 rows.

Next (slot) row: Rib 13 (12) (13) (15), * m. 1, k. 3 tog., m. 1, rib 15 (12) (13) (15); repeat from * once (twice) (twice) (twice); m. 1, k. 3 tog., m. 1, rib to end.

Rib 2 rows.

Next row: Rib until 12 sts. remain, turn and leave remaining 12 sts. on a safety-pin—51 (53) (57) (61) sts.

Change to No. 9 (3¾ mm) needles and work in pattern as follows:

1st row: K. 3 (3) (4) (5), work as 1st row of back from * to ***, k. to end.

2nd and every alternate row: All p.

These 2 rows set the position of the pattern for the right front.

Pattern a further 50 rows.

To slope the front edge: Next row: K. 3 (3) (4) (5), k. 2 tog., y.fwd., k. 1, y.fwd., sl. 1, k. 2 tog., p.s.s.o., pattern to end.

Pattern 3 rows.

Repeat the last 4 rows, once, then the 1st of these rows again—48 (50) (54) (58) sts.

To shape the armhole and continue to slope front edge: Cast off 6 (7) (7) (8) sts., p. to end of row—42 (43) (47) (50) sts.

Dec. 1 st. at armhole edge on the next row and the 2 (3) (3) (4) following alternate rows, *at the same time*, dec. 1 st. at front edge as before on the 1 (2) (2) (2) following 4th row(s)—38 (37) (41) (43) sts.

Work as given for left front from **** to end, noting variation.

THE RIGHT FRONT BORDER: First join shoulder seams. With wrong side of work facing, sl. the 12 sts. at right front on to a No. 11 (3 mm) needle and rib to end.

Work the 2 buttonhole rows, then rib a further 18 rows.

Repeat the last 20 rows twice, then repeat the 2 buttonhole rows again.

Continue in rib until border is long enough when slightly stretched to fit up right front and across to centre back neck, casting off in rib when correct length is assured.

THE LEFT FRONT BORDER: With right side of work facing and using No. 11 (3 mm) needles, work as given for right front border, omitting buttonholes.

THE ARMHOLE BORDERS (both alike): With right side of work facing and using No. 11 (3 mm) needles, pick up and k. 124 (128) (132) (140) sts. all round armhole edge and work 10 rows in single rib. Cast off in rib.

TO MAKE UP THE WAISTCOAT: Do not press. Join side seams, continuing seams across armhole borders. Sew front borders in place, joining tog. at centre back neck. Add buttons. Using 4 strands of yarn tog., make a length of chain 152 cm (60 inches) in length, knot both ends of cord, then thread through slot row to tie at front.

Lace Pattern Waistcoat

Illustrated on page 86

MEASUREMENTS	*in centimetres (and inches, in brackets)*			
To fit bust sizes	86 (34)	91 (36)	97 (38)	102 (40)
All round at underarms, fastened	88 (34½)	94 (37)	100 (39¼)	106 (41¾)
Side seam, including armhole border	36 (14¼)	36 (14¼)	36 (14¼)	36 (14¼)
Length	53 (20¾)	54 (21¼)	55 (21½)	56 (22)

MATERIALS: *Allow the following quantities in 40 g balls of Littlewoods Keynote Continental, (knits as 4-ply): 4 for all sizes. For any one size: A pair each of No. 8 (4 mm) and No. 9 (3¾ mm) knitting needles; 5 buttons.*

TENSION: *Work at a tension of 20 stitches and 32 rows to measure 10 × 10 cm, over the pattern, using No. 8 (4 mm) needles, to obtain measurements given.*

ABBREVIATIONS: To be read before working: *K., knit plain; p., purl; st., stitch; tog., together; dec., decrease (by taking 2 sts. tog.); y.fwd., yarn forward to make a st.; sl., slip; p.s.s.o., pass sl. st. over; single rib is k. 1 and p. 1 alternately.*

NOTE: *The instructions are given for the 86 cm (34 inch) bust size. Where they vary, work figures within first brackets for the 91 cm (36 inch) size; work figures within second brackets for the 97 cm (38 inch) size, and so on.*

THE BACK: With No. 9 (3¾ mm) needles cast on 89 (95) (101) (107) sts. and, beginning odd-numbered rows with k. 1 and even-numbered rows with p. 1, work 14 rows in single rib.

Change to No. 8 (4 mm) needles and work the 4-row pattern.

Continued on page 86

1st pattern row: K. 1, * y.fwd., sl. 1, k. 2 tog., p.s.s.o., y.fwd., k. 3; repeat from * until 4 sts. remain, y.fwd., sl. 1, k. 2 tog., p.s.s.o., y.fwd., k. 1.

2nd row: P. to end.

3rd row: K. 4, * y.fwd., sl. 1, k. 2 tog., p.s.s.o., y.fwd., k. 3; repeat from * until 1 st. remains, k. 1.

4th row: P. to end.

These 4 rows form the pattern; repeat them a further 22 times.

To shape the armholes: Keeping continuity of the pattern where possible, cast off 5 (6) (6) (7) sts. at beginning of next 2 rows, then dec. 1 st. each end of the following 5 (5) (7) (7) rows. Work 1 row then dec. 1 st. each end of next row and the 2 (3) (2) (3) following alternate rows—63 (65) (69) (71) sts.

Pattern 45 (45) (49) (49) rows.

To slope the shoulders: Cast off 6 (6) (6) (7) sts. at beginning of next 2 rows, 6 (6) (7) (7) sts. on next 2 rows, and finally 6 (7) (7) (7) sts. at beginning of following 2 rows.

Cast off remaining 27 (27) (29) (29) sts.

THE LEFT FRONT: With No. 9 (3¾ mm) needles cast on 41 (45) (47) (51) sts. and work 14 rows in single rib as given on back, but decreasing 1 st. at end of last row on the 91 cm and 102 cm sizes only—41 (44) (47) (50) sts. **

Change to No. 8 (4 mm) needles.

1st pattern row: K. 1, * y.fwd., sl. 1, k. 2 tog., p.s.s.o., y.fwd., k. 3; repeat from * until 4 (7) (4) (7) sts. remain, y.fwd., sl. 1, k. 2 tog., p.s.s.o., y.fwd., k. 1 (4) (1) (4).

2nd row: P. to end.

3rd row: K. 4, * y.fwd., sl. 1, k. 2 tog., p.s.s.o., y.fwd., k. 3; repeat from * until 7 (4) (7) (4) sts. remain, y.fwd., sl. 1, k. 2 tog., p.s.s.o., y.fwd., k. 4 (1) (4) (1).

4th row: P. to end.

These 4 rows form the pattern; repeat them a further 22 times.

To shape the armhole and shape front edge: 1st row: Cast off 5 (6) (6) (7) sts., pattern until 2 sts. remain, k. 2 tog.

2nd row: P. to end.

*** Continue to dec. 1 st. at front edge on every 6th row from previous front dec., *at the same time*, dec. 1 st. at armhole edge on each of the next 5 (5) (7) (7) rows, then, the 3 (4) (3) (4) following alternate rows—25 (26) (28) (29) sts.

Pattern 5 (3) (3) (1) row(s), then dec. 1 st. at front edge on next row and the 6 (6) (7) (7) following 6th rows—18 (19) (20) (21) sts.

Pattern 3 (5) (3) (5) rows—pattern 4 (6) (4) (6) rows here when working right front.

To slope the shoulder: Cast off 6 (6) (6) (7) sts. at beginning of next row, then 6 (6) (7) (7) sts. on the following alternate row.

Pattern 1 row, then cast off.

THE RIGHT FRONT: Work as given for left front to **.

Change to No. 8 (4 mm) needles and beginning with the 1st (3rd) (1st) (3rd) pattern row, pattern 92 rows as given for left front.

To shape front edge: Next row: K. 2 tog., pattern to end.

To shape armhole and continue shaping front edge: 1st row: Cast off 5 (6) (6) (7) sts., p. to end.

Work as left front from *** to end, noting variation where indicated.

THE ARMHOLE BORDERS (both alike): First join shoulder seams.

With right side facing, rejoin yarn and using No. 9 (3¾ mm) needles, pick up and k. 102 (108) (114) (120) sts. all round armhole edge and work 6 rows in single rib. Cast off in rib.

THE FRONT BORDER: With No. 9 (3¾ mm) needles cast on 9 sts. and work 4 rows in rib as given on back.

1st buttonhole row: Rib 3, cast off 3, rib to end.

2nd buttonhole row: Rib 3, turn, cast on 3, turn, rib 3.

Rib 22 rows.

Repeat the last 24 rows, 3 times, then the 2 buttonhole rows again.

Continue in rib until border, when slightly stretched, fits up right front, round neck and down left front, casting off in rib when correct length is assured.

TO MAKE UP THE WAISTCOAT: Press very lightly with a warm iron over a dry cloth. Join side seams, continuing across armhole borders. Sew front border into position, placing top buttonhole level with first front shaping on right front. Add buttons.

Above *Lace Pattern Waistcoat (page 85)*
Opposite *Short-sleeved Top (page 88)*

Short-sleeved Top

Illustrated on page 87

MEASUREMENTS To fit bust sizes	*in centimetres (and inches, in brackets)*					
	76 (30)	81 (32)	86 (34)	91 (36)	97 (38)	102 (40)
All round at widest part	80.5 ($31\frac{3}{4}$)	86 (34)	89.5 ($35\frac{1}{2}$)	95 ($37\frac{1}{2}$)	98 ($38\frac{1}{2}$)	103.5 ($40\frac{3}{4}$)
Side seam	33.5 ($13\frac{1}{4}$)	33.5 ($13\frac{1}{4}$)	33.5 ($13\frac{1}{4}$)	33.5 ($13\frac{1}{4}$)	33.5 ($13\frac{1}{4}$)	33.5 ($13\frac{1}{4}$)
Length	50.5 ($19\frac{3}{4}$)	51 (20)	51.5 ($20\frac{1}{4}$)	51.5 ($20\frac{1}{4}$)	52 ($20\frac{1}{2}$)	52 ($20\frac{1}{2}$)
Sleeve seam	10 (4)	10 (4)	10 (4)	10 (4)	10 (4)	10 (4)

MATERIALS: *Allow the following quantities in 25 g balls of Twilleys Lyscordet:* 11 *for the* 76 cm *and* 81 cm *sizes;* 12 *for the* 86 cm *and* 91 cm *sizes;* 13 *for the* 97 cm *and* 102 cm *sizes. For any one size: a pair each of No.* 12 ($2\frac{3}{4}$ mm) *and No.* 13 ($2\frac{1}{4}$ mm) *knitting needles;* 4 *buttons.*

TENSION: *Work at a tension of* 34 *stitches and* 38 *rows to measure* 10 × 10 cm *over the pattern, using No.* 12 ($2\frac{3}{4}$ mm) *needles to obtain the measurements given.*

ABBREVIATIONS: To be read before working: *K., knit plain; p., purl; st., stitch; tog., together; inc., increase (by working twice into same st.); dec., decrease (by working* 2 *sts. tog.); sl., slip; nil, meaning nothing is worked here for this size; single rib is k.* 1 *and p.* 1 *alternately.*

NOTE: *The instructions are given for the* 76 cm (30 inch) *size. Where they vary, work the figures within the first brackets for the* 81 cm (32 inch) *size, and so on.*

THE BACK: With No. 13 ($2\frac{1}{4}$ mm) needles cast on 136 (146) (152) (160) (166) (176) sts., and work 36 rows in single rib increasing 1 st. at the end of the last of these rows on the 76 cm, 91 cm and 97 cm sizes only—137 (146) (152) (161) (167) (176) sts.

Change to No. 12 ($2\frac{3}{4}$ mm) needles and work the 4-row pattern as follows:

1st row: All k.

2nd row: All p.

3rd row: K. 1, * k. 1 winding yarn twice round needle; repeat from * until 1 st. remains, k. 1.

4th row: K. 1, * sl. next 3 sts. from left hand needle on to right hand needle allowing extra loops to fall, sl. these 3 sts. back on to left hand needle and k. 1, p. 1, k. 1 through all 3 sts.; repeat from * until 1st remains, k. 1. ******

Pattern a further 92 rows.

To shape the armholes: Keeping continuity of the pattern, cast off 3 sts. at the beginning of the next 2 rows, then dec. 1 st. at each end of the next 6 rows—119 (128) (134) (143) (149) (158) sts.

Pattern 56 (58) (60) (62) (62) rows.

For shoulders: Cast off 32 (35) (38) (42) (45) (50) sts. at the beginning of the next 2 rows—55 (58) (58) (59) (59) (58) sts.

Cast off.

THE FRONT: Work as given for back to ******.

Pattern a further 29 rows.

To divide for fronts: Next row: Pattern 63 (68) (71) (75) (78) (83) sts. and leave these sts. on a spare needle for right half front, pattern 11 (10) (10) (11) (11) (10) and leave these sts. on a safety-pin for front border, pattern to end and work on these 63 (68) (71) (75) (78) (83) sts. for left half front.

The left half front: Pattern 42 rows.

To shape the neck: Dec. 1 st. at the neck edge on the next row and the 6 following 3rd rows—56 (61) (64) (68) (71) (76) sts.

Work 1 row—work 2 rows here when working right front *******.

To shape the armhole and continue shaping the neck: Next row: Cast off 3 sts., pattern to end.

Next row: Dec., pattern to end.

**** Dec. 1 st. at armhole edge on the next 6 rows, *at the same time,* dec. 1 st. at front edge on the 3rd of these rows and the 13 (15) (15) (15) (15) following 3rd rows—32 (35) (38) (42) (45) (50) sts.

Pattern 20 (16) (18) (18) (20) (20) rows—pattern 21 (17) (19) (19) (21) (21) rows here when working right half front.

For shoulder: Cast off the remaining sts.

The right half front: With right side of work facing, rejoin yarn to inner edge of the 63 (68) (71) (75) (78) (83) sts. left on spare needle and work as given for left half front to *******.

To shape the armhole and continue shaping the neck: Next row: Cast off 3 sts., pattern until 2 sts. remain dec.

Work as given for left half front from ******** to end noting variation.

THE SLEEVES (both alike): With No. 13 ($2\frac{1}{4}$ mm) needles cast on 84 (84) (84) (90) (90) (90) sts. and work 11 rows in single rib, increasing 1 st. at the end of the last of these rows on the 91 cm, 97 cm and 102 cm sizes only— 84 (84) (84) (91) (91) (91) sts.

Next (inc.) row: Rib 4 (4) (4) (3) (3) (3), * inc., rib 3; repeat from * to end—104 (104) (104) (113) (113) (113) sts.

Change to No. 12 ($3\frac{3}{4}$ mm) needles and work 28 rows in pattern as given for back.

To shape the sleeve top: Cast off 3 sts. at the beginning of the next 2 rows, then dec. 1 st. at each end of the next row and the 10 (13) (15) (11) (13) (13) following alternate rows, and then dec. 1 st. at each end of the next 14 (10) (8) (16) (14) (14) rows—48 (50) (50) (51) (51) (51) sts.

Work 1 row. Cast off.

THE FRONT BORDER: First join shoulder seams. With right side of work facing, using No. 13 ($2\frac{1}{4}$ mm) needles, rejoin yarn to the 11 (10) (10) (11) (11) (10) sts. left on safety-pin.

1st rib row: * K. 1, p. 1; repeat from * 3 times, k. 2 tog., p. 1 (k. 1, p. 1) (k. 1, p. 1) (k. 2 tog., p. 1) (k. 2 tog., p. 1) (k. 2, p. 1)—10 sts.

Rib 5 rows.

Next (buttonhole) row: Rib 4, cast off 2 sts. rib 3.

Next (buttonhole) row: Rib 4, cast on 2, rib 4.

Rib 12 rows.

Repeat the last 14 rows, twice, then the 2 buttonhole rows again.

Continue in rib until border fits, when slightly stret-ched, up right front, across back neck and down left front. Cast off.

TO MAKE UP THE BLOUSE: Do not press. Set in sleeves. Join side and sleeve seams. Sew on front border, catch down cast off edge of border behind the buttonhole section. Sew on buttons.

Button-up Cardigan in Mohair

Illustrated on page 90

MEASUREMENTS	*in centimetres (and inches, in brackets)*			
To fit bust sizes	81 (32)	86 (34)	91 (36)	97 (38)
Side seam	42 (16½)	42 (16½)	42 (16½)	42 (16½)
Length	61.5 (24¼)	62 (24½)	63 (24¾)	63.5 (25)
Sleeve seam	47.5 (18¾)	47.5 (18¾)	47.5 (18¾)	47.5 (18¾)

MATERIALS: *Allow the following quantities in 50 g balls of Pingouin Laine et Mohair:* 8 *for* 81 *cm size;* 9 *for* 86 *cm size;* 10 *for* 91 *cm and* 97 *cm sizes. For any one size: a pair each of No.* 8 (4 *mm) and No.* 11 (3 *mm) knitting needles; a cable needle;* 8 *buttons.*

TENSION: *Work at a tension of* 22 *stitches and* 29 *rows to measure* 10 × 10 *cm, over the stocking stitch, using No.* 8 (4 *mm) needles, to obtain measurements given.*

ABBREVIATIONS: To be read before working: *K., knit plain; p., purl; st., stitch; tog., together; inc., increase (by working twice into same st.); dec., decrease (by working* 2 *sts. tog.); c.* 6 *f., cable* 6 *front (slip next* 3 *sts. on to cable needle and leave at front of work, k.* 3, *then k.* 3 *from cable needle); tw.* 3 *rt., twist* 3 *right (slip next st. on to cable needle and leave at back of work, k.* 3, *then p.* 1 *from cable needle); tw.* 3 *lt., twist* 3 *left (slip next* 3 *sts. on to cable needle and leave at front of work, p.* 1, *then k.* 3 *from cable needle); M.B., make a bobble (k.* 1, *p.* 1, *k.* 1, *p.* 1 *and k.* 1 *all into next* 2 *sts. tog., turn and k.* 5, *turn and p.* 5, *turn and k.* 5, *turn and p.* 5, *then pass* 2nd, 3rd, 4th *and* 5th *sts. over first st.); double rib is k.* 2, *p.* 2 *alternately; nil, meaning nothing is worked for this size, s.s., stocking st. (k. on right side and p. on wrong side).*

NOTE: *The instructions are given for the* 81 *cm* (32 *inch) size. Where they vary, work figures within first brackets for* 86 *cm* (34 *inch) size; work figures within second brackets for* 91 *cm* (36 *inch) size, and so on.*

THE BACK: With No. 11 (3 mm) needles cast on 100 (104) (110) (114) sts.

1st rib row: K. 3 (nil) (nil) (2), p. 2 (3) (2) (2), ** k. 2, p. 2; repeat from * until 3 (5) (4) (2) sts. remain, k. 3 (k. 2, p. 3) (k. 2, p. 2) (k. 2).

2nd rib row: P. 3 (nil) (nil) (2), k. 2 (3) (2) (2), ** p. 2, k. 2; repeat from * until 3 (5) (4) (2) sts. remain, p. 3 (p. 2, k. 3) (p. 2, k. 2) (p. 2).

Rib a further 32 rows.

Change to No. 8 (4 mm) needles and work the 34-row pattern as follows:

1st row: K. 11 (13) (16) (18), * p. 10, c. 6 f., p. 10 *, k. 26; repeat from * to * once, k. to end.

2nd row: P. 11 (13) (16) (18), k. 10, p. 6, k. 10, p. 26, k. 10, p. 6, k. 10, p. to end.

3rd to 6th rows: Repeat 1st and 2nd rows, twice.

7th row: K. 11 (13) (16) (18), * p. 9, tw. 3 rt., tw. 3 lt., p. 9 *, k. 26; repeat from * to * once, k. to end.

8th row: P. 11 (13) (16) (18), * k. 9. p. 3, k. 2, p. 3, k. 9 *, p. 26; repeat from * to * once, p. to end.

9th row: K. 11 (13) (16) (18), * p. 8, tw. 3 rt., p. 2, tw. 3 lt., p. 8 *, k. 26; repeat from * to * once, k. to end.

10th row: P. 11 (13) (16) (18), * k. 8, p. 3, k. 4, p. 3, k. 8 *, p. 26; repeat from * to * once, p. to end.

11th row: K. 11 (13) (16) (18), * p. 7, tw. 3 rt., p. 4, tw. 3 lt., p. 7 *, k. 26; repeat from * to * once, k. to end.

12th row: P. 11 (13) (16) (18), * k. 7, p. 3, k. 6, p. 3, k. 7 *, p. 26; repeat from * to * once, p. to end.

13th row: K. 11 (13) (16) (18), * p. 6, tw. 3 rt., p. 6, tw. 3 lt., p. 6 *, k. 26; repeat from * to * once, k. to end.

14th row: P. 11 (13) (16) (18), * k. 6, p. 3, k. 8, p. 3, k. 6 *, p. 26; repeat from * to * once, p. to end.

15th row: K. 11 (13) (16) (18), * p. 5, tw. 3 rt., p. 8, tw. 3 lt., p. 5 *, k. 26; repeat from * to * once, k. to end.

16th row: P. 11 (13) (16) (18), * k. 5, p. 3, k. 10, p. 3, k. 5 *, p. 26; repeat from * to * once, p. to end.

17th row: K. 11 (13) (16) (18), * p. 4, tw. 3 rt., p. 10, tw. 3 lt., p. 4 *, k. 26; repeat from * to * once, k. to end.

18th row: P. 11 (13) (16) (18), * k. 4, p. 3, k. 12, p. 3, k. 4 *, p. 26; repeat from * to * once, p. to end.

19th row: K. 11 (13) (16) (18), * p. 3, tw. 3 rt., p. 5, M.B., p. 5, tw. 3 lt., p. 3 *, k. 26; repeat from * to * once, k. to end.

20th row: P. 11 (13) (16) (18), * k. 3, p. 3, k. 6, k. twice into next st. thus making a st., k. 6, p. 3, k. 3 *, p. 26; repeat from * to * once, p. to end.

21st row: K. 11 (13) (16) (18), * p. 3, tw. 3 lt., p. 12, tw. 3 rt., p. 3 *, k. 26; repeat from * to * once, k. to end.

22nd to 34th rows: As 18th back to 6th rows in that

Continued on page 90

reverse order, *but* reading tw. 3 rt. instead of tw. 3 lt., and tw. 3 lt. instead of tw. 3 rt.

Pattern a further 62 rows.

To shape the armholes: Keeping continuity of the pattern, cast off 8 sts. at beginning of next 2 rows—84 (88) (94) (98) sts.

Pattern 48 (50) (52) (54) rows.

To shape the shoulders: Cast off 10 (11) (11) (12) sts. at beginning of next 2 rows, then 10 (10) (11) (11) sts. on the following 4 rows—24 (26) (28) (30) sts. Leave sts. on a spare needle.

THE LEFT FRONT: With No. 11 (3 mm) needles cast on 50 (52) (55) (57) sts.

1st rib row: K. 3 (nil) (nil) (2), p. 2 (3) (2) (2), * k. 2, p. 2; repeat from * until 5 sts. remain, k. 2, p. 3.

2nd rib row: K. 3, p. 2, * k. 2, p. 2; repeat from * until 5 (3) (2) (4) sts. remain, k. 2 (3) (2) (2), p. 3 (nil) (nil) (2).

Rib a further 32 rows.

Change to No. 8 (4 mm) needles and continue as follows:

1st row: K. 11 (13) (16) (18), p. 10, c. 6 f., p. 10, k. 13.

2nd row: P. 13, k. 10, p. 6, k. 10, p. 11 (13) (16) (18).

** These 2 rows set the position of the pattern panel. Keeping continuity of pattern to match panels on back, work a further 94 rows—work 95 rows here when working right front.

To shape the armhole: Cast off 8 sts. at beginning of next row—42 (44) (47) (49) sts.

Pattern 34 (36) (38) (40) rows.

To shape the neck: Cast off 8 (9) (10) (11) sts. at

Opposite *V-neck Sweater in Mohair (page 92)*
Below *Button-up Cardigan in Mohair (page 89)*

beginning of next row, then dec. 1 st. at neck edge on the following 4 rows—30 (31) (33) (34) sts.

Pattern 10 rows.

To slope the shoulder: Cast off 10 (11) (11) (12) sts. at beginning of next row and 10 (10) (11) (11) sts. on the following alternate row—10 (10) (11) (11) sts.

Pattern 1 row. Cast off.

THE RIGHT FRONT: With No. 11 (3 mm) needles cast on 50 (52) (55) (57) sts.

1st rib row: P. 3, k. 2, * p. 2, k. 2; repeat from * until 5 (3) (2) (4) sts. remain, p. 2, k. 3 (p. 3) (p. 2) (p. 2, k. 2).

2nd rib row: P. 3 (k. 3, p. 2) (k. 2, p. 2) (p. 2), k. 2, * p. 2, k. 2; repeat from * until 5 sts. remain, p. 2, k. 3.

Rib a further 32 rows.

Change to No. 8 (4 mm) needles and continue as follows:

1st row: K. 13, p. 10, c. 6 f., p. 10, k. 11 (13) (16) (18).

2nd row: P. 11 (13) (16) (18), k. 10, p. 6, k. 10, p. 13.

Work as left front from **, noting variation.

THE SLEEVES (both alike): With No. 11 (3 mm) needles cast on 42 (46) (46) (50) sts. and, beginning odd-number rows with k. 2 and even-number rows with p. 2, work 28 rows in double rib.

Change to No. 8 (4 mm) needles and continue as follows:

1st row: K. 8 (10) (10) (12), p. 10, c. 6 f., p. 10, k. 8 (10) (10) (12).

2nd row: P. 8 (10) (10) (12), k. 10, p. 6, k. 10, p. 8 (10) (10) (12).

These 2 rows set the position of the pattern panel. Keeping continuity of pattern to match panels on back and taking extra sts. into the s.s. as they occur, inc. 1 st. each end of next row, then on the 19 (18) (20) (19) following 4th rows—82 (84) (88) (90) sts.

Pattern 37 (41) (33) (37) rows, marking each end of the last of these rows to denote end of sleeve seam.

Pattern a further 12 rows.

Cast off.

THE BUTTONHOLE BAND: With right side of work facing and using No. 11 (3 mm) needles, rejoin yarn and pick up and k. 146 (146) (150) (150) sts. along row ends of right front to beginning of neck shaping.

1st rib row: P. 2, * k. 2, p. 2; repeat from * to end.

2nd rib row: K. 2, * p. 2, k. 2; repeat from * to end.

Rib 1 more row.

1st buttonhole row: Rib 2 (2) (4) (4), * cast off 2, rib a further 17; repeat from * 6 times, cast off 2, rib to end.

2nd buttonhole row: Rib to end, casting on 2 sts. over each group cast off on previous row.

Rib 4 rows. Cast off in rib.

THE BUTTON BAND: Work as buttonhole band, omitting buttonholes.

THE COLLAR: First join shoulder seams. With right side of work facing and using No. 11 (3 mm) needles, rejoin yarn halfway across row ends of buttonhole band and pick up and k. 43 (44) (45) (46) sts. round right front neck, k. 24 (26) (28) (30) sts. across back neck, then pick up and k. 43 (44) (45) (46) round left front neck to centre of row ends of button band—110 (114) (118) (122) sts.

Work 10 rows in rib as for sleeves.

Change to No. 8 (4 mm) needles and rib a further 20 rows.

Cast off in rib.

TO MAKE UP THE CARDIGAN: Do not press. Set in sleeves above markers, then join sleeve and side seams. Add buttons.

V-neck Sweater in Mohair

Illustrated on page 91

MEASUREMENTS	*in centimetres (and inches, in brackets)*			
To fit bust sizes	81 (32)	86 (34)	91 (36)	97 (38)
All round underarms	87 (34¼)	92 (36¼)	97 (38)	102 (40)
Side seam	38.5 (15¼)	38.5 (15¼)	38.5 (15¼)	38.5 (15¼)
Length	57.5 (22½)	58 (22¾)	58.5 (23)	59.5 (23½)
Sleeve seam	43.5 (17)	43.5 (17)	43.5 (17)	43.5 (17)

MATERIALS: *Allow the following quantities in 40 g balls of Littlewoods Keynote Continental (knits as 4-ply): 6 for 81 cm and 86 cm sizes; 7 for 91 cm and 97 cm sizes. For any one size: a pair each of No. 10 (3¼ mm) and No. 12 (2¾ mm) knitting needles.*

TENSION: *Work at a tension of 25 stitches and 32 rows to measure 10 × 10 cm, over the pattern, using No. 10 (3¼ mm) needles, to obtain measurements given.*

ABBREVIATIONS: To be read before working: *K., knit plain; p., purl; st., stitch; tog., together; inc., increase (by working twice into same st.); dec., decrease (by working 2 sts. tog.); k. or p. 2 tog.b., k. or p. 2 tog. through back of sts.;*

s.s., stocking st. (k. on right side, p. on wrong side); y.r.n., yarn round needle to make a st.; single rib is k. 1, p. 1 alternately; nil, meaning nothing is worked here for this size.

NOTE: *The instructions are given for the 81 cm (32 inch) size. Where they vary, work figures within first brackets for 86 cm (34 inch) size; work figures within second brackets for 91 cm (36 inch) size, and so on.*

THE BACK: With No. 12 (2¾ mm) needles cast on 109 (115) (121) (127) sts. and, beginning odd-numbered rows with k. 1 and even-number rows with p. 1, work 21 rows in single rib.

Change to No. 10 (3¼ mm) needles and, beginning with a k. row, s.s. 2 rows.

Work 24-row pattern as follows: 1st row: K. 13 (nil) (3) (6), * k. 2 tog., y.r.n., y.r.n., k. 14; repeat from * until 16 (3) (6) (9) sts. remain, k. 2 tog., y.r.n., y.r.n., k. 14 (1) (4) (7).

2nd row: P. to end, but purling once into "y.r.n., y.r.n.", dropping extra loop off needle.

3rd and 4th rows: S.s.

5th row: K. 11 (k. 2, k. 2 tog., y.r.n., y.r.n., k. 10) (k. 1, k. 2 tog., y.r.n., y.r.n., k. 2, k. 2 tog., y.r.n., y.r.n., k. 10) (k. 4, k. 2 tog., y.r.n., y.r.n., k. 2, k. 2 tog., y.r.n., y.r.n., k. 10), * k. 2 tog., y.r.n., y.r.n., k. 2, k. 2 tog., y.r.n., y.r.n., k. 10; repeat from * until 2 (5) (8) (11) sts. remain, k. 2 (k. 2 tog., y.r.n., y.r.n., k. 3) (k. 2 tog., y.r.n., y.r.n., k. 2) (k. 2 tog., y.r.n., y.r.n., k. 2, k. 2 tog., y.r.n., y.r.n., k. 5).

6th to 8th rows: As 2nd to 4th rows.

9th to 12th rows: As 1st to 4th rows.

13th row: K. 5 (8) (11) (14), * k. 2 tog., y.r.n., y.r.n., k. 14; repeat from * until 8 (11) (14) (17) sts. remain, k. 2 tog., y.r.n., y.r.n., k. 6 (9) (12) (15).

14th to 16th rows: As 2nd to 4th rows.

17th row: K. 3 (6) (9) (12), * k. 2 tog., y.r.n., y.r.n., k. 2, k. 2 tog., y.r.n., y.r.n., k. 10; repeat from * until 10 (13) (16) (19) sts. remain, k. 2 tog., y.r.n., y.r.n., k. 2, k. 2 tog., y.r.n., y.r.n., k. 4 (7) (10) (13).

18th to 20th rows: As 2nd to 4th rows.

21st row: As 13th row.

22nd to 24th rows: As 2nd to 4th rows. **
Pattern a further 82 rows.

To shape the armholes: *** Keeping continuity of pattern, cast off 6 sts. at beginning of next 2 rows, then dec. 1 st. each end of next row and then on the 9 following alternate rows ***—77 (83) (89) (95) sts.

Pattern a further 33 (35) (37) (39) rows.

To slope the shoulders: Cast off 7 (7) (8) (9) sts. at beginning of next 2 (4) (4) (2) rows, then 6 (7) (7) (8) sts. on the following 4 (2) (2) (4) rows—39 (41) (43) (45) sts.

Leave sts. on a spare needle.

THE FRONT: Work as back to **.
Pattern a further 77 rows.

To divide for neck: Next row: Pattern 54 (57) (60) (63) and leave these sts. on a spare needle for right half neck, p. 1 and leave this st. on a safety pin, pattern to end and work on these 54 (57) (60) (63) sts. for left half neck.

The left half neck: Keeping continuity of pattern throughout, dec. 1 st. at neck edge on the next row and on the following 3rd row.

Work 1 row here when working right half neck.

To shape the armhole and continue to shape front neck: Cast off 6 sts. at beginning of next row, work 1 row—omit this row when working right half neck—then dec. 1 st. at armhole edge on the next row and then on the 9 following alternate rows—*at the same time*, continue to dec. at front edge on every following 3rd row from previous front dec.—29 (32) (35) (38) sts.

Pattern 2 rows, then dec. 1 st. at front edge on the next row and then on the 9 (10) (11) (12) following 3rd rows—19 (21) (23) (25) sts.

Pattern 3 (2) (1) nil row(s)—pattern 4 (3) (2) (1) row(s) here when working right half front.

To slope the shoulder: Cast off 7 (7) (8) (9) sts. at beginning of next row and 6 (7) (8) (8) sts. on the following alternate row—6 (7) (7) (8) sts.

Pattern 1 row.
Cast off.

The right half neck. With right side of work facing, rejoin yarn to 54 (57) (60) (63) sts. on spare needle and work as left half neck, noting variations.

THE SLEEVES (both alike): With No. 12 (2¾ mm) needles cast on 57 (59) (63) (65) sts. and work 25 rows in rib as given for back.

Change to No. 10 (3¼ mm) needles and, beginning with a k. row, s.s. 2 rows.

Continue as follows: 1st row: K. 3 (4) (6) (7), * k. 2 tog., y.r.n., y.r.n., k. 14; repeat from * twice, k. 2 tog., y.r.n., y.r.n., k. 4 (5) (7) (8).

2nd row: P. to end, but purling once into "y.r.n., y.r.n.", dropping extra loop off needle.

3rd and 4th rows: S.s..

5th row: K. 1 (2) (4) (5), * k. 2 tog., y.r.n., y.r.n., k. 2, k. 2 tog., y.r.n., y.r.n., k. 10; repeat from * twice, k. 2 tog., y.r.n., y.r.n., k. 2, k. 2 tog., y.r.n., y.r.n., k. 2 (3) (5) (6).

These 5 rows set the position of the pattern. Keeping continuity of pattern to match back and taking extra sts. into the pattern as they occur, work 1 row, then inc. 1 st. each end of next row and then on the 13 following 8th rows—85 (87) (91) (93) sts.

Work 7 rows.

To shape the sleeve top: Work as given for back from *** to ***—53 (55) (59) (61) sts.

Work 1 row. Cast off.

THE NECK BAND: First join right shoulder seam. With right side of work facing and using No. 12 (2¾ mm) needles, rejoin yarn and pick up and k. 68 (70) (72) (74) sts. down left front neck, k. 1. st. from centre front neck, pick up and k. 68 (70) (72) (74) sts. up right front neck, then k. 39 (41) (43) (45) sts. across back neck—176 (182) (188) (194) sts.

1st rib row: K. 1, * p. 1, k. 1; repeat from * to within 2 sts. of centre front st., p. 2 tog., p. 1, p. 2 tog.b., * k. 1, p. 1; repeat from this * to end.

2nd row: Rib to within 2 sts. of centre front st., k. 2 tog.b., k. 1, k. 2 tog., rib to end.

Repeat the last 2 rows, 3 times more, then the first of these rows again.

Cast off in rib, decreasing as before either side of centre front st.

TO MAKE UP THE SWEATER: Press lightly on the wrong side with a warm iron over a dry cloth. Join left shoulder seam, continuing across neck band. Set in sleeves, then join sleeve and side seams.

Tie-waist Sweater

Illustrated opposite

MEASUREMENTS	in centimetres (and inches, in brackets)		
To fit bust sizes	86 (34)	91 (36)	97 (38)
All round at underarms	90 (35½)	95 (37¼)	101 (39¾)
Side seam	37 (14½)	37 (14½)	37 (14½)
Length	60 (23½)	61 (24)	62 (24½)
Sleeve seam	44.5 (17½)	44.5 (17½)	44.5 (17½)

MATERIALS: *Allow the following quantities in 25 g balls of Robin Cloudsoft: 11 each for 86 cm and 91 cm sizes; 12 for 97 cm size. For any one size: a pair each of No. 5 (5½ mm) and No. 7 (4½ mm) knitting needles; a large size crochet hook.*

TENSION: *Work at a tension of 16 stitches and 20 rows to measure 10 × 10 cm, over the pattern, using No. 5 (5½ mm) needles, to obtain measurements given.*

ABBREVIATIONS: To be read before working: *K., knit plain; p., purl; st., stitch; tog., together; y.fwd., yarn forward to make a st.; s.k.p.o., slip 1, k. 1, pass slipped st. over; dec., decrease (by taking 2 sts. tog.); inc., increase (by working twice into next st.); single rib is k. 1 and p. 1 alternately; nil, meaning nothing is worked here for this size.*

NOTE: *The instructions are given for the 86 cm (34 inch) bust size. Where they vary, work figures within first brackets for the 91 cm (36 inch) size; work figures within second brackets for 97 cm (38 inch) size.*

THE BACK: With No. 7 (4½ mm) needles cast on 72 (76) (80) sts. and work 12 rows in single rib, increasing 1 st. at end of last row on the 97 cm size only—72 (76) (81) sts.

Change to No. 5 (5½ mm) needles.

1st pattern row: K. 2 (4) (2), * k. 2 tog., y.fwd., k. 1, y.fwd., s.k.p.o., k. 4; repeat from * ending last repeat with k. 2 (4) (2) instead of k. 4.

2nd row: P. to end.

These two rows form the pattern, repeat them a further 31 times—marking each end of last row to denote end of side seams.

Pattern a further 38 (40) (42) rows.

To slope shoulders: Cast off 6 (6) (7) sts. at beginning of next 6 rows, then 7 (8) (7) sts. on following 2 rows.

Cast off remaining 22 (24) (25) sts.

THE FRONT: Work as back to markers.

Pattern 1 row.

To divide for neck: Next row: P. 36 (38) (40) and leave on a spare needle for right front neck, *for 97 cm size only,* p. next st. and slip it on to a safety-pin, then *for all sizes,* p. to end of row and work on these last 36 (38) (40) sts. for left front neck.

The left front neck: Dec. 1 st. at neck edge on next row and the 10 (11) (11) following 3rd rows—25 (26) (28) sts.

Pattern 5 (4) (6) rows—pattern 6 (5) (7) rows here when working right front neck.

To slope shoulder: Cast off 6 (6) (7) sts. at beginning of next row and 2 following alternate rows.

Work 1 row, then cast off 7 (8) (7) sts.

The right front neck: With right side facing rejoin yarn to sts. on spare needle and work as left front neck, noting variation where indicated.

THE SLEEVES (2 alike): With No. 7 (4½ mm) needles cast on 36 (38) (40) sts. and work 15 rows in single rib.

Inc. row: * Rib 3, inc.; repeat from * until nil (2) (4) sts. remain, rib nil (2) (4)—45 (47) (49) sts.

Change to No. 5 (5½ mm) needles.

· 1st pattern row: K. 2 (3) (4), * k. 2 tog., y fwd., k. 1, y.fwd., s.k.p.o., k. 4; repeat from * ending last repeat with k. 2 (3) (4) instead of k. 4.

2nd row: P. to end.

Repeat last 2 rows, 3 times, then working extra sts. into the pattern as they occur, inc. 1 st. each end of next row and the 7 (8) (8) following 8th rows—61 (65) (67) sts.

Pattern 11 (3) (3) rows.

Cast off.

THE NECK RIBBING: First join right shoulder seam. With right side facing, rejoin yarn and using No. 7 (4½ mm) needles, pick up and k. 44 (46) (48) sts. down left front neck edge, pick up and k. 1 st. in centre, pick up and k. 44 (46) (48) sts. up right front neck edge, and finally 22 (24) (26) sts. across back neck—111 (117) (123) sts.

1st row: * P. 1, k. 1; repeat from * to within 2 sts. of centre front st., p. 2 tog., p. centre front st., p. 2 tog., ** k. 1, p. 1; repeat from ** to end.

2nd row: Rib to within 2 sts. of centre front st., p. 2 tog., k. 1, p. 2 tog., rib to end.

Repeat last 2 rows, twice, then 1st row again. Cast off in rib.

TO MAKE UP THE SWEATER: Do not press. Join right shoulder seam, continuing across neck ribbing. Set in sleeves above markers, then join side and sleeve seams. Using 2 strands of yarn together and a large size crochet hook, make a 145 cm (57 inches) length of chain. Slot through first row of pattern above waist ribbing.

Opposite *Tie-waist Sweater*

Overtop

Illustrated on page 98

MEASUREMENTS	in centimetres *(and inches, in brackets)*					
To fit bust size	86	(34)	91	(36)	97	(38)
Side seam	45.5	(18)	45.5	(18)	45.5	(18)
Length	63.5	(25)	63.5	(25)	64.5	(25½)
Sleeve seam, with cuff turned back	36.5	(14½)	36.5	(14½)	36.5	(14½)

MATERIALS: *Allow the following quantities in 40 g balls of Lister Lee Poodle:* 15 *for* 86 *cm size;* 16 *for* 91 *cm size;* 17 *for* 97 *cm size. For any one size: a pair each of No. 6 (5 mm), No. 7 (4½ mm) and No. 8 (4 mm) knitting needles.*

TENSION: *Work at a tension of* 17 *stitches and* 24 *rows to measure* 10 × 10 *cm, over the stocking stitch, using No. 7 (4½ mm) needles, and* 24 *rows to* 10 *cm in depth over the double rib, using No. 7 (4½ mm) needles, to obtain the measurements given.*

ABBREVIATIONS: To be read before working: *K., knit plain; p., purl; st., stitch; tog., together; dec., decrease (by working 2 sts. tog.); sl., slip; s.k.p.o., sl. 1, k. 1, pass the slipped st. over; g.st., garter st. (k. plain on every row); s.s., stocking st. (k. on the right side and p. on the wrong side); double rib is k. 2 and p. 2 alternately.*

NOTE: *The instructions are given for the 86 cm (34 inch) size. Where they vary, work the figures within the first brackets for the 91 cm (36 inch) size; work the figures within the second brackets for the 97 cm (38 inch) size.*

THE BACK AND FRONT ALIKE: With No. 8 (4 mm) needles cast on 90 (95) (99) sts. and work 7 rows in g.st.

Change to No. 7 needles and s.s 30 rows.

To shape the sides: Next (dec.) row: K. 2, s.k.p.o., k. until 4 sts. remain, k. 2 tog., k. 2.

S.s. 11 rows.

Repeat the last 12 rows, twice and the dec. row again—82 (87) (91) sts.

S.s. 37 rows. Cast off.

THE SLEEVES AND YOKE (worked in one piece beginning at edge of left sleeve): With No. 8 (4 mm) needles cast on 74 (74) (78) sts. and work 44 rows in double rib, beginning odd-numbered rows with p. 2, and even-numbered rows with k. 2.

Change to No. 7 (4½ mm) needles and work a further 68 rows in double rib—mark each end of last row with a coloured thread to denote end of sleeve seam.

Rib 35 (37) (39) rows.

To divide for neck: Next row: Rib 37 (37) (39), and leave these sts. on spare needle for front yoke, rib to end and work on these 37 (37) (39) sts. for back yoke.

The back yoke: Rib 37 (41) (41) rows and leave sts. on spare needle.

The front yoke: With right side of work facing, rejoin yarn to 37 (37) (39) sts. on spare needle and rib 18 (20) (20) rows.

Next row: Cast off 36 (36) (38) sts. in rib—1 st. left on needle—turn and cast on 36 (36) (38) sts.—37 (37) (39) sts.

Rib 17 (19) (19) rows.

Next (joining) row: Rib 37 (37) (39) sts. of front yoke, then rib across 37 (37) (39) sts. of back yoke—74 (74) (78) sts.

Rib 36 (38) (40) rows – mark each end of last row with a coloured thread to denote end of sleeve seam. Rib a further 68 rows.

Change to No. 8 (4 mm) needles and rib 44 rows. Cast off.

THE COLLAR: With right side of work facing and using No. 8 (4 mm) needles, pick up and k. 78 (82) (86) sts. all round neck edge and working in double rib as given on yoke, rib 1 row.

1st and 2nd turning rows: Rib until 30 (31) (32) sts. remain for 1st row, turn, sl. 1, rib until 30 (31) (32) sts. remain for 2nd row, turn.

3rd and 4th turning rows: Sl. 1, rib until 26 (27) (28) sts. remain, turn, sl. 1, rib until 26 (27) (28) sts. remain, turn.

5th and 6th turning rows: Sl. 1, rib until 22 (23) (24) sts. remain, turn, sl. 1, rib until 22 (23) (24) sts. remain, turn.

7th and 8th turning rows: Sl. 1, rib until 18 (19) (20) sts. remain, turn, sl. 1, rib until 18 (19) (20) sts. remain, turn.

Next 2 rows: Rib to end of row.

Rib 6 rows.

Change to No. 7 (4½ mm) needles and rib 16 rows.

Change to No. 6 (5 mm) needles and rib 20 (20) (22) rows. Cast off.

THE POCKETS (make 2): With No. 7 (4½ mm) needles cast on 30 sts. and work in rib as follows:

1st rib row: K. 2, * p. 2, k. 2; repeat from * to end.

2nd rib row: P. 2, * k. 2, p. 2; repeat from * to end.

Repeat these 2 rows, 18 times. Cast off.

TO MAKE UP THE OVERTOP: Do not press. Join side seams of back and front together. Sew sleeve seams up to the coloured markers. Then sew yoke to front and back, using a flat seam. Sew on pockets.

V-neck Aran-style Sweater

Illustrated on page 99

MEASUREMENTS												
To fit bust sizes	86	(34)	91	(36)	97	(38)	102	(40)	107	(42)	112	(44)
Side seam	38	(15)	38	(15)	38	(15)	38	(15)	38	(15)	38	(15)
Length	60.5	(23¾)	61	(24)	62	(24½)	63	(24¾)	63.5	(25)	64.5	(25½)
Sleeve seam	42	(16½)	42	(16½)	42	(16½)	42	(16½)	42	(16½)	42	(16½)

in centimetres (and inches, in brackets)

MATERIALS: *Allow the following quantities in 50 g balls of Lister/Lee Target Special Quality for Aran Knitting: 13 for 86 cm and 91 cm sizes; 14 for 97 cm size; 15 for 102 cm and 107 cm sizes; 16 for 112 cm size. For any one size: a pair each of No. 6 (5 mm) and No. 8 (4 mm) knitting needles; a No. 8 (4 mm) circular needle; a cable needle.*

TENSION: *Work at a tension of 18 stitches and 24 rows to measure 10 × 10 cm, over the double moss st., using No. 6 (5 mm) needles, to obtain the measurements given.*

ABBREVIATIONS: To be read before working: *K., knit plain; p., purl; st., stitch; tog., together; inc., increase (by working twice into same st.); s.s., stocking st. (k. on right side, p. on wrong side); d.m.st., double moss st.; sl., slip; s.k.p.o., sl. 1, k. 1, pass the slipped st. over; c. 4b., cable 4 back (sl. next 2 sts. on to cable needle and leave at back of work, k. 2, then k. 2 from cable needle); c. 4f., cable 4 front (as c. 4b. but leave sts. at front of work); tw. 2 rt., twist 2 right (k. into front of 2nd st. on left-hand needle, then k. into first, slipping both sts. off needle tog.); tw. 2 lt., twist 2 left (sl. next st. on to cable needle and leave at front of work, k. 1, then k. 1 from cable needle); cr. 2 rt., cross 2 right (k. into front of 2nd st. on left-hand needle, then p. into first slipping both sts. off needle tog.); cr. 2 lt., cross 2 left (sl. next st. on cable needle and leave at front of work, p. 1, then k. 1 from cable needle); single rib is k. 1, p. 1 alternately; nil meaning nothing is worked for this size.*

NOTE: *The instructions are given for the 86 cm (34 inch) size. Where they vary, work figures within first brackets for the 91 cm (36 inch) size; work figures within second brackets for the 97 cm (38 inch) size, and so on.*

THE BACK: With No. 8 (4 mm) needles cast on 92 (96) (100) (104) (108) (112) sts. and work 12 rows in single rib.
Change to No. 6 (5 mm) needles and work the 16-row pattern as follows:
1st row: K. 1, *p. 1, k. 1 *; repeat from * to * 1 (2)(3)(4) (5) (6) time(s), p. 3, tw. 2 rt., p. 2, k. 8, p. 2, tw. 2 rt., p. 4, tw. 2 rt., p. 4, tw. 2 rt., p. 3, k. 1, p. 1, k. 1, p. 8, k. 1, p. 1, k. 1, p. 3, tw. 2 lt., p. 4, tw. 2 lt., p. 4, tw. 2 lt., p. 2, k. 8, p. 2, tw. 2 rt., p. 3, k. 1; repeat from * to * to end.
2nd row: P. 1, * k. 1, p. 1 *; repeat from * to * 1 (2)(3) (4)(5)(6) time(s), k. 3, p. 2, k. 2, **p. 8, k. 2, p. 2, k. 4, p. 2, k. 4, p. 2, k. 3, p. 1, k. 1, p. 1, k. 8, p. 1, k. 1, p. 1, k. 3, p. 2, k. 4, p. 2, k. 4, p. 2, k. 2, p. 8, ** k. 2, p. 2, k. 3, p. 1; repeat from * to * to end.
3rd row: * P. 1, k. 1; repeat from * 2 (3) (4) (5) (6) (7) times, p. 2, tw. 2 rt., p. 2, c. 4b., c. 4f., p. 2, tw. 2 rt., p. 3, cr. 2 rt., cr. 2 lt., p. 3, tw. 2 rt., p. 3, cr. 2 lt., p. 6, cr. 2 rt., cr. 2 rt., p. 3, tw. 2 lt., p. 3, cr. 2 rt., cr. 2 lt., p. 3, tw. 2

lt., p. 2, c. 4b., c 4f., p. 2, tw. 2 lt., p. 2, ** k. 1, p. 1; repeat from ** to end.
4th row: * K. 1, p. 1; repeat from * 2 (3) (4) (5) (6) (7) times, k. 2, p. 2, k. 2, p. 8, k. 2, **p. 2, k. 3, p. 1, k. 2, p. 1, k. 3, p. 2 **, k. 4, cr. 2 rt., cr. 2 rt., k. 4, cr. 2 lt., cr. 2 lt., k. 4; repeat from ** to ** once, k. 2, p. 8, k. 2, p. 2, k. 2, * p. 1, k. 1; repeat from this * to end.
These 4 rows set the position of the d.m.st. and twist st. at each end of work. Keeping continuity of the d.m.st. and twist st., continue as follows:
5th row: Pattern 12 (14) (16) (18) (20) (22), k. 8, p. 2, tw. 2 rt., p. 2, cr. 2 rt., p. 2, cr. 2 lt., p. 2, tw. 2 rt., p. 5, cr. 2 lt., cr. 2 lt., p. 2, cr. 2 rt., cr. 2 rt., p. 5, tw. 2 lt., p. 2, cr. 2 rt., p. 2, cr. 2 lt., p. 2, tw. 2 lt., p. 2, k. 8, pattern to end.
6th row: Pattern 12 (14) (16) (18) (20) (22), p. 8, k. 2, p. 2, k. 2, p. 1, k. 4, p. 1, k. 2, p. 2, k. 6, cr. 2 rt., cr. 2 rt., cr. 2 lt., cr. 2 lt., k. 6, p. 2, k. 2, p. 1, k. 4, p. 1, k. 2, p. 2, k. 2, p. 8, pattern to end.
7th row: Pattern 12 (14) (16) (18) (20) (22), c. 4f., c. 4b., p. 2, tw. 2 rt., p. 1, cr. 2 rt., p. 4, cr. 2 lt., p. 1, tw. 2 rt., p. 7, cr. 2 lt., cr. 2 lt., cr. 2 rt., p. 7, tw. 2 lt., p. 1, cr. 2 rt., p. 4, cr. 2 lt., p. 1, tw. 2 lt., p. 2, c 4f., c. 4b., pattern to end.
8th row: Pattern 12 (14) (16) (18) (20) (22), p. 8, k. 2, p. 2, k. 1, p. 1, k. 6, p. 1, k. 1, p. 2, k. 8, cr. 2lt., cr. 2 lt., k. 8, p. 2, k. 1, p. 1, k. 6, p. 1, k. 1, p. 2, k. 2, p. 8, pattern to end.
9th row: Pattern 12 (14) (16) (18) (20) (22), k. 8, p. 2, tw. 2 rt., p. 1, cr. 2 lt., p. 4, cr. 2 rt., p. 1, tw. 2 rt., p. 7, cr. 2 rt., cr. 2 lt., cr. 2 lt., p. 7, tw. 2 lt., p. 1, cr. 2 lt., p. 4, cr. 2 rt., p. 1, tw. 2 lt., p. 2, k. 8, pattern to end.
10th row: Pattern 12 (14) (16) (18) (20) (22), p. 8, k. 2, p. 2, k. 2, p. 1, k. 4, p. 1, k. 2, p. 2, k. 6, cr. 2 lt., cr. 2 rt., k. 6, p. 2, k. 2, p. 1, k. 4, p. 1, k. 2, p. 2, k. 2, p. 8, pattern to end.
11th row: Pattern 12 (14) (16) (18) (20) (22), c. 4b., c. 4f., p. 2, tw. 2 rt., p. 2, cr. 2 lt., p. 2, cr. 2 rt., p. 2, tw. 2 rt., p. 5, cr. 2 rt., cr. 2 rt., p. 2, cr. 2 lt., cr. 2 lt., p. 5, tw. 2 lt., p. 2, cr. 2 lt., p. 2, cr. 2 rt., p. 2, tw. 2 lt., p. 2, c. 4b., c. 4f., pattern to end.
12th row: Pattern 12 (14) (16) (18) (20) (22), p. 8, k. 2, p. 2, k. 3, p. 1, k. 2, p. 1, k. 3, p.2, k. 4, cr. 2 lt., cr. 2 lt., k. 4, cr. 2 rt., cr. 2 rt., k. 4, p. 2, k. 3, p. 1, k. 2, p. 1, k. 3, p. 2, k. 2, p. 8, pattern to end.
13th row: Pattern 12 (14) (16) (18) (20) (22), k. 8, p. 2, tw. 2 rt., p. 3, cr. 2 lt., cr. 2 rt., p. 3, tw. 2 rt., p. 3, cr. 2 rt., cr. 2 rt., p. 6, cr. 2 lt., cr. 2 lt., p. 3, tw. 2 lt., p. 3, cr. 2 lt., cr. 2 rt., p. 3, tw. 2 lt., p. 2, k. 8, pattern to end.
14th row: As 2nd row.
15th row: Pattern 12 (14) (16) (18) (20) (22), c 4f., c. 4b., p. 2, tw. 2 rt., p. 4, tw. 2 rt., p. 4, tw. 2 rt., p. 3, k. 1, p. 1, k. 1, p. 8, k. 1, p. 1, k. 1, p. 3, tw. 2 lt., p. 4, tw. 2 lt., p. 4, tw. 2 lt., p. 2, c. 4f., c. 4b., pattern to end.

Continued on page 100

Opposite *Overtop (page 96).*   Above *V-neck Aran-style Sweater (page 97)*

16th row: Pattern 12 (14) (16) (18) (20) (22), work as 2nd row from ** to **, pattern to end.

Pattern a further 64 rows.

To shape the armholes: Cast off 4 (4) (4) (6) (6) (6) sts. at beginning of next 2 rows—84 (88) (92) (92) (96) (100) sts. ***

Pattern 46 (48) (50) (52) (54) (56) rows.

To slope the shoulders: Cast off 9 (10) (10) (10) (10) (11) sts. at beginning of next 2 (2) (4) (4) (2) (2) rows, then 9 (9) (9) (9) (10) (10) sts. on the following 4 (4) (2) (2) (4) (4) rows—30 (32) (34) (34) (36) (38) sts.

Leave sts. on a stitch-holder.

THE FRONT: Work as back to ***.

Pattern 1 row.

To divide for neck: Pattern 38 (40) (42) (42) (44) (46) and leave these sts. on a spare needle for right half neck, cast off 8 sts., pattern to end and work on these 38 (40) (42) (42) (44) (46) sts. for left half neck.

The left half neck: 1st row: Pattern until 3 sts. remain, k. 2 tog., k. 1.

2nd row: P. 2, pattern to end.

Repeat last 2 rows once, then the 1st row again.

Next row: As 2nd row.

Next row: Pattern until 2 sts. remain, k. 2.

Next row: As 2nd row.

Next row: As 1st row.

**** Repeat last 4 rows 7 (8) (9) (9) (10) (11) times—27 (28) (29) (29) (30) (31) sts.

Keeping 2 sts. at neck edge in s.s., pattern 7 (5) (3) (5) (3) (1) row(s) straight—pattern 8 (6) (4) (6) (4) (2) rows here when working right half neck.

To slope the shoulder: Cast off 9 (10) (10) (10) (10) (11) sts. at the beginning of the next row, then 9 (9) (10) (10) (10) (10) sts. on the following alternate row—9 (9) (9) (9) (10) (10) sts.

Pattern 1 row, then cast off.

The right half neck: With right side of work facing, rejoin yarn to sts. on spare needle.

1st row: K. 1, s.k.p.o., pattern to end.

2nd row: Pattern until 2 sts. remain, p. 2.

Repeat last 2 rows once, then the 1st row again.

Next row: As 2nd row.

Next row: K. 2, pattern to end.

Next row: As 2nd row.

Next row: As 1st row.

Work as left half neck from ****, noting variation.

THE SLEEVES (2 alike): With No. 8 (4 mm) needles cast on 41 (43) (45) (47) (49) (51) sts. and, beginning odd-number rows with k. 1, and even-number rows with p. 1, work 18 rows in single rib.

Change to No. 6 (5 mm) needles.

Inc. row: Rib nil (3) (1) (7) (6) (5), * inc., rib 3 (2) (2) (1) (1) (1); repeat from * 9 (11) (13) (15) (17) (19) times, inc., rib nil (3) (1) (7) (6) (5)—52 (56) (60) (64) (68) (72) sts.

Foundation row: * K. 1, p. 1; repeat from * 1 (2) (3) (4) (5) (6) time(s), k. 2, p. 2, k. 4, p. 2, k. 4, p. 2, k. 2, p. 8, k. 2, p. 2, k. 4, p. 2, k. 4, p. 2, k. 2, * p. 1, k. 1; repeat from this * to end.

1st row: * K. 1, p. 1; repeat from * 1 (2) (3) (4) (5) (6) time(s), p. 2, tw. 2 rt., p. 4, tw. 2 rt., p. 4, tw. 2 rt., p. 2, k. 8, p. 2, tw. 2 lt., p. 4, tw. 2 lt., p. 4, tw. 2 lt., p. 3, k. 1, * p. 1, k. 1; repeat from this * to end.

2nd row: P. 1, * k. 1, p. 1; repeat from * nil (1) (2) (3) (4) (5) time(s), k. 3, p. 2, k. 4, p. 2, k. 4, p. 2, k. 2, p. 8, k. 2, p. 2, k. 4, p. 2, k. 4, p. 2, k. 3, p. 1, * k. 1, p. 1; repeat from this * to end.

3rd row: * P. 1, k. 1; repeat from * 1 (2) (3) (4) (5) (6) time(s), p. 2, tw. 2 rt., p. 3, cr. 2 rt., cr. 2 lt., p. 3, tw. 2 rt., p. 2, c. 4b., c. 4f., p. 2, tw. 2 lt., p. 3, cr. 2 rt., cr. 2 lt., p. 3, tw. 2 lt., p. 2, * k. 1, p. 1; repeat from this * to end.

4th row: * K. 1, p. 1; repeat from * 1 (2) (3) (4) (5) (6) time(s), k. 2, p. 2, k. 3, p. 1, k. 2, p. 1, k. 3, p. 2, k. 2, p. 8, k. 2, p. 2, k. 3, p. 1, k. 2, p. 1, k. 3, p. 2, k. 2, * p. 1, k. 1; repeat from this * to end.

These 4 rows set the position of the 16-row pattern. Keeping continuity of pattern, work 12 rows, then, taking extra sts. into d.m.st. as they occur, inc. 1 st. each end of the next row, then on the 11 following 6th rows—76 (80) (84) (88) (92) (96) sts.

Pattern 9 rows. Cast off.

THE NECK BAND: First join shoulder seams. With right side of work facing and using No. 8 (4 mm) circular needle, rejoin yarn at centre front and pick up and k. 41 (43) (45) (47) (49) (51) sts. up right front neck edge, k. across sts. of back, then pick up and k. 41 (43) (45) (47) (49) (51) sts. down left front neck edge, leaving 8 cast off sts. free at centre front—112 (118) (124) (128) (134) (140) sts.

Working backwards and forwards in rows, work 8 rows in single rib.

Cast off in rib.

TO MAKE UP THE SWEATER: Press with a warm iron over a damp cloth. Set last 9 rows of sleeves into armholes, then join sleeve and side seams. Placing right front neck band over left front neck band, join row ends to 8 cast off sts. at front.

Aran-style Jacket

Illustrated on page 103

MEASUREMENTS To fit bust sizes	*in centimetres (and inches, in brackets)*			
	81 (32)	86 (34)	91 (36)	97 (38)
Side seam	43.5 (17)	43.5 (17)	43.5 (17)	43.5 (17)
Length	62.5 (24½)	63.5 (25)	64.5 (25¼)	65 (25½)
Sleeve seam	40.5 (16)	40.5 (16)	40.5 (16)	40.5 (16)

MATERIALS: *Allow the following quantities in 50 g balls of Phildar Shoot:* 13 *for 81 cm size;* 14 *for 86 cm size;* 16 *for 91 cm size;* 17 *for 97 cm size. For any one size: a pair each of No. 6 (5 mm) and No. 8 (4 mm) knitting needles; cable needle; 7 buttons.*

TENSION: *Work at a tension of 11 sts. to 6 cm in width and 25 rows to 10 cm in depth over the double moss stitch, using No. 6 (5 mm) needles, to obtain the measurements given.*

ABBREVIATIONS: To be read before working: *K., knit plain; p., purl; st., stitch; tog., together; inc., increase (by working twice into same st.); dec., decrease (by taking 2 sts. tog.); s.s., stocking st. (k. on the right side and p. on the wrong side); single rib is k. 1 and p. 1 alternately; p. 2 tog.b., p. 2 sts. tog. through back of loops; sl., slip; d.m.st., double moss stitch; cr. 2 rt., cross 2 right (sl. next st. on to cable needle and leave at back of work. k. 1, then p. 1 from cable needle); cr. 2 lt., cross 2 left (sl. next st. on to cable needle and leave at front of work, p. 1, then k. 1 from cable needle); c. 4b., cable 4 back (sl. next 2 sts. on to a cable needle and leave at back of work, k. 2 then k. 2 from cable needle); c. 4f., cable 4 front (work as given for c. 4b., but leave cable needle at front of work); inc. k., inc. 1 st. k.wise.*

NOTE: *The instructions are given for the 81 cm (32 inch) size. Where they vary, work the figures within the first brackets for the 86 cm (34 inch) size; work the figures within the second brackets for the 91 cm (36 inch) size, and so on.*

THE BACK: With No. 8 (4 mm) needles cast on 73 (77) (83) (87) sts. and beginning odd-numbered rows with p. 1 and even-numbered rows with k. 1, work 10 rows in single rib.

Change to No. 6 (5 mm) needles.

1st (foundation and increase) row: For d.m.st. k. 1, * p. 1, k. 1; repeat from * 4 (4) (5) (6) times, ** p. 2, inc. k., inc. k., p. 3, inc. k., k. 1, inc. k., p. 3, inc. k., inc. k., p. 2 **, for d.m.st. k. 1, * p. 1, k. 1; repeat from this * 7 (9) (10) (10) times, repeat from ** to ** once, for d.m.st. k. 1, * p. 1, k. 1; repeat from this * 4 (4) (5) (6) times—85 (89) (95) (99) sts.

2nd (foundation) row: For d.m.st. p. 1, * k. 1, p. 1; repeat from * 4 (4) (5) (6) times, ** k. 2, p. 4, k. 4, p. 3, k. 4, p. 4, k. 2 **, for d.m.st. p. 1, * k. 1, p. 1; repeat from this * 7 (9) (10) (10) times, repeat from ** to ** once, for d.m.st. p. 1, * k. 1, p. 1; repeat from this * 4 (4) (5) (6) times.

1st (pattern) row: For d.m.st. p. 1, * k. 1, p. 1; repeat from * 4 (4) (5) (6) times, ** p. 2, k. 4, p. 3, cr. 2 rt., k. 1, cr. 2 lt., p. 3, k. 4, p. 2 **, for d.m.st. p. 1, * k. 1, p. 1; repeat from this * 7 (9) (10) (10) times, repeat from ** to ** once, for d.m.st. p. 1, * k. 1, p. 1; repeat from this * 4 (4) (5) (6) times.

2nd row: For d.m.st. k. 1, * p. 1, k. 1; repeat from * 4 (4) (5) (6) times, ** k. 2, p. 4, k. 3, p. 1, k. 1, p. 1, k. 1, p. 1, k. 3, p. 4, k. 2 **, for d.m.st. k. 1, * p. 1, k. 1; repeat from this * 7 (9) (10) (10) times, repeat from ** to ** once, for d.m.st. k. 1, * p. 1, k. 1; repeat from this * to end.

3rd row: For d.m.st. k. 1, * p. 1, k. 1; repeat from * 4 (4) (5) (6) times, ** p. 2, c. 4b., p. 2, cr. 2 rt., p. 1, k. 1, p. 1, cr. 2 lt., p. 2, c. 4f., p. 2 **, for d.m.st. k. 1, * p. 1, k. 1; repeat from this * 7 (9) (10) (10) times, repeat from ** to ** once, for d.m.st. k. 1, * p. 1, k. 1; repeat from * to end.

4th row: For d.m.st. p. 1, * k. 1, p. 1; repeat from * 4 (4) (5) (6) times, ** k. 2, p. 4, k. 2, p. 1, k. 2, p. 1, k. 2, p. 1, k. 2, p. 4, k. 2 **, for d.m.st. p. 1, * k. 1, p. 1; repeat from this * 7 (9) (10) (10) times, repeat from ** to ** once, for d.m.st. p. 1, * k. 1, p. 1; repeat from this * to end.

These 4 rows from the d.m.st. Keeping continuity of d.m.st. in centre and at each end, continue working pattern panels as follows:

5th row: D.m.st. 11 (11) (13) (15), ** p. 2, k. 4, p. 1, cr. 2 rt., p. 2, k. 1, p. 2, cr. 2 lt., p. 1, k. 4, p. 2 **, d.m.st. 17 (21) (23) (23), repeat from ** to ** once, d.m.st. 11 (11) (13) (15).

6th row: D.m.st. 11 (11) (13) (15), ** k. 2, p. 4, k. 1, p. 1, k. 3, p. 1, k. 3, p. 1, k. 1, p. 4, k. 2 **, d.m.st. 17 (21) (23) (23), repeat from ** to ** once, d.m.st. 11 (11) (13) (15).

7th row: D.m.st. 11 (11) (13) (15), work from ** to ** as given on 1st pattern row once, d.m.st. 17 (21) (23) (23), work from ** to ** as given on 1st pattern row once, d.m.st. 11 (11) (13) (15).

8th row: D.m.st. 11 (11) (13) (15), work from ** to ** as given on 2nd pattern row once, d.m.st. 17 (21) (23) (23), work from ** to ** as given on 2nd pattern row once, d.m.st. 11 (11) (13) (15).

9th row: D.m.st. 11 (11) (13) (15), work from ** to ** as given on 3rd row once, d.m.st. 17 (21) (23) (23), work from ** to ** as given on 3rd row once, d.m.st. 11 (11) (13) (15).

10th row: D.m.st. 11 (11) (13) (15), work from ** to ** as given on 4th row once, d.m.st. 17 (21) (23) (23), work from ** to ** as given on 4th row once, d.m.st. 11 (11) (13) (15).

11th row: D.m.st. 11 (11) (13) (15), work from ** to ** as given on 5th row once, d.m.st. 17 (21) (23) (23), work from ** to ** as given on 5th row once, d.m.st. 11 (11) (13) (15).

12th row; D.m.st. 11 (11) (13) (15), work from ** to ** as given on 6th row once, d.m.st. 17 (21) (23) (23), work from ** to ** as given on 6th row once, d.m.st. 11 (11) (13) (15).

These 12 rows form the pattern, keeping continuity of pattern, work 86 rows.

Continued on page 102

To shape the armholes: 1st and 2nd rows: Cast off 3 (3) (4) (4) sts., pattern to end.

3rd row: P. 1, k. 1, p. 2 tog., pattern until 4 sts. remain, p. 2 tog.b., k. 1, p. 1.

4th row: K. 1, p. 1, k. 1, pattern until 3 sts. remain, k. 1, p. 1, k. 1.

Repeat the 3rd and 4th rows, 22 (23) (24) (25) times more—33 (35) (37) (39) sts.

Cast off.

THE POCKET BACKS (2 alike): With No. 6 (5 mm) needles cast on 19 sts. and s.s. 24 rows.

Next row: P. 1, work from ** to ** as given on 1st foundation and increase row of back, p. 1—25 sts.

Next row: K. 3, p. 4, k. 4, p. 3, k. 4, p. 4, k. 3

Break yarn and leave sts. on a stitch-holder.

THE LEFT FRONT: With No. 8 (4 mm) needles cast on 43 (45) (49) (51) sts. and work 10 rows in rib as given on back.

Change to No. 6 (5 mm) needles.

1st (foundation and increase) row: For d.m.st. k. 1, * p. 1, k. 1; repeat from * 4 (4) (5) (6) times, work from ** to ** as given on 1st foundation and increase row on back, for d.m.st. * k. 1, p. 1; repeat from this * 3 (4) (5) (5) times, turn, leave remaining 7 sts. on a safety-pin for the button band.

Continue to work on these 42 (44) (48) (50) sts. as follows:

2nd (foundation) row: For d.m.st. * k. 1, p. 1; repeat from * 3 (4) (5) (5) times, work from ** to ** as given on 2nd foundation row on back, for d.m.st. p. 1, * k. 1, p. 1; repeat from this * 4 (4) (5) (6) times.

1st (pattern) row: For d.m.st. p. 1, * k. 1, p. 1; repeat from * 4 (4) (5) (6) times, work from ** to ** as given on 1st pattern row on back, for d.m.st. * p. 1, k. 1; repeat from this * 3 (4) (5) (5) times.

2nd row: For d.m.st. * p. 1, k. 1; repeat from * 3 (4) (5) (5) times, work from ** to ** as given on 2nd pattern row of back, for d.m.st. k. 1, * p. 1, k. 1; repeat from this * 4 (4) (5) (6) times.

These 2 rows set the position of the pattern for the left front, keeping continuity of pattern to match back, work a further 22 rows.

Next (pocket) row: D.m.st. 10 (10) (12) (14), sl. next 25 sts. on to a stitch-holder and in their place, work across pocket back thus: p. 1, work from ** to ** as given on 1st pattern row of back, p. 1, then d.m.st. 7 (9) (11) (11).

Pattern 73 rows.

To shape the armhole: 1st row: Cast off 3 (3) (4) (4) sts., work to end.

2nd row: Pattern until 3 sts. remain, k. 1, p. 1, k. 1.

3rd row: P. 1, k. 1, p. 2 tog., pattern to end.

Repeat the 2nd and 3rd rows, 14 times more—24 (26) (29) (31) sts.

To shape the neck: 1st row: Cast off 6 (6) (7) (7) sts., pattern until 3 sts. remain, k. 1, p. 1, k. 1.

2nd row: P. 1, k. 1, p. 2 tog., pattern until 2 sts. remain, p. 2 tog.

3rd row: Pattern until 3 sts. remain, k. 1, p. 1, k. 1.

Repeat the 2nd and 3rd rows, 5 (6) (7) (8) times more—6 sts.

Next row: P. 1, k. 1, p. 2 tog., p. 2 tog.—4 sts.

Next row: K. 2, p. 1, k. 1.

Next row: P. 1, k. 1, p. 2 tog.—3 sts.

K. 3 tog., and fasten off.

THE RIGHT FRONT: With No. 8 (4 mm) needles cast

on 43 (45) (49) (51) sts. and work 6 rows in rib as given on back.

1st (buttonhole) row: Rib 3, cast off 2 sts., rib to end.

2nd (buttonhole) row: Rib to end, casting on 2 sts. over those cast off on previous row.

Rib a further 2 rows.

Next row: Rib 7 and leave these sts. on a safety-pin for buttonhole band. Change to No. 6 (5 mm) needles and work as follows across the 36 (38) (42) (44) sts. thus: * p. 1, k. 1; repeat from * 3 (4) (5) (5) times, work from ** to ** on 1st foundation and increase row on back, then for d.m.st. k. 1, * p. 1, k. 1; repeat from this * 4 (4) (5) (6) times—42 (44) (48) (50) sts.

2nd (foundation) row: For d.m.st. p. 1, * k. 1, p. 1; repeat from * 4 (4) (5) (6) times, work from ** to ** as given on 2nd foundation row on back, * p. 1, k. 1; repeat from this * 3 (4) (5) (5) times.

1st (pattern) row: For d.m.st. * k. 1, p. 1; repeat from * 3 (4) (5) (5) times, work from ** to ** as given on 1st pattern row on back, for d.m.st. p. 1, * k. 1, p. 1; repeat from this * 4 (4) (5) (6) times.

2nd row: For d.m.st. k. 1, * p. 1, k. 1; repeat from * 4 (4) (5) (6) times, work from ** to ** on 2nd pattern row on back, for d.m.st. * p. 1, k. 1; repeat from this to end.

These 2 rows set the position of the pattern for the right front, keeping continuity of pattern to match back, work a further 22 rows.

Next (pocket) row: D.m.st. 7 (9) (11) (11), sl. next 25 sts. on to a stitch-holder and in their place work across pocket back thus: p. 1, work from ** to ** as given on 1st pattern row of back, p. 1, then d.m.st. 7 (9) (11) (11).

Pattern 74 rows.

To shape the armhole: 1st row: Cast off 3 (3) (4) (4) sts., pattern to end.

2nd row: Pattern until 4 sts. remain, p. 2 tog.b., k. 1, p. 1.

3rd row: K. 1, p. 1, k. 1, pattern to end.

Repeat the 2nd and 3rd rows, 14 times more—24 (26) (29) (31) sts.

To shape the neck: 1st row: Cast off 6 (6) (7) (7) sts., pattern until 4 sts. remain, p. 2 tog.b., k. 1, p. 1.

2nd row: K. 1, p. 1, k. 1, pattern to end.

3rd row: P. 2 tog., pattern until 4 sts. remain, p. 2 tog.b., k. 1, p. 1.

Repeat 2nd and 3rd rows, 5 (6) (7) (8) times—5 sts.

Next row: K. 1, p. 1, k. 1, p. 2.

Next row: P. 2 tog., p. 2 tog.b., p. 1—3 sts.

Work 1 row.

Take remaining 3 sts. tog. and fasten off.

THE SLEEVES (both alike): With No. 8 (4 mm) needles cast on 33 (33) (37) (37) sts. and work 10 rows in rib as given on back.

Change to No. 6 (5 mm) needles.

1st (foundation and increase) row: For d.m.st. * k. 1, p. 1; repeat from * 3 (3) (4) (4) times, work from ** to ** as given on 1st foundation and increase row on back once, for d.m.st. * p. 1, k. 1; repeat from this * 3 (3) (4) (4) times—39 (39) (43) (43) sts.

2nd (foundation) row: For d.m.st. * p. 1, k. 1; repeat from * 3 (3) (4) (4) times, work from ** to ** as given on 2nd foundation row on back once, for d.m.st. * k. 1, p. 1; work from this * 3 (3) (4) (4) times.

1st (pattern) row: For d.m.st. * p. 1, k. 1; repeat from * 3 (3) (4) (4) times, work from ** to ** on 1st pattern row of back, once, for d.m.st. * k. 1, p. 1; repeat from this * 3 (3) (4) (4) times.

Continued on page 104

Above *Aran-style jacket (page 101)*

2nd row: For d.m.st. * k. 1, p. 1; repeat from * 3 (3) (4) (4) times, work from ** to ** as given on 2nd row of back once, for d.m.st. * p. 1, k. 1; repeat from this * 3 (3) (4) (4) times.

These 2 rows set the position of the pattern for the sleeves, keeping continuity of pattern to match back and working extra sts. into d.m.st. as they occur, inc. 1 st. each end of the next row and 9 (10) (9) (10) following 6th rows—59 (61) (63) (65) sts.

Pattern 33 (27) (33) (27) rows—mark each end of the last row with a coloured thread to denote end of sleeve seam.

Pattern 4 (4) (6) (6) rows.

1st row: P. 1, k. 1, p. 2 tog., pattern until 4 sts. remain, p. 2 tog.b., k. 1, p. 1.

2nd row: K. 1, p. 1, k. 1, pattern until 3 sts. remain, k. 1, p. 1, k. 1.

Repeat these 2 rows, 22 (23) (24) (25) times.

Cast off remaining 13 sts.

THE BUTTON BAND: With right side of work facing, rejoin yarn and using No. 8 (4 mm) needles, inc. in first st., rib to end—8 sts.

Rib 121 rows. Cast off in rib.

THE BUTTONHOLE BAND: With wrong side of work facing, rejoin yarn and using No. 8 (4 mm) needles, inc. in first st., rib to end—8 sts.

Rib 14 rows.

1st (buttonhole) row: Rib 3, cast off 2 sts., rib to end.

2nd (buttonhole) row: Rib to end, casting on 2 sts. over those cast off on previous row.

Rib 18 rows.

Repeat the last 20 rows, 4 times and the 2 buttonhole rows again.

Rib 4 rows. Cast off in rib.

THE POCKET TOPS (both alike): With right side of work facing rejoin yarn and using No. 8 (4 mm) needles work thus: inc. k., * p. 1, k. 1; repeat from * until 2 sts. remain, p. 1, inc. k—27 sts.

Next row: K. 1, * p. 1, k. 1; repeat from * to end.

Rib a further 4 rows.

Cast off in rib.

THE COLLAR: With No. 8 (4 mm) needles cast on 33 (35) (37) (39) sts. and rib 1 row as given on back.

Keeping continuity of rib, cast on 4 (6) (6) (6) sts. at the beginning of the next 4 (4) (6) (2) rows, then cast on 6 (6) (8) (8) sts. at the beginning of the next 6 (6) (4) (8) rows—85 (95) (105) (115) sts.

Rib a further 19 rows.

Cast off loosely in rib.

TO MAKE UP THE JACKET: Press with a cool iron over a dry cloth. Join raglan seams, setting 4 (4) (6) (6) rows above markers to sts. cast off on back and fronts. Join sleeve and side seams. Sew on front bands. Stitch collar all round neck beginning and ending in centre of front bands and placing cast on group to back neck. Catch pocket backs to wrong side and row end of pocket tops to right side. Sew on buttons.

Lacy, Square-neck Jersey

Illustrated opposite

MEASUREMENTS	*in centimetres (and inches, in brackets)*				
To fit bust sizes	86 (34)	91 (36)	97 (38)	102 (40)	107 (42)
All round at underarms	91 (36)	95 (37$\frac{1}{4}$)	101 (39$\frac{3}{4}$)	107 (42)	111 (43$\frac{3}{4}$)
Side seam	37 (14$\frac{1}{2}$)	37 (14$\frac{1}{2}$)	37 (14$\frac{1}{2}$)	37 (14$\frac{1}{2}$)	37 (14$\frac{1}{2}$)
Length	59.5 (23$\frac{1}{2}$)	59.5 (23$\frac{1}{2}$)	59.5 (23$\frac{1}{2}$)	59.5 (23$\frac{1}{2}$)	61.5 (24$\frac{1}{4}$)
Sleeve seam	53 (21)	53 (21)	53 (21)	53 (21)	53 (21)
To fit bust sizes	112 (44)	117 (46)	122 (48)	127 (50)	
All round at underarms	117 (46)	121 (47$\frac{1}{2}$)	127 (50)	133 (52$\frac{1}{4}$)	
Side seam	37 (14$\frac{1}{2}$)	37 (14$\frac{1}{2}$)	37 (14$\frac{1}{2}$)	37 (14$\frac{1}{2}$)	
Length	61.5 (24$\frac{1}{4}$)	61.5 (24$\frac{1}{4}$)	61.5 (24$\frac{1}{4}$)	61.5 (24$\frac{1}{4}$)	
Sleeve seam	53 (21)	53 (21)	53 (21)	53 (21)	

MATERIALS: *Allow the following quantities in 50 g balls of 3 Suisses Aubretia: 9 for 86 cm size; 10 for 91 and 97 cm sizes; 11 for 102 cm size; 12 for 107 and 112 cm sizes; 13 for 117 cm size; 14 for 122 and 127 cm sizes. For any one size: a pair each of No. 8 (4 mm) and No. 10 (3$\frac{1}{4}$ mm) knitting needles.*

TENSION: *Work at a tension of 20 stitches and 26 rows to measure 10 × 10 cm, over the pattern, using No. 8 (4 mm) needles, to obtain measurements given.*

ABBREVIATIONS: To be read before working: *K., knit plain; p., purl; st., stitch; tog., together; inc., increase (by working twice into next st.); y.fwd., yarn forward to make a st.; sl., slip; p.s.s.o., pass sl. st. over; k. or p. 2 tog.b., k. or p. 2 tog. through back of sts.; single rib is k. 1. p. 1 alternately.*

NOTE: *The instructions are given for the 86 cm (34 inch) size. Where they vary work figures within first brackets for 91 cm (36 inch) size; work figures within second brackets for 97 cm (38 inch) size, and so on.*

THE BACK: With No. 10 (3¼ mm) needles cast on 91 (95) (101) (107) (111) (117) (121) (127) (133) sts. and, beginning odd-number rows with k. 1 and even-number rows with p. 1, work 11 rows in single rib.

Change to No. 8 (4 mm) needles and work the 8-row pattern as follows:

1st row: K. 1 (3) (1) (4) (1) (4) (1) (4) (2), * y.fwd., k. 3, sl. 1, k. 2 tog., p.s.s.o., k. 3, y.fwd., k. 1; repeat from * ending last repeat with k. 1 (3) (1) (4) (1) (4) (1) (4) (2), instead of k. 1.

2nd and alternate rows: All p.

3rd row: K. 2 (4) (2) (5) (2) (5) (2) (5) (3) * y.fwd., k. 2, sl. 1, k. 2 tog., p.s.s.o., k. 2, y.fwd., k. 3; repeat from * ending last repeat with k. 2 (4) (2) (5) (2) (5) (2) (5) (3), instead of k. 3.

5th row: K. 3 (5) (3) (6) (3) (6) (3) (6) (4), * y.fwd., k. 1, sl. 1, k. 2 tog., p.s.s.o., k. 1, y.fwd., k. 5; repeat from * ending last repeat with k. 3 (5) (3) (6) (3) (6) (3) (6) (4), instead of k. 5.

7th row: K. 4 (6) (4) (7) (4) (7) (4) (7) (5), * y.fwd., sl. 1, k. 2 tog., p.s.s.o., y.fwd., k. 7; repeat from * ending last repeat with k. 4 (6) (4) (7) (4) (7) (4) (7) (5), instead of k. 7.

8th row: All p.

Pattern a further 78 rows, marking each end of the last of these rows to denote end of side seams. **

Pattern 52 (52) (52) (52) (58) (58) (58) (58) (58) rows.

To slope the shoulders: Cast off 7 (8) (9) (9) (10) (11) (11) (12) (13) sts. at beginning of next 4 rows, then 7 (7) (8) (10) (10) (11) (12) (13) (14) sts. on the following 2 rows—49 (49) (49) (51) (51) (51) (53) (53) (53) sts. remain.

Leave sts. on a spare needle.

THE FRONT: Work as back until ** has been reached.

Pattern 17 (17) (17) (17) (23) (23) (23) (23) (23) rows.

To divide for neck: Next row: P. 21 (23) (26) (28) (30) (33) (34) (37) (40) and leave these sts. on a spare needle for right half neck, p. 49 (49) (49) (51) (51) (51) (53) (53) (53) and leave these sts. on a stitch-holder, p. to end and work on these 21 (23) (26) (28) (30) (33) (34) (37) (40) sts. for left half neck.

The left half neck: Keeping continuity of pattern where possible, work 34 rows—work 35 rows here when working right half neck.

To slope the shoulder: Cast off 7 (8) (9) (9) (10) (11) (11) (12) (13) sts. at beginning of next row, and the following alternate row—7 (7) (8) (10) (10) (11) (12) (13) (14) sts.

Work 1 row, then cast off.

The right half neck: With right side of work facing rejoin yarn to inner end of sts. on spare needle and work as left half neck, noting variation.

THE SLEEVES (both alike): With No. 10 (3¼ mm) needles cast on 41 (41) (41) (41) (47) (47) (47) (47) (47) sts. and work 20 rows in rib as given for back.

Inc. row: K. 1 (1) (1) (1) (3) (3) (3) (3) (3), * inc.; repeat from * to end—81 (81) (81) (81) (91) (91) (91) (91) (91) sts.

Change to No. 8 (4 mm) needles.

Continuing to work in pattern for all sizes as given for the 86 cm (34 inch) size on back, pattern 120 rows.

Cast off.

THE NECK RIBBING: First join right shoulder seam.

With right side of work facing and using No. 10 (3¼ mm) needles, rejoin yarn and pick up and k. 39 sts. down left half neck, pick up 1 st. from corner and k. into back of it, k. 49 (49) (49) (51) (51) (51) (53) (53) (53) across front neck, pick up 1 st. from corner and k. into back of it, pick up and k. 39 sts. up left half neck, then k. 49 (49) (49) (51) (51) (51) (53) (53) (53) sts. across back neck—178 (178) (178) (182) (182) (182) (186) (186) (186) sts.

1st rib row: * K. 1, p. 1 *; repeat from * to * to within 2 sts. of first corner st., k. 2 tog., p. 1, k. 2 tog.b., p. 1, repeat from * to * to within 2 sts. of second corner st., k. 2 tog., p. 1, k. 2 tog.b., p. 1, repeat from * to * to end.

2nd rib row: * Rib to within 2 sts. of corner st., p. 2 tog.b., k. 1, p. 2 tog., repeat from * once, rib to end.

Rib a further 5 rows decreasing as before on each row.

Cast off in rib, decreasing as before at corners.

TO MAKE UP THE SWEATER: Do not press. Join left shoulder seam, continuing seam across neck ribbing. Set in sleeves between markers on back and fronts, then join sleeve and side seams.

Button-up Bomber Jacket
Illustrated opposite

MEASUREMENTS	*in centimetres (and inches, in brackets)*					
To fit loosely bust sizes	86 to 91	(34 to 36)	97	(38)	102 to 107	(40 to 42)
All round at underarms, fastened	100	(39½)	106.5	(41¾)	113	(44½)
Side seam	39	(15¼)	39	(15¼)	39	(15¼)
Length	61.5	(24¼)	62	(24½)	63	(24¾)
Sleeve seam	49	(19¼)	49	(19¼)	49	(19¼)

MATERIALS: *Allow the following quantities in 50 g balls of Sirdar Astrakhan and Sirdar Majestic D.K.: 10 Astrakhan and 2 D.K. for the 86 to 91 cm size; 11 Astrakhan and 3 D.K. for the 97 cm size; 12 Astrakhan and 3 D.K. for the 102 to 107 cm size. For any one size: a pair each of No. 8 (4 mm) and No. 10 (3¼ mm) knitting needles.*

TENSION: *Work at a tension of 17 stitches and 28 rows to measure 10 × 10 cm, over the reversed stocking stitch, using No. 8 (4 mm) needles, to obtain the measurements given.*

ABBREVIATIONS: To be read before working: *K., knit plain; p., purl; st., stitch; tog., together; inc., increase (by working twice into next st.); dec., decrease (by taking 2 sts. tog.); up 1, pick up loop lying between needles and k. into the back of it; y.fwd., yarn forward to make a st.; single rib is k. 1 and p. 1 alternately; r.s.s., reverse stocking st. (p. on the right side and k. on the wrong side); g.st., garter st. (k. plain on every row); nil, meaning nothing is worked here for this size: A., Astrakhan; D.K., Double Knitting.*

NOTE: *The instructions are given for the 86 to 91 cm (34 to 36 inch) size. Where they vary, work the figures within the first brackets for the 97 cm (38 inch) size; work the figures within the second brackets for the 102 to 107 cm (40 to 42 inch) size.*

THE BACK: With No. 10 (3¼ mm) needles and D.K. cast on 102 (108) (114) sts. and work 33 rows in single rib.

Next (dec.) row: Rib 5 (8) (11), * dec., rib 8; repeat from * until 7 (10) (13) sts. remain, dec., rib to end—92 (98) (104) sts. Break off D.K., join in A.

Change to No. 8 (4 mm) needles and with A., beginning with a p. row, r.s.s. 82 rows.

To shape the raglan armholes: Cast off 5 (6) (7) sts. at the beginning of each of the next 2 rows.

** Dec. 1 st. at each end of the next row and the 4 following alternate rows.

R.s.s. 3 rows. **

Repeat from ** to ** 4 times (4 times, then the 1st 2 rows again) (4 times, then the 1st 4 rows again)—32 (34) (36) sts.

Leave sts. on a spare needle.

THE LEFT FRONT: With No. 10 (3¼ mm) needles and D.K. cast on 54 (58) (62) sts. and work 33 rows in rib as given for back.

Next (dec.) row: Rib 6 and leave these sts. on a safety pin for border, rib 1 (2) (nil), * rib 4, dec., rib 3 (rib 3, dec., rib 3) (rib 3, dec., rib 3); repeat from * until 2 (2) (nil) sts. remain, rib to end—43 (46) (49) sts.

Break off D.K., join in A.

Change to No. 8 (4 mm) needles and with A., r.s.s. 82 rows.

*** **To shape the raglan armhole:** Cast off 5 (6) (7) sts. at the beginning of the next row. Work 1 row—omit this row when working right front.

Dec. 1 st. at armhole edge on the next row and the 4 following alternate rows.

R.s.s. 3 rows.

Repeat the last 12 rows, once.

Dec. 1 st. at armhole edge on the next row and the 2 (3) (4) following alternate rows. ***

To shape the neck and continue shaping raglan armhole: 1st row: K. 6 (7) (8) and leave these sts. on a safety pin, k. to end.

For the 86 to 91 cm size only: 2nd row: Dec., p. until 2 sts. remain, dec.

3rd row: All k.

4th row: Dec., p. to end.

5th row: All k.

6th row: P. until 2 sts. remain, dec.

7th row: All k.—15 sts.

For the 97 cm size only: 2nd and 3rd rows: As 2nd and 3rd rows on the 86 to 91 cm size.

4th row: All p.

5th row: All k.—17 sts.

For the 102 to 107 cm size only: 2nd row: P. until 2 sts. remain, dec.

3rd row: All k.—18 sts.

For all sizes: Dec. 1 st. at armhole edge on the next row and the 4 following alternate rows, *at the same time*, dec. 1 st. at neck edge on the 4th row from previous dec. and then on every following 4th row—8 (9) (11) sts.

R.s.s. 3 rows, decreasing 1 st. at neck edge on the 2nd of these rows on the 86 to 91 cm and 102 to 107 cm sizes only—7 (9) (9) sts.

This completes neck shaping for the 86 to 91 cm size only.

Dec. 1 st. at armhole edge on the next row and the 4 following alternate rows, *at the same time*, dec. 1 st. at neck edge on the 1st of these rows for the 97 cm size and on the 3rd of these rows for the 102 to 107 cm size—2 (7) (7) sts.

*** **For the 86 to 91 cm size only:** Work 2 rows, then take remaining 2 sts. tog. and fasten off.

For the 97 cm and 102 to 107 cm sizes only: R.s.s. 3 rows.

Dec. 1 st. at armhole edge only on the next row and the nil (1) following alternate row(s).

Take remaining 2 sts. tog. and fasten off.

Continued on page 108

Opposite *Button-up Bomber Jacket*

THE RIGHT FRONT: With No. 10 (3¼ mm) needles and D.K. cast on 54 (58) (62) sts. and work 2 rows in rib as given for back.

Buttonhole row: Rib 2, k. 2 tog., y.fwd., k. 1, p. 1, rib to end.

Rib 11 rows.

Repeat the last 12 rows, once, then the buttonhole row again.

Rib 7 rows.

Next (dec.) row: Rib 2 (2) (nil), * rib 3, dec., rib 4 (3) (3); repeat from * until 7 (8) (6) sts. remain, rib 1 (2) (nil), turn and leave the remaining 6 sts. on a safety pin for front border—43 (46) (49) sts. Break off D.K., join in A.

Change to No. 8 (4 mm) needles and with A., r.s.s. 83 rows.

Work as given for left front from *** to ***.

Work 1 row.

To shape the neck and continue shaping raglan armhole: For the 86 to 91 cm and 97 cm sizes only: 1st row: P. 6 (7) and leave these sts. on a safety pin, p. until 2 sts. remain, dec.

For the 102 to 107 cm size only: 1st row: P. 8 and leave these sts. on a safety pin, p. to end.

For the 86 to 91 cm size only: 2nd row: All k.

3rd row: Dec., p. until 2 sts. remain, dec.

4th to 6th rows: R.s.s. 3 rows—16 sts.

For the 97 cm size only: 2nd row: All k.

3rd row: Dec., p. to end.

4th row: All k.—17 sts.

For the 102 to 107 cm size only: 2nd row: All k.—19 sts.

For all sizes: Dec. 1 st. at armhole edge only on the next row and the 4 following alternate rows, *at the same time*, dec. 1 st. at neck edge on the 4th row from previous dec. and then on every following 4th row—8 (10) (12) sts.

R.s.s. 3 rows decreasing 1 st. at neck edge on the 2nd of these rows on the 97 cm and 102 to 107 cm sizes only—8 (9) (11) sts.

Dec. 1 st. at armhole edge on the next row and the 4 following alternate rows, *at the same time*, dec. 1 st. at neck edge on the 1st (3rd) (3rd and 7th) of these rows—2 (3) (4) sts.

Work as given for left front from **** to end.

THE SLEEVES (both alike): With No. 10 (3¼ mm) needles and D.K. cast on 44 (48) (52) sts. and work 33 rows in rib as given for back.

Next (inc.) row: Rib 4 (6) (8), * inc., rib 3; repeat from * until 4 (6) (8) sts. remain, inc., rib to end—54 (58) (62) sts. Break off D.K., join in A.

Change to No. 8 (4 mm) needles and with A., r.s.s. 8 rows.

Continuing in r.s.s., inc. 1 st. at each end of the next row and the 7 following 8th rows—70 (74) (78) sts.

R.s.s. 45 rows.

To shape the raglan sleeve top: Work exactly as given for raglan shaping on back when 10 sts. will remain. Leave sts. on a safety pin.

THE RIGHT FRONT BORDER: With wrong side of work facing and using No. 10 (3¼ mm) needles join D.K. to 6 sts. on safety pin at right front and rib 12 rows.

Buttonhole row: Rib 2, k. 2 tog., y.fwd., k. 1, p. 1.

Rib 21 rows.

Repeat the last 22 rows, 3 times, then the buttonhole row again.

Rib a further 20 (22) (24) rows. Cast off 2 sts. Leave 4 sts. on a safety pin. Sew border in position.

THE LEFT FRONT BORDER: With right side of work facing, and using No. 10 (3¼ mm) needles, join D.K. to sts. left on safety pin at left front and rib 121 (123) (125) rows. Cast off 2 sts. Leave 4 sts. on a safety pin. Sew border in position.

THE COLLAR: First join raglan seams. With right side of work facing, and using No. 10 (3¼ mm) needles and A., k. across the 6 (7) (8) sts. on right front safety pin, pick up and k. 19 sts. up right front neck edge, k. across the 10 sts. at top of right sleeve, k. across the 32 (34) (36) sts. at back neck, k. the 10 sts. at top of left sleeve, pick up and k. 19 sts. down left front neck edge, then k. across the 6 (7) (8) sts. on left front safety pin—102 (106) (110) sts.

1st (dec.) row: P. 2, * p. 2 tog., p. 2; repeat from * to end—77 (80) (83) sts.

2nd row: All k.

3rd row: All p.

4th row: K. 4, up 1, k. until 4 sts. remain, up 1, k. 4.

5th row: All p.

Repeat the last 4 rows, once—81 (84) (87) sts.

Change to No. 8 (4 mm) needles and repeat the last 4 rows, 5 times—91 (94) (97) sts.

Work 7 rows in g.st. Cast off.

THE RIGHT COLLAR EDGING: With wrong side of work facing and using No. 10 (3¼ mm) needles and D.K., work across the 4 sts. on safety pin as follows:

1st row: K. 1, p. 1, k. 1, p. 1.

2nd row: K. 1, p. 1, k. 2.

Repeat the last 2 rows until edging is long enough when slightly stretched to fit up row ends of collar, casting off in rib when correct length is assured. Sew collar edging in place.

THE LEFT COLLAR EDGING: With right side of work facing and using No. 10 (3¼ mm) needles and D.K., work across the sts. on safety pin as follows:

1st row: K. 2, p. 1, k. 1.

2nd row: P. 1, k. 1, p. 1, k. 1.

Work as given for right collar edging to end. Sew collar edging in place.

TO MAKE UP JACKET: Do not press. Join sleeve and side seams. Add buttons.

Lacy twin-set

Illustrated on page 111

MEASUREMENTS	*in centimetres (and inches, in brackets)*					
To fit bust sizes	102 (40)	107 (42)	112 (44)	117 (46)	122 (48)	127 (50)
JERSEY						
All round at underarms	102.5 (40¼)	107 (42)	113.5 (44¾)	118.5 (46¾)	125 (49¼)	131.5 (51¾)
Side seam	34.5 (13½)	34.5 (13½)	34.5 (13½)	34.5 (13½)	34.5 (13½)	34.5 (13½)
Length	56 (22)	57.5 (22¾)	58.5 (23)	59.5 (23½)	60.5 (23¾)	62 (24½)
Sleeve seam	7.5 (3)	7.5 (3)	7.5 (3)	7.5 (3)	7.5 (3)	7.5 (3)
CARDIGAN						
All round at underarms, fastened	108.5 (42¾)	113 (44½)	119.5 (47)	124.5 (49)	131 (51½)	137.5 (54¼)
Side seam	36.5 (14½)	36.5 (14¼)	36.5 (14¼)	36.5 (14¼)	36.5 (14¼)	36.5 (14¼)
Length	59.5 (23½)	61 (24)	62 (24½)	63 (24¾)	64 (25¼)	65.5 (25¾)
Sleeve seam	44.5 (17½)	44.5 (17½)	44.5 (17½)	44.5 (17½)	44.5 (17½)	44.5 (17½)

MATERIALS: *Allow the following quantities in 50 g balls of Lister-Lee Motoravia 4-ply wool: JERSEY: 5 for 102 cm size; 6 for 107 cm and 112 cm sizes; 7 for 117 cm and 122 cm sizes; 8 for 127 cm size. CARDIGAN: 8 for 102 cm size; 9 for 107 and 112 cm sizes; 10 for 117 cm and 122 cm sizes; 11 for 127 cm size. For any one size of either garment: A pair each of No. 10 (3¼ mm) and No. 12 (2¾ mm) knitting needles; a 10 cm (4 inch) slide fastener for jersey; 5 buttons for cardigan.*

TENSION: *Work at a tension of 22 stitches to measure 9 cm in width and 39 rows to measure 10 cm in depth, over the pattern, using No. 10 (3¼ mm) needles, to obtain measurements given.*

ABBREVIATIONS: To be read before working: *K., knit plain; p., purl; st., stitch; tog., together; p. 2 tog.b., p. 2 tog. through back of sts.; inc., increase (by working twice into same st.); dec., decrease (by taking 2 sts. tog.); sl., slip; p. 2 s.s.o., pass 2 sl. sts. over the k. st.; s.k.p.o., sl. 1, k. 1, pass sl. st. over; y. fwd.; yarn forward to make a st.; single rib is k. 1 and p. 1 alternately; nil, meaning nothing is worked here for this size; up 1, pick up loop lying between needles and k. or p. into back of it; p.s.s.o., pass sl. st. over; sl. 2, slip 2 tog. as if about to k. 2 tog.*

NOTE: *The instructions are given for the 102 cm (40 inch) size. Where they vary, work figures within first brackets for the 107 cm (42 inch) size, and so on.*

THE JERSEY

THE BACK: With No. 12 (2¾ mm) needles cast on 125 (131) (139) (145) (153) (161) sts.

Beginning the odd-numbered rows with k. 1 and even-numbered rows with p. 1, work 6 rows in single rib.

Change to No. 10 (3¼ mm) needles.

1st pattern row: K. 5 (4) (4) (3) (3) (3), * y.fwd., sl. 2 k. 1, p. 2 s.s.o., y.fwd., k. 5; repeat from * ending last repeat with k. 5 (4) (4) (3) (3) (3) instead of k. 5.

2nd and alternate rows: P. to end.

3rd row: K. 2 (1) (1) (nil) (nil) (nil), s.k.p.o., k. 1, y.fwd., k. 3, * y.fwd., k. 1, sl. 2, k. 1, p. 2 s.s.o., k. 1, y.fwd., k. 3; repeat from * until 5 (4) (4) (3) (3) (3) sts. remain, y.fwd., k. 1, k. 2 tog. then, k. 2 (1) (1) (nil) (nil) (nil).

5th row: K. 2 (1) (1) (nil) (nil) (nil), s.k.p.o., y.fwd., k. 5, * y. fwd., sl. 2, k. 1, p. 2 s.s.o., y. fwd, k. 5; repeat from * until 4 (3) (3) (2) (2) (2) sts. remain, y.fwd., k. 2 tog. then, k. 2 (1) (1) (nil) (nil) (nil).

7th row: K. 4 (3) (3) (2) (2) (2), * y.fwd., k. 1, sl. 2, k. 1, p. 2 s.s.o., k. 1, y.fwd., k. 3; repeat from * ending last repeat with k. 4 (3) (3) (2) (2) (2) instead of k. 3.

8th row: P. to end.

These 8 rows form the pattern. Pattern a further 120 rows—read 128 rows here when working cardigan back.

To shape raglan armholes: 1st and 2nd rows: Cast off 7 (7) (8) (8) (9) (9) sts., pattern to end.

3rd row: K. 1, s.k.p.o., pattern until 3 sts. remain, k. 2 tog., k. 1.

4th row: P. 1, p. 2 tog., p. until 3 sts., remain, p. 2 tog.b., p. 1.

Repeat 3rd and 4th rows, nil (nil) (nil) (nil) (once) (twice).

Next row: As 3rd row.

Next row: P. to end. **

Repeat last 2 rows, 21 (24) (26) (28) (29) (31) times, then 1st of these rows again 61 (61) (63) (65) (65) (65) sts.

To divide for back opening: Next row: P. 28 (28) (29) (30) (30) (30), k. 2, and leave these 30 (30) (31) (32) (32) (32) sts. on a spare needle for left half back, k. 2 tog., k. 1, p. to end and work on these last sts. for right half back.

The right half back: 1st row: K. 1, s.k.p.o., pattern until 2 sts. remain, k. 2.

2nd row: K. 2, p. to end.

Repeat last 2 rows, 16 times more.

Break yarn and leave remaining 13 (13) (14) (15) (15) (15) sts. on stitch-holder.

The left half back: With right side facing, rejoin yarn to inner end of sts. on spare needle.

1st row: K. 2, pattern until 3 sts. remain, k. 2 tog., k. 1.

2nd row: P. until 2 sts. remain, k. 2.

Repeat last 2 rows, 16 times more.

Break yarn and leave remaining 13 (13) (14) (15) (15) (15) sts. on a stitch-holder.

THE FRONT: Work as back to **.

Repeat last 2 rows, 28 (31) (33) (35) (36) (38) times, then

Continued on page 110

1st of these rows again—47 (47) (49) (51) (51) (51) sts.

To divide for neck: Next row: P. 17 (17) (18) (18) (18) (18) and leave these sts. on a spare needle for right front neck, p. 13 (13) (13) (15) (15) (15) and leave these sts. on a stitch-holder, p. to end and work on these last 17 (17) (18) (18) (18) (18) sts. for left half neck.

The left half neck: Keep continuity of the decreases at armhole edge as before, *at the same time* dec. 1 st. at neck edge on next row and the 4 (4) (5) (5) (5) (5) following alternate rows—7 (7) (6) (6) (6) (6) sts.

Work 1 row, then dec. at armhole edge only as before on next row and the 4 (4) (3) (3) (3) (3) following alternate rows—2 sts.

P. 1 row, then take remaining 2 sts. tog. and fasten off.

The right half neck: With right side facing, rejoin yarn to inner end of sts. on a spare needle, and work as given for left half neck, to end.

THE SLEEVES (2 alike): With No. 12 (2¾ mm) needles cast on 93 (99) (105) (111) (117) (123) sts. and work 5 rows in rib as given on back.

Inc. row: Rib 5 (4) (3) (6) (4) (3), up 1, * rib 12 (13) (11) (11) (10) (9), up 1; repeat from * until 4 (4) (3) (6) (3) (3) sts. remain, rib to end—101 (107) (115) (121) (129) (137) sts.

Change to No. 10 (3¼ mm) needles, and repeat the 8 pattern rows given on back, 3 times.

To shape raglan sleeve top: Work as given for raglan armhole shaping on back, until ** is reached.

Repeat last 2 rows, 38 (41) (44) (46) (47) (49) times more.

For 102 cm and 107 cm sizes only: 1st row: K. 1, sl. 1, k. 2 tog., p.s.s.o., k. 1.

2nd row: P. to end.

For all sizes: Break yarn and leave remaining 3 (3) (5) (7) (7) (7) sts. on a safety-pin.

THE NECK RIBBING: First join raglan seams, leaving sts. at top of sleeves free to form part of neck edge.

With right side facing, rejoin yarn and using No. 12 (2¾ mm) needles, increasing 1 st., k. across sts. of left half back, and top of left sleeve, pick up and k. 22 sts. from row ends of left front neck, increasing 2 sts., k. across sts. at centre front, pick up and k. 22 sts. from row ends of right front neck, k. across st. at top of right sleeve, then increasing 1 st., k. across right half back—93 (93) (99) (107) (107) (107) sts.

Keeping 2 sts. all k. at each end work 8 rows in rib as given on back.

Cast off in rib.

TO MAKE UP THE JERSEY: Press with a warm iron over a damp cloth. Join side and sleeve seams. Fold neck ribbing in half and catch to inside. Insert slide fastener.

THE CARDIGAN

THE BACK: With No. 12 (2¾ mm) needles cast on 133 (139) (147) (153) (161) (169) sts. and work as given for jersey back to **, noting variation—113 (119) (125) (131) (133) (137) sts.

Repeat last 2 rows, 42 (45) (47) (49) (50) (52) times more.

Cast off remaining 29 (29) (31) (33) (33) (33) sts.

THE LEFT FRONT: With No. 12 (2¾ mm) needles cast on 64 (66) (70) (74) (78) (82) sts. and work 6 rows in single

rib increasing 1 st. at end of last row on the 107 cm and 112 cm sizes only—64 (67) (71) (74) (78) (82) sts.

Change to No. 10 (3¼ mm) needles.

1st pattern row: K. 5 (4) (4) (3) (3) (3), y.fwd., sl. 2, k. 1, p. 2 s.s.o., * y. fwd., k. 5, y.fwd., sl. 2, k. 1, p. 2 s.s.o.; repeat from * until 8 (4) (8) (4) (8) (4) sts. remain, y.fwd, then k. 5, y.fwd., k. 2 tog., k. 1 (k. 4) (k. 5, y.fwd., k. 2 tog., k. 1) (k. 4) (k. 5, y.fwd., k. 2 tog., k. 1) (k. 4).

2nd row: P. to end.

3rd row: K. 2 (1) (1) (nil) (nil) (nil), s.k.p.o., k. 1, y.fwd., k. 3, * y.fwd., k. 1, sl. 2, k. 1, p. 2 s.s.o., k. 1, y.fwd., k. 3; repeat from * until nil (4) (nil) (4) (nil) (4) sts. remain, nil (y.fwd., k. 1, k. 2 tog., k. 1) (nil) (y.fwd., k. 1, k. 2 tog., k. 1) (nil) (y.fwd., k. 1, k. 2 tog., k. 1).

4th row: P. to end.

These 4 rows set the position of the pattern. Keeping continuity of the pattern to match jersey back, pattern a further 126 rows.

To shape front edge: 1st row: Pattern until 3 sts. remain, k. 2 tog., k. 1.

Pattern 5 rows.

To shape raglan armhole and continue shaping front edge: 1st row: Cast off 7 (7) (8) (8) (9) (9) sts., pattern to end.

2nd row: P. to end.

Next row: K. 1, s.k.p.o., pattern until 3 sts. remain, k. 2 tog., k. 1.

Next row: P. until 3 sts. remain, p. 2 tog. b., p. 1.

*** Working all decreases 1 st. in from edges as before, dec. 1 st. at armhole edge on next 1 (1) (1) (1) (3) (5) row(s), then the 41 (44) (46) (48) (49) (51) following alternate rows, *at the same time*, dec. 1 st. at front edge on the 7th of these rows, then the 8 (8) (9) (10) (10) (10) following 8th rows—2 sts.

P. 1 row, then take remaining 2 sts. tog. and fasten off.

THE RIGHT FRONT: Work as given for left front until pattern is reached.

Change to No. 10 (3¼ mm) needles.

1st pattern row: K. 1 (4) (1) (4) (1) (4), then s.k.p.o., y.fwd., k. 5 (nil) (s.k.p.o., y.fwd., k. 5) (nil) (s.k.p.o., y.fwd., k. 5) (nil). * y.fwd., sl. 2, k. 1, p. 2 s.s.o., y.fwd., k. 5; repeat from * ending last repeat with k. 5 (4) (4) (3) (3) (3) instead of k. 5.

2nd row: P. to end.

3rd row: K. 3 (k. 1, s.k.p.o., k. 1, y.fwd., k. 3) (k. 3) (k. 1, s.k.p.o., k. 1, y.fwd., k. 3) (k. 3) (k. 1, s.k.p.o., k. 1, y.fwd., k. 3) * y.fwd., k. 1, sl. 2, k. 1, p. 2 s.s.o., k. 1, y.fwd., k. 3; repeat from * until 5 (4) (4) (3) (3) (3) sts. remain, y fwd., k. 1, k. 2 tog., then k. 2 (1) (1) (nil) (nil) (nil).

4th row: P. to end.

These 4 rows set the position of the pattern, keeping continuity of the pattern to match back, pattern a further 126 rows.

To shape front edge: 1st row: K. 1, s.k.p.o., pattern to end.

Pattern 6 rows.

To shape raglan armhole and continue shaping front edge: 1st row: Cast off 7 (7) (8) (8) (9) (9) sts., pattern to end.

2nd row: K. 1, s.k.p.o., pattern until 3 sts. remain, k. 2 tog., k. 1.

3rd row: P. 1, p. 2 tog., p. to end.

Work as left front from *** to end.

THE SLEEVES (2 alike): With No. 12 (2¾ mm) needles cast on 61 (67) (75) (81) (89) (97) sts. and work 8 rows in rib as given on jersey back.

Change to No. 10 (3¼ mm) needles and work the 8 pattern rows of jersey back, once.

Keeping continuity of pattern, and working extra sts. into pattern as they occur, inc. 1 st. each end of next row and the 23 following 6th rows—109 (115) (123) (129) (137) (145) sts.

Pattern 21 rows.

To shape raglan sleeve top: Work as given for raglan armholes on back.

Cast off 5 (5) (7) (9) (9) (9) sts.

THE BUTTONHOLE BORDER: First join raglan seams.

With right side facing, rejoin yarn to lower edge of right front, and using No. 12 (2¾ mm) needles, pick up and k. 95 sts. up front edge to 1st front dec. then 90 (94) (100) (106) (110) (116) sts. to centre back neck—185 (189) (195) (201) (205) (211) sts.

Work 2 rows in rib as given on jersey back.

1st buttonhole row: Rib 91 (95) (101) (107) (111) (117), cast off 3,* rib a further 18 sts., cast off 3; repeat from * 3 times, rib 2.

2nd buttonhole row: Rib to end, casting on 3 sts. over each group cast off on previous row.

Rib 1 row, then cast off in rib.

THE BUTTON BORDER: Work as given for buttonhole border, omitting buttonholes and beginning pick up at centre back neck.

TO MAKE UP CARDIGAN: Press as for jersey. Join side and sleeve seams. Join row ends of front borders at centre back neck. Add buttons.

Below *Lacy twin-set (page 109)*

Turtle-neck Sweater and Shaped Jacket

Illustrated on page 114

MEASUREMENTS	*in centimetres (and inches, in brackets)*					
To fit bust size	102 (40)	107 (42)	112 (44)	117 (46)	122 (48)	127 (50)
SWEATER						
All round at underarms	104.5 (41)	110 (43¼)	115.5 (45½)	120.5 (47½)	126 (49½)	131.5 (51¾)
Side seam	39.5 (15½)	39.5 (15½)	39.5 (15½)	39.5 (15½)	39.5 (15½)	39.5 (15½)
Length	62.5 (24½)	63 (24¾)	63.5 (25)	64 (25¼)	64.5 (25½)	65 (25¾)
Sleeve seam	39.5 (15½)	39.5 (15½)	39.5 (15½)	39.5 (15½)	39.5 (15½)	39.5 (15½)
JACKET						
All round at underarms	109.5 (43)	114.5 (45)	119.5 (47)	124.5 (49)	129.5 (51)	134.5 (53)
Side seam	49 (19¼)	49 (19¼)	49 (19¼)	49 (19¼)	49 (19¼)	49 (19¼)
Length	71.5 (28¼)	72.5 (28½)	73.5 (29)	74.5 (29¼)	75.5 (29¾)	76.5 (30¼)
Sleeve seam, with cuff turned back	43 (17)	43 (17)	43 (17)	43 (17)	43 (17)	43 (17)

MATERIALS: SWEATER: *Allow the following quantities in 50 g balls of Sirdar Majestic 4-ply: 10 balls for 102 cm size; 11 balls for 107 cm size; 11 balls for 112 cm size; 12 balls for 117 cm size; 12 balls for 122 cm size; 13 balls for 127 cm size. For any one size: a pair each of No. 10 (3¼ mm) and No. 12 (2¾ mm) knitting needles; a slide fastener of appropriate length.*

JACKET: *Allow the following quantities in 50 g balls of Sirdar Majestic Double Knitting: 15 balls for 102 cm size; 16 balls for 107 cm size; 16 balls for 112 cm size; 17 balls for 117 cm size; 18 balls for 122 cm size; 18 balls for 127 cm size. For any one size: a pair each of No. 8 (4 mm) and No. 10 (3¼ mm) knitting needles; 5 buttons.*

TENSION: *Work at a tension of 30 stitches and 39 rows to measure 10 × 10 cm, using 4-ply and No. 10 (3¼ mm) needles and 24 stitches and 31 rows to measure 10 × 10 cm, using double knitting and No. 8 (4 mm) needles, to obtain measurements given.*

ABBREVIATIONS: To be read before working: *K., knit plain; p., purl; st., stitch; tog., together; k. 2 or 3 tog.b., k. 2 or 3 tog. through back of sts.; s.s., stocking st. (k. on the right side and p. on the wrong side); g.st., garter st. (k. plain on every row); up 1 p., pick up loop lying between needles and p. into back of it; inc., increase (by working twice into same st.); dec., decrease (by working 2 sts. tog.); w., white; n., navy; single rib is k. 1 and p. 1 alternately.*

NOTE: *The instructions are given for the 102 cm (40 inch) size. Where they vary, work the figures within the first brackets for the 107 cm (42 inch) size; work the figures within the second brackets for the 112 cm (44 inch) size, and so on.*

THE SWEATER

THE BACK: With No. 12 (2¾ mm) needles and w. cast on 147 (155) (163) (171) (179) (187) sts. and, beginning odd-numbered rows with k. 1 and even-numbered rows with p. 1, work 25 rows in single rib.

Inc. row: Rib 1 (5) (9) (13) (17) (21), inc., * rib 15, inc.; repeat from * 8 times, rib to end—157 (165) (173) (181) (189) (197) sts.

Change to No. 10 (3¼ mm) needles and, beginning with a k. row, s.s. 134 rows.

To shape the armholes: Cast off 10 (11) (12) (13) (14) (15) sts. at beginning of next 2 rows, then dec. 1 st. at each end of the following 9 (9) (11) (11) (13) (13) rows.

Work 1 row, then dec. 1 st. at each end of the next row and the 5 (6) (5) (6) (5) (6) following alternate rows—107 (111) (115) (119) (123) (127) sts. ******

S.s. 30 (30) (32) (32) (34) (34) rows.

To divide for opening: Next row: P. 53 (55) (57) (59) (61) (63) and leave on spare needle for left back shoulder, cast off 1 st., p. to end and work on these 53 (55) (57) (59) (61) (63) sts. for the right back shoulder.

The right back shoulder: S.s. 28 rows—s.s. 29 rows here when working left back shoulder.

To slope shoulder: Cast off 11 (11) (12) (12) (13) (13) sts. at beginning of next row and following alternate row, then 11 (12) (11) (13) (12) (13) sts. on next alternate row.

Work 1 row—omit this row when working left back shoulder.

Break yarn and leave 20 (21) (22) (22) (23) (24) sts. on a stitch-holder.

The left back shoulder: With right side facing, rejoin yarn to 53 (55) (57) (59) (61) (63) sts. on spare needle and work as right back shoulder, noting variations where indicated.

THE FRONT: Work as back to ******.

S.s. 28 (28) (30) (30) (32) (32) rows.

To divide for neck: Next row: P. 39 (40) (41) (43) (44) (45) and leave on spare needle for right front shoulder, p. 29 (31) (33) (33) (35) (37) and leave on stitch-holder, p. to end and work on these last 39 (40) (41) (43) (44) (45) sts. for left front shoulder.

The left front shoulder: Dec. 1 st. at neck edge on each of the next 6 rows—33 (34) (35) (37) (38) (39) sts.

S.s 24 rows—s.s. 25 rows here when working right front shoulder.

To slope the shoulder: Cast off 11 (11) (12) (12) (13) (13) sts. at beginning of next row and following alternate row.

Work 1 row, then cast off.

The right front shoulder: With right side facing, rejoin yarn to inner end of sts. on spare needle and work as left front shoulder, noting variation where indicated.

THE SLEEVES (2 alike): With No. 12 (2¾ mm) needles and w. cast on 65 (67) (69) (71) (73) (77) sts. and work 39 rows in single rib.

Inc. row: Rib 4 (5) (6) (7) (8) (10) inc., ★ rib 7, inc.; repeat from ★ 6 times, rib to end—73 (75) (77) (79) (81) (85) sts.

Change to No. 10 (3¼ mm) needles; s.s. 8 rows.

Still working in s.s., inc. 1 st. at each end of next row and the 17 (18) (19) (20) (21) (21) following 6th (5th) (5th) (5th) (5th) (5th) rows—109 (113) (117) (121) (125) (129) sts.

S.s. 9 (21) (16) (11) (6) (6) rows.

To shape sleeve top: Cast off 10 (11) (12) (13) (14) (15) sts. at beginning of next 2 rows, then dec. 1 st. at each end of the next row and the 19 (20) (21) (22) (23) (24) following alternate rows—49 sts.

Work 1 row, then dec. 1 st. at each end of the next 8 rows. Cast off 33 sts.

THE NECK RIBBING: Join shoulder seams. With right side facing, rejoin w. yarn and with No. 12 (2¾ mm) needles, k. 20 (21) (22) (22) (23) (24) sts. of left back neck, pick up and k. 25 sts. from row ends of left front neck, k. across 29 (31) (33) (33) (35) (37) sts. at front, pick up and k. 25 sts. from row ends of right front neck, and finally, k. 20 (21) (22) (22) (23) (24) sts. from right back neck—119 (123) (127) (127) (131) (135) sts.

Beginning with a wrong-side row, work 26 rows in rib as on back.

Cast off in rib.

TO MAKE UP THE SWEATER: Press on wrong side with a warm iron over a damp cloth. Set in sleeves, then join side and sleeve seams. Insert slide fastener.

THE JACKET

THE BACK: With No. 10 (3¼ mm) needles and n. cast on 146 (152) (158) (164) (170) (176) sts. and k. 14 rows.

Inc. row: P. 20 (21) (21) (22) (22) (23), up 1 p., ★ p. 21 (22) (23) (24) (25) (26), up 1 p.; repeat from ★ 4 times, p. 21 (21) (22) (22) (23) (23)—152 (158) (164) (170) (176) (182) sts.

Change to No. 8 (4 mm) needles and, beginning with a k. row, s.s. 20 rows.

1st dec. row: K. 7, 2 tog.b., k. 24, k. 3 tog.b., k. until 36 sts. remain, k. 3 tog., k. 24, k. 2 tog., k. 7.

S.s. 21 rows.

Repeat the last 22 rows, twice, then the dec. row again, working 2 sts. less between decreases on each successive repeat—128 (134) (140) (146) (152) (158) sts.

S.s. 57 rows.

To shape the armholes: Cast off 9 (10) (10) (10) (12) (13) sts. at beginning of next 2 rows, then dec. 1 st. at each end of the following 7 (7) (9) (9) (9) (9) rows.

Work 1 row, then dec. 1 st. at each end of the next row and the 5 (5) (5) (6) (6) (6) following alternate rows—84 (88) (90) (94) (96) (100) sts.

S.s. 43 (47) (47) (49) (51) (55) sts.

To slope the shoulders: Cast off 9 (9) (9) (10) (10) (10) sts. at beginning of next 4 rows, then 8 (9) (10) (9) (10) (11) sts. on the following 2 rows.

Cast off 32 (34) (34) (36) (36) (38) sts.

THE LEFT FRONT: With No. 10 (3¼ mm) needles and n. cast on 77 (80) (83) (86) (89) (92) sts. and k. 14 rows.

Inc. row: K. 9, and leave on safety-pin for front band, p. 5 (6) (6) (7) (7) (8), up 1 p., ★ p. 21 (22) (23) (24) (25) (26), up 1 p.; repeat from ★ to last p. 21 (21) (22) (22) (23) (23)—71 (74) (77) (80) (83) (86) sts.

Change to No. 8 (4 mm) needles.

Beginning with a k. row, s.s. 20 rows.

1st dec. row: K. 7, k. 2 tog.b., k. 24, k. 3 tog.b., k. to end.

S.s. 21 rows.

Repeat the last 22 rows, twice, then the dec. row again, working 2 sts. less between decreases on each successive repeat—59 (62) (65) (68) (71) (74) sts.

★★ S.s. 57 rows—s.s. 58 rows here when working right front.

To shape the armhole: Cast off 9 (10) (10) (10) (12) (13) sts. at beginning of next row.

P. 1 row—omit this row when working right front.

Dec. 1 st. at armhole edge on each of the next 7 (7) (9) (9) (9) (9) rows.

Work 1 row, then dec. 1 st. at armhole edge on the next row and the following 5 (5) (5) (6) (6) (6) alternate rows—37 (39) (40) (42) (43) (45) sts.

S.s. 18 (22) (22) (24) (26) (30) rows—s.s. 19 (23) (23) (25) (27) (31) rows here when working right front.

To shape the neck: Cast off 6 (7) (7) (8) (8) (9) sts. at beginning of next row, then, dec. 1 st. at neck edge on each of the following 5 rows—26 (27) (28) (29) (30) (31) sts.

S.s. 19 rows.

To slope the shoulder: Cast off 9 (9) (9) (10) (10) (10) sts. at beginning of next row and following alternate row.

Work 1 row, then cast off 8 (9) (10) (9) (10) (11) sts.

THE RIGHT FRONT: With No. 10 (3¼ mm) needles and n. cast on 77 (80) (83) (86) (89) (92) sts. and k. 14 rows.

Inc. row: P. 20 (21) (21) (22) (22) (23), up 1 p., ★ p. 21 (22) (23) (24) (25) (26), up 1 p.; repeat from ★ once, p. 6 (6) (7) (7) (8) (8) turn, leaving remaining 9 sts. on safety-pin—71 (74) (77) (80) (83) (86) sts.

Change to No. 8 (4 mm) needles.

Beginning with a k. row, s.s. 20 rows.

1st dec. row: K. until 36 sts. remain, k. 3 tog., k. 24, k. 2 tog., k. 7.

S.s. 21 rows.

Repeat the last 22 rows, twice, then dec. row again, working 2 sts. less between decreases on each successive repeat—59 (62) (65) (68) (71) (74) sts.

Work as given for left front from ★★ to end, noting variations where indicated.

THE SLEEVES (2 alike): With No. 10 (3¼ mm) needles and n. cast on 62 (64) (64) (66) (66) (68) sts. and k. 62 rows.

Change to No. 8 (4 mm) needles and, beginning with a k. row, s.s. 18 rows.

Continue in s.s. and inc. 1 st. at each end of next row and the 13 (14) (15) (16) (17) (18) following 6th (6th) (6th) (5th) (5th) (5th) rows—90 (94) (96) (100) (102) (106) sts.

S.s. 23 (17) (11) (21) (16) (11) rows—mark each end of last row to denote end of sleeve seam.

To shape the sleeve top: S.s. a further 12 (14) (14) (14) (16) (16) rows.

Dec. 1 st. at each end of next row and the 11 (12) (13) (14) (15) (16) following alternate rows.

Work 1 row, then dec. 1 st. at each end of the next 8 rows.

Cast off 50 (52) (52) (54) (54) (56) sts.

Continued on page 114

THE LEFT FRONT BAND: With right side facing, rejoin n. yarn to inner end of 9 sts. on safety-pin and using No. 10 (3¼ mm) needles, work in g.st. until band fits up left front to neck, finishing at inner end. Break yarn and leave.

THE RIGHT FRONT BAND: With wrong side facing, rejoin n. to inner end of 9 sts. on safety-pin and using No. 10 (3¼ mm) needles, work in g.st. until band fits up right front to neck, finishing at outer edge. Do not break yarn.

THE NECK BAND: First join shoulder seams. With right side facing and using No. 10 (3¼ mm) needles, return to right front band, and using yarn attached, k. these 9 sts., pick up and k. 24 (25) (25) (26) (26) (27) sts. from right front neck edge, 27 (29) (29) (31) (31) (33) sts. across back neck, 24 (25) (25) (26) (26) (27) sts. from left front neck edge, and finally, k. 9 sts. from other front band—93 (97) (97) (101) (101) (105) sts.

K. 22 rows. Cast off.

THE BRAID TRIMMING (2 pieces alike): With No. 10 (3¼ mm) needles and n. cast on 135 sts. and k. 2 rows. Cast off loosely.

TO MAKE UP THE JACKET: Press as for sweater, set in sleeves, setting row ends above markers to sts. cast-off at underarms. Join side and sleeve seams. Sew front bands into place. Sew braid trimming to top half of fronts inside front border edges, forming 5 loops at equal intervals. Make 5 button-loops along edge of right front and sew buttons to left front to correspond. Fold 7.5 cm (3 inches) of g.st. at lower edge of sleeve to right side to form cuff.

Opposite *Sweater with Diagonal Design (page 116)*
Below *Turtle-neck Sweater and Shaped Jacket (page 112)*

Sweater with Diagonal Design

Illustrated on page 115

MEASUREMENTS	in centimetres (and inches, in brackets)			
Bust sizes	81 (32)	86 (34)	91 (36)	97 (38)
All round at underarms	87 (34½)	92 (36¼)	97.5 (38¼)	102.5 (40¼)
Side seam	47.5 (18¾)	48.5 (19)	50 (19½)	51.5 (20¼)
Length	66 (26)	68.5 (27)	71.5 (28)	74 (29)
Sleeve seam	47 (18½)	47 (18½)	47 (18½)	47 (18½)

MATERIALS: *Allow the following quantities in 50 g balls of Patons Clansman Double Knitting: 5 dark and 5 light for the 81 cm and 86 cm sizes; 6 dark and 6 light for the 91 cm and 97 cm sizes. For any one size: a pair each of No. 8 (4 mm) and No. 10 (3¼ mm) knitting needles.*

TENSION: *Work at a tension of 23 stitches and 29 rows to measure 10 × 10 cm, over the stocking stitch, using No. 8 (4 mm) needles, to obtain the measurements given.*

ABBREVIATIONS: To be read before working: *K., knit plain; p., purl; st., stitch; tog., together; inc., increase (by working twice into next st.); dec., decrease (by taking 2 sts. tog.); s.s., stocking st. (k. on the right side and p. on the wrong side); single rib is k. 1 and p. 1 alternately; dk., dark; lt., light.*

NOTE: *The instructions are given for the 81 cm (32 inch) size. Where they vary, work the figures within the first brackets for the 86 cm (34 inch) size; work the figures within the second brackets for the 91 cm (36 inch) size, and so on.*

THE BACK: With No. 10 (3¼ mm) needles and dk. cast on 97 (105) (113) (121) sts.

1st row: K. 2, * p. 1, k. 1; repeat from * until 1 st. remains, k. 1.

2nd row: K. 1, * p. 1, k. 1; repeat from * to end.

Rib a further 18 rows, increasing 1 st. at the end of the last row—98 (106) (114) (122) sts.

Change to No. 8 (4 mm) needles and beginning with a k. row, s.s. 8 (6) (4) (2) rows.

Joining in and breaking off colours as required and working in s.s. beginning with a k. row, so only the colour details are give, work border pattern as follows:

1st and 2nd rows: 2 lt., * 6 dk., 2 lt.; repeat from * to end.

3rd and 4th rows: 4 lt., * 2 dk., 6 lt.; repeat from * until 6 sts. remain, 2 dk., 4 lt.

5th to 12th rows: Repeat 1st to 4th rows twice, increasing 1 st. at each end of the last row on the 81 cm size and decreasing 2 sts. on the last row on 91 cm size and decreasing 4 sts. on the last row on the 97 cm size—100 (106) (112) (118) sts. **

Work the diagonal stripe pattern as follows, which is worked in s.s. so only the colour details are given and taking care when changing from one colour to another to wind yarn round the one just used, to avoid a gap.

1st row: 2 dk., 98 (104) (110) (116) lt.

2nd row: 98 (104) (110) (116) lt., 2 dk.

3rd row: 4 dk., 96 (102) (108) (114) lt.

4th row: 96 (102) (108) (114) lt., 4 dk.

5th row: 6 dk., 94 (100) (106) (112) lt.

6th row: 94 (100) (106) (112) lt., 6 dk.

7th row: 8 dk., 92 (98) (104) (110) lt.

8th row: 92 (98) (104) (110) lt., 8 dk.

Continuing in this way, working 2 sts. more in dk. and 2 sts. less in lt. on the next and every following alternate row throughout, pattern a further 91 (97) (103) (109) rows, marking each end of the last row to denote end of side seams. Break off lt. With dk., s.s. 48 (52) (56) (60) rows.

To slope the shoulders: Cast off 12 (12) (13) (14) sts. at the beginning of each of the next 4 rows, then 11 (13) (13) (13) sts. at the beginning of each of the next 2 rows. Leave remaining 30 (32) (34) (36) sts. on a spare needle.

THE FRONT: Work as given for back to **.

Work the diagonal stripe pattern as follows:

1st row: 98 (104) (110) (116) lt., 2 dk.

2nd row: 2 dk., 98 (104) (110) (116) lt.

These 2 rows set the diagonal pattern for the front.

Continuing in this way, working 2 sts. more in dk. and 2 sts. less in lt. on the next and every following alternate row, pattern a further 97 (103) (109) (115) rows marking each end of the last row to denote end of side seams. Break off lt.

With dk., s.s. 27 (29) (31) (33) rows.

Divide sts. for front neck: Next row: P. 40 (42) (44) (46) and leave these sts. on a spare needle for right front neck, p. the next 20 (22) (24) (26) and leave these sts. on a stitch-holder for neck band p. to end and work on these 40 (42) (44) (46) sts. for left front neck.

The left front neck: Dec. 1 st. at neck edge on each of the next 5 rows—35 (37) (39) (41) sts.

S.s. 15 (17) (19) (21) rows—s.s. 16 (18) (20) (22) rows here when working right front neck.

To slope the shoulder: Cast off 12 (12) (13) (14) sts. at the beginning of the next row and the following alternate row—11 (13) (13) (13) sts.

Work 1 row, then cast off.

The right front neck: With right side of work facing, rejoin yarn to inner end of sts. on spare needle and work as given for left front neck, noting variation.

THE SLEEVES (both alike): With No. 8 (4 mm) needles and dk. cast on 74 (82) (90) (98) sts. for sleeve top and s.s. 2 rows.

Work the 12 rows of border pattern as given for back. Break off dk.

Continuing in s.s. with lt., work 8 rows.

Dec. 1 st. at each end of the next row and the 8 (9) (10) (11) following 10th (10th) (8th) (6th) rows—56 (62) (68) (74) sts.

S.s. 12 (2) (12) (26) rows.

Next (dec.) row: P. 12 (9) (6) (3), * p. 2 tog., p. 1; repeat from * until 14 (11) (8) (5) sts. remain, p. 2 tog., p. 12 (9) (6) (3)—45 (47) (49) (51) sts.

Change to No. 10 (3¼ mm) needles and, beginning odd-numbered rows with k. 1 and even-numbered rows with p. 1, work 22 rows in single rib. Cast off in rib.

THE NECKBAND: First join right shoulder seam. With right side of work facing and using No. 10 (3¼mm) needles and dk., pick up and k. 23 sts. down left front neck edge, k. across the 20 (22) (24) (26) sts. at centre front, pick up and k. 23 sts. up right front neck edge and finally, k. across the 30 (32) (34) (36) sts. at back neck—96 (100) (104) (108) sts.

Work 20 rows in single rib. Cast off in rib.

TO MAKE UP THE SWEATER: Press work lightly on the wrong side, using a warm iron over a damp cloth. Join left shoulder seam, continuing seam across neckband. Set in sleeves between markers, then join sleeve and side seams. Fold neckband in half to wrong side and slip st. in place on the inside.

Sweater in Three Colours

Illustrated on page 119

MEASUREMENTS	in centimetres (and inches, in brackets)					
To fit bust sizes	86	(34)	91	(36)	97	(38)
All round underarms	90.5	(35½)	95	(37½)	100	(39½)
Side seam	35	(13¾)	35	(13¾)	35	(13¾)
Length	56	(22)	57	(22½)	57.5	(22¾)
Sleeve seam	51	(20)	51	(20)	51	(20)

MATERIALS: *Allow the following quantities in 50 g balls of Sirdar Country Style Double Knitting:* 5 cream, 2 navy, 1 red for 86 cm size; 5 cream, 3 navy, 1 red for 91 cm size; 6 cream, 3 navy, 1 red for 97 cm size. For any one size: a pair each of No. 8 (4 mm) and No. 10 (3¼ mm) knitting needles; a 3.50 crochet hook; 2 buttons.

TENSION: *Work at a tension of 25 stitches and 30 rows to measure 10 × 10 cm, over the plain stocking stitch, using No. 8 (4 mm) needles, to obtain measurements given.*

ABBREVIATIONS: To be read before working: *K., knit plain; p., purl; st., stitch; tog., together; inc., increase (by working twice into next st.); dec., decrease (by working 2 sts. tog.); s.s., slip; c., cream; n., navy; r., red; d.c., double crochet; double rib is k. 2, p. 2 alternately; nil, meaning nothing is worked here for this size.*

NOTE: *The instructions are given for the 86 cm (34 inch) size. Where they vary, work figures within first brackets for 91 cm (36 inch) size; work figures within second brackets for 97 cm (38 inch) size.*

THE BACK: With No. 10 (3¼ mm) needles and n. cast on 112 (116) (124) sts. and work 26 rows in double rib, increasing 1 (3) (1) st(s). evenly across the last of these rows—113 (119) (125) sts.

Break off n., join in c. **
Change to No. 8 (4 mm) needles and, beginning with a k. row, s.s. 84 rows.

To shape the armholes: Cast off 8 sts. at beginning of next 2 rows—97 (103) (109) sts. S.s. 24 (26) (28) rows.

Joining and breaking colours as required, work the 24-row pattern as follows, which is worked entirely in s.s., beginning with a k. row, so only the colour details are given:

1st row: 1 r. (9 c., 1 r.) (1 r.), 11 c., * 1 r., 11 c.; repeat from * until 1 (10) (1) st(s)., remain(s), 1 r. (1 r., 9 c.) (1 r.).

2nd row: 2 r. (8 c., 3 r.) (2 r.), * 9 c., 3 r.; repeat from * until 11 (8) (11) sts. remain, 9 c., 2 r. (8 c.) (9 c., 2 r.).

3rd row: 3 r. (7 c., 5 r.) (3 r.), * 7 c., 5 r.; repeat from * until 10 (7) (10) sts. remain, 7 c., 3 r. (7 c.) (7 c., 3 r.).

4th row: 1 n. (1 r., 5 c., 3 r., 1 n.) (1 n.), * 3 r., 5 c., 3 r., 1 n.; repeat from * to end (until 9 sts. remain, 3 r., 5 c., 1 r.) (to end).

5th row: 2 n. (2 r., 3 c., 3 r., 3 n.) (2 n.), * 3 r., 3 c., 3 r., 3 n.; repeat from * until 11 (8) (11) sts. remain, 3 r., 3 c., 3 r., 2 n. (3 r., 3 c., 2 r.) (3 r., 3 c., 3 r., 2 n.).

6th row: 3 n. (3 r., 1 c., 3 r., 5 n.) (3 n.), * 3 r., 1 c., 3 r., 5 n.; repeat from * until 10 (7) (10) sts. remain, 3 r., 1 c., 3 r., 3 n. (3 r., 1 c., 3 r.) (3 r., 1 c., 3 r., 3 n.).

7th row: 1 c. (1 n., 5 r., 3 n., 1 c.) (1 c.), * 3 n., 5 r., 3 n., 1 c.; repeat from * to end (until 9 sts. remain, 3 n., 5 r., 1 n.) (to end).

8th row: 2 c. (2 n., 3 r., 3 n., 3 c.) (2 c.), * 3 n., 3 r., 3 n., 3 c.; repeat from * until 11 (8) (11) sts. remain, 3 n., 3 r., 3 n., 2 c. (3 n., 3 r., 2 n.) (3 n., 3 r., 3 n., 2 c.).

9th row: 3 c. (3 n., 1 r., 3 n., 5 c.) (3 c.), * 3 n., 1 r., 3 n., 5 c.; repeat from * until 10 (7) (10) sts. remain, 3 n., 1 r., 3 n., 3 c. (3 n., 1 r., 3 n.) (3 n., 1 r., 3 n., 3 c.).

10th row: 4 c. (1 c., 5 n., 7 c.) (4 c.), * 5 n., 7 c.; repeat from * until 9 (6) (9) sts. remain, 5 n., 4 (1) (4) c.

11th row: 1 r. (2 c., 3 n., 4 c., 1 r.) (1 r.), * 4 c., 3 n., 4 c., 1 r.; repeat from * to end (until 9 sts. remain, 4 c., 3 n., 2 c.) (to end).

12th row: 2 r. (3 c., 1 n., 4 c., 3 r.) (2 r.), * 4 c., 1 n., 4 c., 3 r.; repeat from * until 11 (8) (11) sts. remain, 4 c., 1 n., 4 c., 2 r. (4 c., 1 n. 3 c.) (4 c., 1 n., 4 c., 2 r.).

13th row: As 3rd row.

14th row: 4 r. (1 r., 5 c., 7 r.) (4 r.), * 5 c., 7 r.; repeat from * until 9 (6) (9) sts. remain, 5 c., 4 (1) (4) r.

15th row: 5 r. (2 r., 3 c., 9 r.) (5 r.), * 3 c., 9 r.; repeat from * until 8 (5) (8) sts. remain, 3 c., 5 (2) (5) r.

16th row: 1 n. (3 r., 1 c., 5 r., 1 n.) (1 n.), * 5 r., 1 c., 5 r., 1 n.; repeat from * to end (until 9 sts. remain, 5 r., 1 c., 3 r.) (to end).

Continued on page 118

17th row: 2 n. (8 r., 3 n.) (2 n.), * 9 r., 3 n.; repeat from * until 11 (8) (11) sts. remain, 9 r., 2 n. (8 r.) (9 r., 2 n.).

18th row: 3 n. (7 r., 5 n.) (3 n.), * 7 n., 5 n.; repeat from * until 10 (7) (10) sts. remain, 7 r., 3 n. (7 r.) (7 r., 3 n.).

19th to 22nd rows: As 7th to 10th rows.

23rd row: 5 c., 3 n. (2 c., 3 n.) (5 c., 3 n.); * 9 c., 3 n.; repeat from * until 5 (2) (5) sts. remain, 5 (2) (5) c.

24th row: 6 c., 1 n. (3 c., 1 n.) (6 c., 1 n.); * 11 c., 1 n.; repeat from * until 6 (3) (6) sts. remain, 6 (3) (6) c.

S.s. 2 rows in r.

Break off r. and c. and continue with n. yarn only.

Change back to No. 10 (3¼ mm) needles.

Inc. row: K. 6 (2) (6), * inc. k. 6 (6) (5); repeat from * until 7 (3) (7) sts. remain, inc., k. to end—110 (118) (126) sts.

Beginning odd-number rows with p. 2 and even-numbered rows with k. 2, work 13 rows in double rib.

Cast off in rib.

THE FRONT: Work as back to **.

Change to No. 8 (4 mm) needles and, beginning with a k. row, s.s. 81 rows.

To divide for neck: Next row: P. 54 (57) (60) and leave these sts. on a spare needle for right half front, cast off 5, p. to end and work on these 54 (57) (60) sts. for left half front.

The left half front: S.s. 2 rows—s.s. 3 rows here when working right half front.

To shape the armhole: Cast off 8 sts. at beginning of next row—46 (49) (52) sts.

S.s. 17 (19) (21) rows—s.s. 16 (18) (20) rows here when working right half front.

To shape the neck: Dec. 1 st. at neck edge on next row, then on the 3 following alternate rows—42 (45) (48) sts. P. 1 row. ***

Joining and breaking colours as required continue as follows:

1st row: 1 r. (9 c., 1 r.) (1 r.), * 11 c., 1 r.; repeat from * until 5 (11) (11) sts. remain, 3 (9) (9) c., k. 2 tog., with c.

2nd row: 3 (9) (9) c., * 3 r., 9 c.; repeat from * until 2 (11) (2) sts. remain, 2 r. (3 r., 8 c.) (2 r.).

3rd row: 3 (nil) (3) r., * 7 c., 5 r.; repeat from * until 2 (8) (8) sts. remain, nil (6) (6) c., k. 2 tog. with c.

4th row: 3 (1) (1) r., nil (5) (5) c., nil (3) (3) r., * 1 n., 3 r., 5 c., 3 r.; repeat from * until 1 (10) (1) st(s). remain(s), 1 n. (1 n., 3 r., 5 c., 1 r.) (1 n.).

**** These 4 rows set the position of the pattern, keeping continuity of pattern to match back, dec. 1 st. at neck edge on the next row, then on the 9 following alternate rows—30 (33) (36) sts. Work 1 row.

S.s. 2 rows in r. Break off r. and c. and continue with n.

Change back to No. 10 (3¼ mm) needles.

Inc. row: K. 6 (4) (3), * inc., k. 5; repeat from * until 6 (5) (3) sts. remain, inc., k. to end—34 (38) (42) sts.

Beginning odd-number rows with k. 2 and even-number rows with p. 2, work 13 rows in double rib—work 14 rows here when working right-half front.

Cast off in rib.

The right half front: Work as left half front to ***, noting variations.

1st row: K. 2 tog. with c., 3 (9) (9) c., * 1 r., 11 c.; repeat from * until 1 (10) (1) st(s). remain(s), 1 r. (1 r., 9 c.) (1 r.).

2nd row: 2 (nil) (2) r., 9 (8) (9) c., * 3 r., 9 c.; repeat from * until 6 (12) (12) sts. remain, 3 r., 3 (9) (9) c.

3rd row: K. 2 tog. with c., nil (6) (6) c., * 5 r., 7 c.; repeat from * until 3 sts. remain, 3 r. (to end) (until 3 sts. remain, 3 r.).

4th row: 1 (nil) (1) n., 3 (1) (3) r., * 5 c., 3 r., 1 n., 3 r.; repeat from * to end (until 6 sts. remain, 5 c., 1 r.) (until 6 sts. remain, 5 c., 1 r.).

Work as left half front from ****, noting variation.

THE SLEEVES (both alike): With No. 10 (3¼ mm) needles and n. cast on 52 (52) (56) sts. and work 25 rows in double rib.

Inc. row: Rib 6 (5) (8), * inc., rib 7 (5) (7); repeat from * until 6 (5) (8) sts. remain, inc., rib to end—58 (60) (62) sts. Break off n., join in c.

Change to No. 8 (4 mm) needles and, beginning with a k. row, s.s. 6 rows, then inc. 1 st. each end of next row and then on the 12 following 8th rows—84 (86) (88) sts.

S.s. 29 rows.

To shape sleeve top: Cast off 4 sts. at beginning of next 16 rows—20 (22) (24) sts. Cast off.

THE COLLAR: With No. 10 (3¼ mm) needles and n. cast on 114 (118) (122) sts. and, beginning odd-number rows with k. 2 and even-number rows with p. 2, work 28 rows, in double rib. Cast off in rib.

THE LEFT FRONT BORDER AND REVERS: With No. 10 (3¼ mm) needles and n. cast on 50 sts.

***** **1st and 2nd turning rows:** P. 2, k. 2, turn, sl. 1, rib to end for 2nd turning row.

3rd and 4th turning rows: * P. 2, k. 2; repeat from * once, turn, sl. 1, rib to end for 4th turning row.

5th and 6th turning rows: * P. 2, k. 2; repeat from * twice, turn, sl. 1, rib to end for 6th turning row.

Continue in this way, working 4 sts. more before turn, for a further 10 rows. *****

Work 10 rows in double rib across all sts. Cast off in rib.

THE RIGHT FRONT BORDER AND REVERS: With No. 10 (3¼ mm) needles and n. cast on 50 sts.

1st row: P. 2, * k. 2, p. 2; repeat from * to end.

Work as left front border and revers from ***** to *****, but reading k. for p., and p. for k.

Work 3 rows in double rib across all sts.

1st buttonhole row: Rib 3, cast off 3, rib 7, cast off 3, rib to end.

2nd buttonhole row: Rib to end, casting on 3 sts. over both groups cast off on previous row.

Rib a further 4 rows. Cast off in rib.

THE ARMHOLE BORDERS (both alike): First join shoulder seams, leaving centre 42 sts. at back free. With right side of work facing and using No. 10 (3¼ mm) needles, rejoin n. and pick up and k. 114 (118) (122) sts. evenly along row ends of armhole.

Work 11 rows in rib as for collar. Cast off in rib.

TO MAKE UP THE SWEATER: Press with a warm iron over a dry cloth. Set in sleeves, catching down row ends of armhole borders to cast off groups at underarms, then join sleeve and side seams. Sew down shaped edges of front borders and revers to their respective fronts, then placing left front border behind right front border, sew down row ends to cast off group at front neck. Sew cast off edge of collar round remainder of neck, then join row ends of collar and revers for 2.5 cm (1 in.). With right side of work facing and using size 3.50 crochet hook, rejoin n. and work a row of d.c. evenly round remaining row ends of collar and revers. Add buttons. Using 2 strands of yarn tog., embroider 'V' sts. on front with r. and n., as in photo.

Opposite *Sweater in Three Colours (page 117)*

Geometric-design Sweater

Illustrated on page 122

MEASUREMENTS	in centimetres *(and inches, in brackets)*					
To fit bust sizes, loosely	86	(34)	91	(36)	97	(38)
All round at underarms	97.5	(38¼)	102.5	(40¼)	107.5	(42¼)
Side seam	40.5	(16)	40.5	(16)	40.5	(16)
Length	65.5	(25¾)	66	(26)	67	(26½)
Sleeve seam	52.5	(20½)	52.5	(20½)	52.5	(20½)

MATERIALS: *Allow the following quantities in 50 g balls of Hayfield Falkland D.K.: 8 cream, 2 grey, 2 rust, 1 pink for the 86 cm size; 8 cream, 3 grey, 2 rust, 2 pink for the 91 cm size; 8 cream, 3 grey, 3 rust, 2 pink for the 97 cm size. For any one size: a pair each of No. 8 (4 mm) and No. 10 (3¼ mm) knitting needles.*

TENSION: *Work at a tension of 24 stitches and 24 rows to measure 10 × 10 cm, over the stocking stitch, using No. 8 (4 mm) needles, to obtain the measurements given.*

ABBREVIATIONS: To be read before working: *K., knit plain; p., purl; st., stitch; tog., together; dec., decrease (by working 2 sts. tog.); inc., increase (by working twice into same st.); up 1, pick up loop lying between needles and k. or p. into the back of it; nil, meaning nothing is worked here for this size; cr., cream; gr., grey; pk., pink; r., rust; s.s. stocking st. (k. on right side and p. on wrong side); single rib is k. 1 and p. 1 alternately; sl., slip.*

NOTE: *The instructions are given for the 86 cm (34 inch) size. Where they vary, work the figures within the first brackets for the 91 cm (36 inch) size; work the figures within the second brackets for the 97 cm (38 inch) size.*

THE BACK: With no. 10 (3¼ mm) needles and cr., cast on 104 (110) (116) sts. and work 23 rows in single rib.

Next (increase) row: Rib 4 (7) (4), up 1, * rib 8 (8) (9), up 1; repeat from * 11 times, rib 4 (7) (4)—117 (123) (129) sts.

Change to No. 8 (4 mm) needles and work the 14-row pattern as follows, which is worked entirely in s.s. beginning with a k. row so only the colour details are given.

1st row: 3 cr. (1 gr., 5 cr.) (nil), * 3 cr., 5 cr., 1 gr., 1 cr., 1 gr., 1 cr., 1 gr., 5 cr.; repeat from * until 6 (9) (3) sts. remain, 3 gr., then 3 cr. (5 cr., 1 gr.) (nil).

2nd row: 2 (5) (nil) cr., 2 (2) (1) gr., 1 cr., 2 gr., * 5 cr., 3 gr., 5 cr., 2 gr., 1 cr., 2 gr.; repeat from * until 2 (5) (17) sts. remain, 2 cr. (5 cr.) (5 cr., 3 gr., 5 cr., 2 gr., 1 cr., 1 gr).

3rd row: 1 cr. (1 gr., 3 cr.) (3 cr., 2 gr., 3 cr., 1 gr., 1 cr., 1 gr., 1 cr., 1 gr., 3 cr.), * 2 gr., 3 cr., 2 gr., 3 cr., 1 gr., 1 cr., 1 gr., 1 cr., 1 gr., 3 cr.; repeat from * until 8 (11) (5) sts. remain, 2 gr., 3 cr., then 2 gr., 1 cr. (2 gr., 3 cr., 1 gr.) (nil).

4th to 6th rows: As 3rd row back to 1st row in that reverse order.

7th row: 4 cr. (1 cr., 1 pk., 5 cr.) (1 cr.), * 1 pk., 5 cr., 1 pk., 1 cr., 3 pk., 1 cr., 1 pk., 5 cr.; repeat from * until 5 (8) (2) sts. remain, 1 pk., then 4 cr. (5 cr., 1 pk., 1 cr.) (1 cr.).

8th row: Nil (2 cr., 1 pk.) (6 cr., 1 pk., 7 cr., 1 pk.), * 9 cr., 1 pk., 7 cr., 1 pk.; repeat from * until 9 (12) (6) sts. remain, 9 cr. (9 cr., 1 pk., 2 cr.) (6 cr.).

9th row: Nil (3 cr.) (3 cr.), * 3 r., 3 cr.; repeat from * until 3 (nil) (nil) sts. remain, 3 (nil) (nil) r.

10th row: 1 cr., 2 r. (1 r., 3 cr., 2 r.) (nil), * 3 cr., 2 r., 3 cr., 2 r., 1 cr., 2 r., 3 cr., 2 r.; repeat from * until 6 (9) (3) sts. remain, 3 cr., then 2 r., 1 cr. (2 r., 3 cr., 1 r.) (nil).

11th and 12th rows: Repeat 10th row then 9th row.

13th and 14th rows: Repeat 8th row then 7th row.

Pattern a further 66 rows.

To shape the armholes: Keeping continuity of the pattern, cast off 8 sts. at the beginning of each of the next 2 rows—101 (107) (113) sts. **

Pattern a further 50 (52) (54) rows.

To slope the shoulders: Cast off 8 sts. at the beginning of each of the next 6 rows, then 8 (10) (12) sts. at the beginning of the following 2 rows—37 (39) (41) sts.

Leave these sts. on a spare needle.

THE FRONT: Work as given for back to **.

Pattern a further 41 (43) (43) rows.

To divide for neck: Next row: Pattern 38 (40) (44), work 2 tog. and leave these 39 (41) (45) sts. on a spare needle for right half neck, pattern 21 (23) (21) and leave these sts. on a stitch-holder for neckband, work 2 tog., pattern to end and work on these 39 (41) (45) sts. for left half neck.

The left half neck: Dec 1 st. at neck edge on each of the next 7 (7) (9) rows—32 (34) (36) sts.

Pattern 1 row—pattern 2 rows here when working right half neck.

To slope the shoulder: Cast off 8 sts. at the beginning of the next row and the 2 following alternate rows—8 (10) (12) sts.

Pattern 1 row.

Cast off.

The right half neck: With right side of work facing, rejoin appropriate yarn to the 39 (41) (45) sts. left on spare needle and work as given for left half neck, noting variation.

THE SLEEVES (both alike): With No. 10 (3¼ mm) needles and cr., cast on 50 (56) (62) sts. and work 19 rows in single rib.

Next (increase) row: Rib 1 (4) (1), up 1, * rib 4 (4) (5), up 1; repeat from * 11 times, rib 1 (4) (1)—63 (69) (75) sts.

Change to No. 8 (4 mm) needles and work 4 rows in pattern exactly as given on back.

Maintaining continuity of pattern to match back, and taking extra sts. into pattern as they occur, inc. 1 st. at each end of the next row and the 20 following 4th rows—105 (111) (117) sts.

Pattern a further 25 rows.

Mark each end of last row to denote end of sleeve seam.

Pattern a further 8 rows.

Cast off.

THE NECKBAND: First join right shoulder seam. With

right side of work facing, using No. 10 (3¼ mm) needles and cr. pick up and k. 14 (14) (16) sts. down left side of neck, k. across the 21 (23) (21) sts. at centre front, pick up and k. 14 (14) (16) sts. up right side of neck, and finally k. across the 37 (39) (41) sts. at back neck—86 (90) (94) sts.

Next (inc.) row: K. 2 (6) (8), * inc., rib 6; repeat from * until nil (nil) (2) sts. remain, rib nil (nil) (2)—98 (102) (106) sts.

Work 15 rows in single rib.
Cast off loosely in rib.

TO MAKE UP THE SWEATER: Press on the wrong side with a warm iron over a damp cloth.

Join the left shoulder seam, continuing the seam across neck ribbing. Set sleeves into armholes, sewing the last 8 row ends of sleeve to the sts. cast off at underarms. Join side and sleeve seams. Fold neckband in half to wrong side and sl.st. into place.

Lightly press all seams.

Aran-style Sweater

Illustrated on page 123

MEASUREMENTS						
To fit bust sizes	*in centimetres (and inches, in brackets)*					
	81 (32)	86 (34)	91 (36)	97 (38)	102 (40)	107 (42)
Side seam	44.5 (17½)	44.5 (17½)	44.5 (17½)	44.5 (17½)	44.5 (17½)	44.5 (17½)
Length	64 (25¼)	65.5 (25¾)	65.5 (25¾)	66.5 (26¼)	66.5 (26¼)	68 (26¾)
Sleeve seam	42.5 (16¾)	42.5 (16¾)	42.5 (16¾)	42.5 (16¾)	42.5 (16¾)	42.5 (16¾)

MATERIALS: *Allow the following quantities in 50 g balls of Emu Aran: 15 for 81 cm size; 16 for 86 cm size; 17 for 91 cm size; 18 for 97 cm size; 19 for 102 cm size; 20 for 107 cm size. For any one size: a pair each of No. 8 (4 mm) and No. 10 (3¼ mm) needles; a cable needle.*

TENSION: *Work at a tension of 10 stitches to measure 5 cm in width and 29 rows to measure 10 cm in depth, over the double moss stitch and the centre 33-stitch panel to measure 12 cm in width, using No. 8 (4 mm) needles, to obtain measurements given.*

ABBREVIATIONS: To be read before working: *K., knit plain; p., purl; st., stitch; tog., together; inc., increase (by working twice into next st.); sl., slip; up 1, pick up loop lying between needles and k. or p. into back of it; dec., decrease (by working 2 sts. tog.); c. 6 f., cable 6 forward (sl. next 3 sts. on to cable needle and leave at front of work, k. 3, then k. 3 from cable needle); c. 6 b., cable 6 back (as c. 6 f. but leave cable needle at back of work); c. 4 b., cable 4 back (sl. next 2 sts. on to cable needle and leave at back of work, k. 2, then k. 2 from cable needle); c. 4 f., cable 4 front (as c. 4 b., but leave sts. at front of work); tw. 2 lt., twist 2 left (sl. next st. on to cable needle and leave at front of work, p. 1, then k. st. from cable needle); tw. 2 rt., twist 2 right (sl. next st. on to cable needle and leave at back of work, k. 1, then p. st. from cable needle); cr. 5 b., cross 5 back (sl. next 3 sts. on to cable needle and leave at back of work, k. 2, sl. the p. st. from cable needle back on to left-hand needle, p. this st., then k. 2 from cable needle); cr. 3 f., cross 3 forward (sl. next 2 sts. on to cable needle and leave at front of work, p. 1, then k. 2 from cable needle); cr. 3 b., cross 3 back (sl. next st. on to cable needle and leave at back of work, k. 2, then p. st. from cable needle); y. fwd., yarn forward to make a st.; cr. 5 f., cross 5 front (sl. next 3 sts. on to cable needle and leave at front of work, k. 2, sl. p. st. from cable needle back on to left-hand needle, p. this st., then k. 2 from cable needle); m.b., make a bobble (k. 1, y.fwd., k. 1, y.fwd., k. 1 all into next st., turn, p. 5, turn, k. 5, then sl. 2nd, 3rd, 4th and 5th sts. over first st., leaving first on right-hand needle); d.m.st., double moss st.; single rib is k. 1, p. 1 alternately.*

NOTE: *The instructions are given for the 81 cm (32 inch) size. Where they vary, work figures within first brackets for 86 cm (34 inch) size; work figures within second brackets for 91 cm (36 inch) size, and so on.*

THE BACK: With No. 10 (3¼ mm) needles cast on 80 (86) (92) (98) (104) (110) sts. and work 16 rows in single rib.

Increase row: Rib 4 (4) (10) (10) (4) (3), up 1, * rib 3 (3) (3) (3) (4) (4), up 1; repeat from * until 4 (4) (10) (10) (4) (3) sts. remain, rib to end—105 (113) (117) (125) (129) (137) sts.

Change to No. 8 (4 mm) needles.

Foundation row: * K. 1, p. 1 *; repeat from * to * 4 (6) (7) (9) (10) (12) times, k. 3, ** p. 6, k. 3, p. 1, repeat from * to * 5 times, k. 3, p. 6 **, k. 4, p. 2, k. 2, p. 2, k. 1, p. 2, k. 2, p. 2, k. 4, repeat from ** to ** once, k. 3, p. 1, repeat from * to * until 1 st. remains, k. 1.

Work pattern as follows: **1st row (right side):** * P. 1, k. 1 *; repeat from * to * 4 (6) (7) (9) (10) (12) times, p. 3, k. 6, p. 3, tw. 2 lt., tw. 2 lt., tw. 2 lt., p. 8, k. 6, p. 4, k. 2, p. 2, cr. 5 b., p. 2, k. 2, p. 4, k. 6, p. 8, tw. 2 rt., tw. 2 rt., tw. 2 rt., p. 3, k. 6, p. 3, k. 1, repeat from * to * 4 (6) (7) (9) (10) (12) times, p. 1.

2nd row: P. 1, * k. 1, p. 1 *; repeat from * to * 4 (6) (7) (9) (10) (12) times, k. 2, p. 6, k. 4, p. 1, k. 1, p. 1, k. 1, p. 1, k. 8, p. 6, k. 4, p. 2, k. 2, p. 2, k. 1, p. 2, k. 2, p. 2, k. 4, p. 6, k. 8, p. 1, k. 1, p. 1, k. 1, p. 1, k. 4, p. 6, k. 2, p. 1, repeat from * to end.

3rd row: K. 1, * p. 1, k. 1 *; repeat from * to * 4 (6) (7) (9) (10) (12) times, p. 2, c. 6 f., p. 4, tw. 2 lt., tw. 2 lt., tw. 2 lt., p. 2, m.b., p. 4, c. 6 f., p. 4, cr. 3 f., cr. 3 b., p. 1, cr. 3 f., cr. 3 b., p. 4, c. 6 b., p. 4, m.b., p. 2, tw. 2 rt., tw. 2 rt., tw. 2 rt., p. 4, c. 6 b., p. 2, k. 1, repeat from * to * to end.

4th row: * K. 1, p. 1 *; repeat from * to * 4 (6) (7) (9) (10) (12) times, k. 3, p. 6, k. 5, p. 1, k. 1, p. 1, k. 1, p. 1, k. 7, p. 6, k. 5, p. 4, k. 3, p. 4, k. 5, p. 6, k. 7, p. 1, k. 1, p. 1, k. 1, p. 1, k. 5, p. 6, k. 3, p. 1, repeat from * to * until 1 st. remains, k. 1.

Continued on page 124

Opposite *Geometric-design Sweater (page 120).*   Above *Aran-style Sweater (page 121)*

The first and last 11 (15) (17) (21) (23) (27) sts. of the 1st to 4th rows form the d.m.st. pattern. Keeping continuity of d.m.st., continue as follows:

5th row: D.m.st. 11 (15) (17) (21) (23) (27), p. 2, k. 6, p. 5, tw. 2 lt., tw. 2 lt., tw. 2 lt., p. 6, k. 6, p. 5, c. 4 b., p. 3, c. 4 f., p. 5, k. 6, p. 6, tw. 2 rt., tw. 2 rt., tw. 2 rt., p. 5, k. 6, p. 2, d.m.st. to end.

6th row: D.m.st. 11 (15) (17) (21) (23) (27), k. 2, p. 6, k. 6, p. 1, k. 1, p. 1, k. 1, p. 1, k. 6, p. 6, k. 5, p. 4, k. 3, p. 4, k. 5, p. 6, k. 6, p. 1, k. 1, p. 1, k. 1, p. 1, k. 6, p. 6, k. 2, d.m.st. to end.

7th row: D.m.st. 11 (15) (17) (21) (23) (27), p. 2, k. 6, p. 6, tw. 2 lt., tw. 2 lt., tw. 2 lt., p. 5, k. 6, p. 4, cr. 3 b., cr. 3 f., p. 1, cr. 3 b., cr. 3 f., p. 4, k. 6, p. 5, tw. 2 rt., tw. 2 rt., tw. 2 rt., p. 6, k. 6, p. 2, d.m.st. to end.

8th row: D.m.st. 11 (15) (17) (21) (23) (27), k. 2, p. 6, k. 7, p. 1, k. 1, p. 1, k. 1, p. 1, k. 5, p. 6, k. 4, p. 2, k. 2, p. 2, k. 1, p. 2, k. 2, p. 2, k. 4, p. 6, k. 5, p. 1, k. 1, p. 1, k. 1, p. 1, k. 7, p. 6, k. 2, d.m.st. to end.

The 1st to 8th rows form the cable pattern at each side, within d.m.st. Keeping continuity of d.m.st. and cable patterns, continue as follows:

9th row: Pattern 19 (23) (25) (29) (31) (35), p. 4, m.b., p. 2, tw. 2 lt., tw. 2 lt., tw. 2 lt., p. 4, k. 6, p. 4, k. 2, p. 2, cr. 5 f., p. 2, k. 2, p. 4, k. 6, p. 4, tw. 2 rt., tw. 2 rt., tw. 2 rt., p. 2, m.b., p. 4, pattern to end.

10th row: Pattern 19 (23) (25) (29) (31) (35), k. 8, p. 1, k. 1, p. 1, k. 1, p. 1, k. 4, p. 6, k. 4, p. 2, k. 2, p. 2, k. 1, p. 2, k. 2, p. 2, k. 4, p. 6, k. 4, p. 1, k. 1, p. 1, k. 1, p. 1, k. 8, pattern to end.

11th row: Pattern 19 (23) (25) (29) (31) (35), p. 8, tw. 2 lt., tw. 2 lt., tw. 2 lt., p. 3, c. 6 f., p. 4, cr. 3 f., cr. 3 b., p. 1, cr. 3 f., cr. 3 b., p. 4, c. 6 b., p. 3, tw. 2 rt, tw. 2 rt., tw. 2 rt., p. 8, pattern to end.

12th row: Pattern 19 (23) (25) (29) (31) (35), k. 3, p. 1, * k. 1, p. 1 *; repeat from * to * 4 times, k. 3, p. 6, k. 5, p. 4, k. 3, p. 4, k. 5, p. 6, k. 3, p. 1, repeat from * to * 5 times, k. 3, pattern to end.

The 1st to 12th rows form the bobble patterns. Keeping continuity of d.m.st., bobble patterns, and cables each side of bobble patterns, continue centre panel as follows:

13th row: Pattern 42 (46) (48) (52) (54) (58), p. 5, c. 4 b., p. 3, c. 4 f., p. 5, pattern to end.

14th row: Pattern 42 (46) (48) (52) (54) (58), k. 5, p. 4, k. 3, p. 4, k. 5, pattern to end.

15th row: Pattern 42 (46) (48) (52) (54) (58), p. 4, cr. 3 b., cr. 3 f., p. 1, cr. 3 b., cr. 3 f., p. 4, pattern to end.

16th row: Pattern 42 (46) (48) (52) (54) (58), k. 4, p. 2, k. 2, p. 2, k. 1, p. 2, k. 2, p. 2, k. 4, pattern to end.

The 1st to 16th rows form the centre lattice pattern panel.

Keeping continuity of all pattern panels as set, work a further 96 rows.

To shape the armholes: Keeping continuity of pattern panels, cast off 3 sts. at beginning of next 2 rows, then dec. 1 st. each end of next row and then on the 6 (8) (8) (10) (10) (12) following alternate rows—85 (89) (93) (97) (101) (105) sts. **★★**

Work 35 rows.

To slope the shoulders: Cast off 8 (9) (9) (10) (10) (11) sts. at beginning of next 4 (2) (4) (2) (4) (2) rows, then 7 (8) (8) (9) (9) (10) sts. on the following 2 (4) (2) (4) (2) (4) rows—39 (39) (41) (41) (43) (43) sts.

Leave sts. on a spare needle.

THE FRONT: Work as back to **★★**.

Work 20 rows.

To divide for neck: Next row: Work 31 (33) (34) (36) (37) (39) and leave these sts. on a spare needle for right half neck, work 23 (23) (25) (25) (27) (27) and leave these sts. on a stitch-holder, work to end and continue on these 31 (33) (34) (36) (37) (39) sts. for left half neck.

The left half neck: Dec. 1 st. at neck edge on the next 8 rows—23 (25) (26) (28) (29) (31) sts.

Work 6 rows—work 7 rows here when working right half neck.

To slope the shoulder: Cast off 8 (9) (9) (10) (10) (11) sts. at beginning of next row, then 8 (8) (9) (9) (10) (10) sts. on the following alternate row—7 (8) (8) (9) (9) (10) sts.

Work 1 row. Cast off.

The right half neck: With right side of work facing, rejoin yarn to sts. on spare needle and work as left half neck, noting variation.

THE SLEEVES (both alike): With No. 10 (3¼ mm) needles cast on 38 (42) (42) (46) (46) (50) sts. and work 16 rows in single rib.

Increase row: Rib 7 (9) (9) (11) (11) (13), up 1, * rib 2, up 1; repeat from * 11 times, rib to end—51 (55) (55) (59) (59) (63) sts.

Change to No. 8 (4 mm) needles.

Foundation row: * K. 1, p. 1 *; repeat from * to * 2 (3) (3) (4) (4) (5) times, k. 3, p. 6, k. 4, p. 2, k. 2, p. 2, k. 1, p. 2, k. 2, p. 2, k. 4, p. 6, k. 3, p. 1, repeat from * to * until 1 st. remains, k. 1.

Work pattern as follows:

1st row (right side): * P. 1, k. 1 *; repeat from * to * 2 (3) (3) (4) (4) (5) times, p. 3, k. 6, p. 4, k. 2, p. 2, cr. 5 b., p. 2, k. 2, p. 4, k. 6, p. 3, k. 1, repeat from * to * until 1 st. remains, p. 1.

2nd row: P. 1, * k. 1, p. 1 *; repeat from * to * 2 (3) (3) (4) (4) (5) times, k. 2, p. 6, k. 4, p. 2, k. 2, p. 2, k. 1, p. 2, k. 2, p. 2, k. 4, p. 6, k. 2, p. 1, repeat from * to * to end.

3rd row: K. 1, * p. 1, k. 1 *; repeat from * to * 2 (3) (3) (4) (4) (5) times, p. 2, c. 6 f., p. 4, cr. 3 f., cr. 3 b., p. 1, cr. 3 f., cr. 3 b., p. 4, c. 6 b., p. 2, k. 1, repeat from * to * to end.

4th row: * K. 1, p. 1 *; repeat from * to * 2 (3) (3) (4) (4) (5) times, k. 3, p. 6, k. 5, p. 4, k. 3, p. 4, k. 5, p. 6, k. 3, ** p. 1, k. 1 **; repeat from ** to **, to end.

These 4 rows set the position of the d.m.st., cable and lattice panels. Keeping continuity of panels to match back and taking extra sts. into the d.m.st. as they occur, inc. 1 st. each end of next row, then on the 8 following 10th rows—69 (73) (73) (77) (77) (81) sts.

Work 21 rows.

To shape the sleeve top: Cast off 3 sts. at beginning of next 2 rows, then dec. 1 st. each end of next row and the 4 (6) (6) (8) (8) (10) following alternate rows.

Pattern 1 row—53 sts.

Dec. 1 st. each end of next 16 rows—21 sts. Cast off.

THE NECK BAND: First join right shoulder seam. With right side of work facing and using No. 10 (3¼ mm) needles, rejoin yarn and pick up and k. 16 sts. down left half neck; decreasing 3 sts. evenly, k. across sts. at front; pick up and k. 16 sts. up right half neck; decreasing 5 sts. evenly, k. across back—86 (86) (90) (90) (94) (94) sts.

Single rib 20 rows.

Cast off fairly loosely in rib.

TO MAKE UP THE SWEATER: Press with a warm iron over a dry cloth. Join right shoulder seam, continuing seam across neck band. Set in sleeves, then join sleeve and side seams. Fold neck band in half to wrong side and catch into place.

Long-line Cardigan

Illustrated on page 126

MEASUREMENTS	*in centimetres (and inches, in brackets)*					
To fit bust sizes	86–91	(34–36)	97	(38)	102	(40)
All round widest part	101.5	(39¾)	106	(41¾)	109	(43)
Side seam	49	(19¼)	49	(19¼)	49	(19¼)
Length	70	(27½)	70.5	(27¾)	71.5	(28¼)
Sleeve seam	45.5	(17¾)	45.5	(17¾)	45.5	(17¾)

MATERIALS: *Allow the following quantities in 40 g balls of Argyll Ferndale Chunky:* 19 *for* 86–91 *cm and* 97 *cm sizes;* 20 *for the* 102 *cm size. For any one size: a pair each of* No. 7 (4½ mm) *and* No. 9 (3¾ mm) *knitting needles,* 5 *buttons.*

TENSION: *Work at a tension of* 18 *stitches and* 28 *rows to measure* 10 × 10 *cm over the pattern, using* No. 7 (4½ mm) *needles to obtain the measurements given.*

ABBREVIATIONS: To be read before working: *K., knit plain; p., purl; st., stitch; sl., slip; tog., together; dec., decrease (by working 2 sts. tog.); inc., increase (by working twice into same st.); y.fwd., yarn forward to make a st.; y.o.n., yarn over needle; r.s.s., reverse stocking st. (p. on the right side and k. on the wrong side); single rib is k. 1 and p. 1 alternately.*

NOTE: *The instructions are given for the* 86–91 *cm (34–36 inch) size. Where they vary, work the figures within the first brackets for the* 97 *cm (38 inch) size; work figures within the second brackets for the* 102 *cm (40 inch) size.*

THE BACK: With No. 9 (3¾ mm) needles cast on 87 (91) (95) sts.

1st rib row: K. 2, * p. 1, k. 1; repeat from * until 1 st. remains, k. 1.

2nd row: K. 1, * p. 1, k. 1; repeat from * to end. Repeat these 2 rows 3 times.

Change to No. 7 (4½ mm) needles and work the 2 row pattern as follows:

1st row: K. 1, * k. 1, y.fwd., sl. 1 p. wise, y.o.n.; repeat from * until 2 sts. remain, k. 2.

2nd row: K. 1, p. 1, * k. 2 tog., p. 1; repeat from * until 1 st. remains, k. 1.

Pattern a further 126 rows.

To shape the armholes: Keeping continuity of pattern, cast off 4 sts. at the beginning of the next 2 rows, then dec. 1 st. at each end of the next row and the 5 following alternate rows—67 (71) (75) sts.

Pattern 45 (47) (49) rows straight.

Cast off.

THE POCKET LININGS (make 2): With No. 9 (3¾ mm) needles cast on 21 sts. and beginning with a p. row, r.s.s. 28 rows.

Leave sts. on a spare needle.

THE LEFT FRONT: With No. 9 (3¾ mm) needles cast on 45 (47) (49) sts. and work 8 rows in rib as given for back.

Change to No. 7 (4½ mm) needles and work 32 rows in pattern as given for back.

Next (pocket) row: Pattern 12 (13) (14), sl. the next 21 sts. on to a stitch-holder and leave at front of work, pattern across the 21 sts. of one pocket lining, pattern 12 (13) (14)—45 (47) (49) sts.

Pattern 41 rows.

To slope the front: Dec. 1 st. at the *end* of next row—read *beginning* here when working right front—then dec. 1 st. at front edge on the 8 following 6th rows—36 (38) (40) sts.

Pattern 5 rows. **

To shape the armholes: Next row: Cast off 4 sts., pattern until 2 sts. remain, dec.

Pattern 1 row.

*** Dec. 1 st. at armhole edge on the next row and the 5 following alternate rows, at the same time dec. 1 st. at neck edge on the 6th row from previous front dec., then on the 5 (6) (7) following 6th rows—19 (20) (21) sts.

Pattern 21 (17) (13) rows.

Cast off.

THE RIGHT FRONT: Work as given for left front to **.

Next row: Dec., pattern to end.

To shape the armhole: Next row: Cast off 4 sts., pattern to end.

Complete as given for left front from *** to end.

THE SLEEVES (both alike): With No. 9 (3¾ mm) needles cast on 43 (45) (47) sts. and work 8 rows in rib as given for back.

Change to No. 7 (4½ mm) needles and work 8 rows in pattern as given for back.

Maintaining continuity of pattern and taking extra sts. into pattern as they occur, inc. 1 st. at each end of the next row and the 8 following 10th rows—61 (63) (65) sts.

Pattern 29 rows.

To shape the sleeve top: Cast off 4 sts. at the beginning of the next 2 rows, then dec. 1 st. at each end of the next row and the 15 (16) (17) following alternate rows—21 sts.

Pattern 1 row.

Cast off.

THE BUTTONHOLE BORDER: First join shoulder seams leaving the 29 (31) (33) sts. at centre back free. With right side of work facing, using No. 9 (3¾ mm) needles, pick up and k. 42 sts. up right side of front to first front dec., 66 (68) (70) sts. up right front neck edge and finally 14 (15) (16) sts. to centre back neck—122 (125) (128) sts.

Work 3 rows in single rib.

Next (buttonhole) row: Rib 4, y.fwd., * k. 2 tog., rib 7, y.fwd; repeat from * 3 times more, k. 2 tog., rib to end.

Rib 2 rows.

Cast off in rib.

THE BUTTON BORDER: With right side of work facing, using No. 9 (3¾ mm) needles, pick up and k. 14 (15)

Continued on page 127

Above *Long-line Cardigan (page 125)*

(16) sts. across second half of back neck, 66 (68) (70) sts. down left front edge to first front dec., and finally 42 sts. down left front to cast on edge—122 (125) (128) sts.

Work as given for buttonhole border omitting buttonholes.

THE POCKET TOPS (both alike): With right side of work facing, using No. 9 (3¾ mm) needles, rejoin yarn to the 21 sts. left on stitch-holder and beginning odd-numbered rows with k. 1 and even-numbered rows with p. 1, single rib 6 rows.

Cast off in rib.

TO MAKE UP THE CARDIGAN: Do not press. Set in sleeves. Join side and sleeve seams. Sew pocket linings to wrong side of work and pocket tops to right side. Join borders at centre back neck. Sew on buttons.

Norwegian-style Cardigan

Illustrated on page 130

MEASUREMENTS	*in centimetres (and inches, in brackets)*					
To fit bust sizes	86	(34)	91	(36)	97	(38)
All round underarms, fastened	91	(36)	95.5	(37½)	100	(39¼)
Side seam	41.5	(16¼)	41.5	(16¼)	41.5	(16¼)
Length	60	(23½)	60	(23½)	61.5	(24¼)
Sleeve seam	42	(16½)	42	(16½)	42	(16½)

MATERIALS: *Allow the following quantities in 50 g balls of Sirdar Majestic DK: 7 red, 4 navy, 2 white for 86 cm and 91 cm sizes; 8 red, 5 navy, 3 white for 97 cm size. For any one size: a pair each of No. 8 (4 mm) and No. 10 (3¼ mm) knitting needles; 9 buttons.*

TENSION: *Work at a tension of 26 stitches and 29 rows to measure 10 × 10 cm, over the pattern, using No. 8 (4 mm) needles, to obtain measurements given.*

ABBREVIATIONS: To be read before working: *K., knit plain; p., purl; st., stitch; tog., together; inc., increase (by working twice into next st.); dec., decrease (by working 2 sts. tog.); s.s., stocking st. (k. on right side and p. on wrong side); r., red; n., navy; w., white; single rib is k. 1 and p. 1 alternately; nil, meaning nothing is worked here for this size.*

NOTE: *The instructions are given for the 86 cm (34 inch) size. Where they vary, work figures within first brackets for 91 cm (36 inch) size; work figures within second brackets for 97 cm (38 inch) size.*

THE BACK: With No. 10 (3¼ mm) needles and n. cast on 93 (99) (105) sts. and beginning odd-numbered rows with k. 1 and even-numbered rows with p. 1, work 21 rows in single rib.

Inc. row: Rib 4 (7) (10), inc., * rib 3, inc.; repeat from * until 4 (7) (10) sts. remain, rib 4 (7) (10)—115 (121) (127) sts.

Change to No. 8 (4 mm) needles.

Joining and breaking colours as required, work the 13-row lower pattern band as follows, which is worked entirely in s.s., beginning with a k. row, so only the colour details are given.

**** 1st row: All w.

2nd row: 3 (nil) (3) w., * 1 n., 5 w.; repeat from * until 4 (1) (4) st(s). remain(s), 1 n., then 3 (nil) (3) w.

3rd row: 2 (nil) (2) w., 3 (2) (3) n., * 3 w., 3 n.; repeat from * until 2 (5) (2) sts. remain, 2 (3) (2) w., nil (2) (nil) n.

4th row: 1 w., * 2 n., 1 w.; repeat from * to end.

5th row: 2 (nil) (2) n., 3 (2) (3) w., * 3 n., 3 w.; repeat

from * until 2 (5) (2) sts. remain, 2 (3) (2) n., nil (2) (nil) w.

6th row: Nil (3) (nil) w., * 1 n., 5 w.; repeat from * until 1 (4) (1) st(s). remain(s), 1 n., then nil (3) (nil) w.

7th row: All w.

8th row: All r.

9th row: 1 r. (nil) (3 r.), * 1 n., 3 r.; repeat from * until 2 (1) (nil) st(s). remain(s), 1 n., 1 r., (1 n.) (nil).

10th row: 2 r. (2 n., 3 r.) (2 r., 3 n., 3 r.), * 1 n., 1 r., 1 n., 3 r., 3 n., 3 r.; repeat from * until 5 (8) (11) sts. remain, 1 n., 1 r., 1 n., then 2 r. (3 r., 2 n.) (3 r., 3 n., 2 r.).

11th row: Nil (3 n.) (1 r., 5 n.), * 3 r., 1 n., 3 r., 5 n.; repeat from * until 7 (10) (1) st(s). remain(s), 3 r., 1 n., 3 r. (3 r., 1 n., 3 r., 3 n.) (1 r.).

12th row: As 10th row.

13th row: As 9th row.

Work the 6-row main pattern as follows: **1st and 2nd rows:** All r.

3rd row: 3 (nil) (3) r., * 1 n., 5 r.; repeat from * until 4 (1) (4) st(s). remain(s), 1 n., then 3 (nil) (3) r.

4th and 5th rows: All r.

6th row: Nil (3) (nil) r., * 1 n., 5 r.; repeat from * until 1 (4) (1) st(s). remain(s), 1 n., then nil (3) (nil) r. ********

Keeping continuity of main pattern, work a further 77 rows.

Work 9th to 12th rows of lower border pattern.

To shape the armholes: 1st row: Keeping continuity of pattern to match 13th row of lower border, cast off 6 sts., work to end.

2nd row: With r., cast off 6 sts., work to end—103 (109) (115) sts.

With r., s.s. 2 rows.

***** Work the yoke pattern as follows:

1st and 2nd rows: Nil (3) (nil) r., * 1 w., 5 r.; repeat from * until 1 (4) (1) st(s). remain(s), 1 w., then nil (3) (nil) r.

3rd row: All w.

Continued on page 128

4th row: 3 (nil) (3) w., * 1 n., 5 w.; repeat from * until 4 (1) (4) st(s). remain(s), 1 n., then 3 (nil) (3) w.

5th row: 3 w. (2 n., 4 w.) (2 w., 3 n., 4 w.), * 2 n., 3 w., 2 n., 4 w., 3 n., 4 w.; repeat from * until 10 (13) (16) sts. remain, 2 n., 3 w., 2 n., then 3 w. (4 w., 2 n.) (4 w., 3 n., 2 w.).

6th row: 3 w. (1 n., 5 w.) (3 w., 1 n., 5 w.), * 3 n., 1 w., 3 n., 5 w., 1 n., 5 w.; repeat from * until 10 (13) (16) sts. remain, 3 n., 1 w., 3 n., then 3 w. (5 w., 1 n.) (5 w., 1 n., 3 w.).

7th row: 2 n. (2 w., 3 n.) (2 n., 3 w., 3 n.), * 2 w., 2 n., 1 w., 2 n., 2 w., 3 n., 3 w., 3 n.; repeat from * until 11 (14) (17) sts. remain, 2 w., 2 n., 1 w., 2 n., 2 w., then 2 n. (3 n., 2 w.) (3 n., 3 w., 2 n.).

8th row: Nil (3 w.) (1 n., 5 w.), * 3 n., 2 w., 1 n., 1 w., 1 n., 2 w., 3 n., 5 w.; repeat from * until 13 (16) (19) sts. remain, 3 n., 2 w., 1 n., 1 w., 1 n., then 3 n. (3 n., 3 w.) (3 n., 5 w., 1 n).

9th row: 1 w. (1 n., 3 w.) (3 w., 1 n., 3 w.), * 3 n., 2 w., 1 n., 2 w., 3 n., 3 w., 1 n., 3 w.; repeat from * until 12 (15) (18) sts. remain, 3 n., 2 w., 1 n., 2 w., 3 n., then 1 w. (3 w., 1 n.) (3 w., 1 n., 3 w.).

10th row: 5 (nil) (2) w., 3 (2) (3) n., * 6 w., 3 n.; repeat from * until 5 (8) (2) sts. remain, 5 w. (6 w., 2 n.) (2 w.).

11th to 17th rows: As 9th row back to 3rd row in that reverse order.

18th and 19th rows: As 1st and 2nd rows.

20th and 21st rows: 3 (nil) (3) r., * 1 w., 5 r.; repeat from * until 4 (1) (4) st(s). remain(s), 1 w., 3 (nil) (3) r.
*****

22nd row: 3 (nil) (3) w., * 1 n., 5 w.; repeat from * until 4 (1) (4) st(s). remain(s), 1 n., then 3 (nil) (3) w.

23rd row: 2 w. (2 n., 3 w.) (2 w.), * 3 n., 3 w.; repeat from * until 5 (2) (5) sts. remain, 3 (2) (3) n., 2 (nil) (2) w.

24th row: 1 w., * 2 n., 1 w.; repeat from * to end.

25th row: 2 n. (2 w., 3 n.) (2 n.), * 3 w., 3 n.; repeat from * until 5 (2) (5) sts. remain, 3 (2) (3) w., 2 (nil) (2) n.

26th row: 1 n., * 2 w., 1 n.; repeat from * to end.

Keeping continuity of pattern as set between 23rd to 26th rows, work a further 16 (16) (20) rows.

To slope the shoulders: Cast off 9 (9) (10) sts. at beginning of next 4 rows, then 8 (9) (9) sts. on the following 4 rows—35 (37) (39) sts.

Leave sts. on a spare needle.

THE LEFT FRONT: With No. 10 (3¼ mm) needles and n. cast on 47 (49) (51) sts. and work 21 rows in rib as given for back.

Inc. row: Rib 3 (2) (1), inc., * rib 3, inc.; repeat from * until 3 (2) (1) st(s). remain(s), rib 3 (2) (1)—58 (61) (64) sts.

Change to No. 8 (4 mm) needles and work the 13-row lower pattern band as follows:

** **1st row:** All w.

2nd row: * 1 n., 5 w.; repeat from * until 4 (1) (4) st(s). remain(s), 1 n., then 3 (nil) (3) w.

3rd row: 2 w. (2 n., 3 w.) (2 w.), * 3 n., 3 w.; repeat from * until 2 sts. remain, then 2 n.

4th row: 1 w., * 2 n., 1 w.; repeat from * to end.

5th row: 2 n. (2 w., 3 n.) (2 n.), * 3 w., 3 n.; repeat from * until 2 sts. remain, 2 w.

6th row: 3 w., * 1 n., 5 w.; repeat from * until 1 (4) (1) st(s). remain(s), 1 n., nil (3) (nil) w.

7th row: All w.

8th row: All r.

9th row: 1 r. (1 n., 3 r.) (3 r., 1 n., 3 r.), 1 n., * 3 r., 1 n.; repeat from * to end.

10th row: 2 n., * 3 r., 1 n., 1 r., 1 n., 3 r., 3 n.; repeat from * until 8 (11) (14) sts. remain, 3 r., 1 n., 1 r., 1 n., then 2 r. (3 r., 2 n.) (3 r., 3 n., 2 r.).

11th row: 3 r. (3 n., 3 r.) (1 r., 5 n., 3 r.), * 1 n., 3 r., 5 n., 3 r.; repeat from * until 7 sts. remain, 1 n., 3 r., 3 n.

12th row: As 10th row.

13th row: As 9th row.

Work the 6-row main pattern as follows:

1st and 2nd rows: All r.

3rd row: 1 n., * 5 r., 1 n.; repeat from * until 3 (nil) (3) sts. remain, 3 (nil) (3) r.

4th and 5th rows: All r.

6th row: Nil (3) (nil) r., * 1 n., 5 r.; repeat from * until 4 sts. remain, 1 n., 3 r.

Keeping continuity of main pattern, work a further 77 rows.

Work 9th to 12th rows of lower border pattern.

To shape the armhole: Keeping continuity of pattern to match 13th row of lower border, cast off 6 sts., work to end—52 (55) (58) sts.

With r., s.s. 3 rows.

Work the yoke pattern as follows: 1st row: Nil (3) (nil) r., * 1 w., 5 r.; repeat from * until 4 sts. remain 1 w., 3 r.

2nd row: 3 r., * 1 w., 5 r.; repeat from * until 1 (4) (1) st(s). remain(s), 1 w., nil (3) (nil) r.

3rd row: All w.

4th row: * 1 n., 5 w.; repeat from * until 4 (1) (4) st(s). remain(s), 1 n., 3 (nil) (3) w.

5th row: 3 w. (2 n., 4 w.) (2 w., 3 n., 4 w.), * 2 n., 3 w., 2 n., 4 w., 3 n., 4 w.; repeat from * until 13 sts. remain, 2 n., 3 w., 2 n., 4 w., 2 n.

6th row: * 1 n., 5 w., 3 n., 1 w., 3 n., 5 w.; repeat from * until 10 (13) (16) sts. remain, 3 n., 1 w., 3 n., then 3 w. (5 w., 1 n.) (5 w., 1 n., 3 w.).

*** These 6 rows set the position of the yoke pattern. Keeping continuity of pattern to match back, work a further 25 (25) (29) rows—work 26 (26) (30) rows here when working right front.

To shape neck: Cast off 8 (9) (10) sts. at beginning of next row, then dec. 1 st. at neck edge on the following 10 rows—34 (36) (38) sts.

To slope the shoulder: Cast off 9 (9) (10) sts. at beginning of next row and following alternate row, then 8 (9) (9) sts. on the next alternate row—8 (9) (9) sts.

Work 1 row, then cast off.

THE RIGHT FRONT: Work as left front to **.

1st row: All w.

2nd row: 3 (nil) (3) w., 1 n., * 5 w., 1 n.; repeat from * to end.

3rd row: 2 n., * 3 w., 3 n.; repeat from * until 2 (5) (2) sts. remain, 2 w. (3 w., 2 n.) (2 w.).

4th row: 1 w., * 2 n., 1 w; repeat from * to end.

5th row: 2 w., * 3 n., 3 w.; repeat from * until 2 (5) (2) sts. remain, 2 n. (3 n., 2 w.) (2 n.).

6th row: 1 n. (3 w., 1 n.) (1 n.), * 5 w., 1 n.; repeat from * until 3 sts. remain, 3 w.

7th row: All w.

8th row: All r.

9th row: * 1 n., 3 r.; repeat from * until 2 (1) (nil) st(s). remain(s), 1 n., 1 r. (1 n.) (nil).

10th row: 2 r. (2 n., 3 r.) (2 r., 3 n., 3 r.), * 1 n., 1 r., 1 n., 3 r., 3 n., 3 r.; repeat from * until 8 sts. remain, 1 n., 1 r., 1 n., 3 r., 2 n.

11th row: 3 n., * 3 r., 1 n., 3 r., 5 n; repeat from * until 7

(10) (13) sts. remain, 3 r., 1 n., then 3 r. (3 r., 3 n.) (3 r., 5 n., 1 r.).

12th row: As 10th row.

13th row: As 9th row.

Work the 6-row main pattern as follows:

1st and 2nd rows: All r.

3rd row: 3 (nil) (3) r., * 1 n., 5 r.; repeat from * until 1 st. remains, 1 n.

4th and 5th rows: All r.

6th row: 3 r., 1 n., * 5 r., 1 n.; repeat from * until nil (3) (nil) sts. remain, nil (3) (nil) r.

Keeping continuity of main pattern, work a further 77 rows.

Work 9th to 13th rows of lower border pattern.

To shape the armhole: With r., cast off 6 sts., work to end—52 (55) (58) sts.

With r., s.s. 2 rows.

Work the yoke pattern as follows: 1st row: 3 r., * 1 w., 5 r.; repeat from * until 1 (4) (1) st(s). remain(s), 1 w., nil (3) (nil) r.

2nd row: Nil (3) (nil) r., * 1 w., 5 r.; repeat from * until 4 sts. remain, 1 w., 3 r.

3rd row: All w.

4th row: 3 w. (1 n., 5 w.) (3 w., 1 n., 5 w.), 1 n., * 5 w., 1 n.; repeat from * to end.

5th row: 2 n., * 4 w., 2 n., 3 w., 2 n., 4 w., 3 n.; repeat from * until 14 (17) (20) sts. remain, 4 w., 2 n., 3 w., 2 n., then 3 w. (4 w., 2 n.) (4 w., 3 n., 2 w.).

6th row: 3 w. (1 n., 5 w.) (3 w., 1 n., 5 w.), * 3 n., 1 w., 3 n., 5 w., 1 n., 5 w.; repeat from * once, 3 n., 1 w., 3 n., 5 w., 1 n.

Work as left front from *** to end.

THE SLEEVES (both alike): With No. 10 (3¼ mm) needles and n. cast on 45 (45) (49) sts. and work 21 rows in rib as given for back.

Inc. row: Rib 8 (8) (9), inc. into each of next 28 (28) (30) sts., rib to end—73 (73) (79) sts.

Change to No. 8 (4 mm) needles.

Work in pattern as given on back from **** to **** but reading instructions as given for the second (second) (third) size.

Keeping continuity of main pattern and taking extra sts. into the pattern as they occur, work 1 row, then inc. 1 st. each end of next row and then on the 8 following 6th rows—91 (91) (97) sts.

Pattern 12 rows straight.

Work top pattern as follows: 1st row: 2 (2) (1) r., * 1 n., 3 r.; repeat from * until 1 (1) (nil) st. remains, 1 (1) (nil) n.

2nd row: 2 n. (2 n.) (2 r., 3 n.), * 3 r., 1 n., 1 r., 1 n., 3 r., 3 n.; repeat from * until 5 (5) (8) sts. remain, 3 r., 1 n., then 1 r. (1 r.) (1 r., 1 n., 2 r.).

3rd row: 1 n. (1 n.) (3 r., 1 n.), 3 r., * 5 n., 3 r., 1 n., 3 r.; repeat from * until 3 (3) (6) sts. remain, 3 n. (3 n.) (5 n., 1 r.).

4th row: As 2nd row.

5th row: As 1st row.

With r., s.s. 3 rows.

Work in pattern as given on back from ***** to ***** but reading instructions as given for the second (second) (third) size and marking each end of the 13th row to denote end of sleeve seam. Cast off.

THE NECK BAND: First join shoulder seams. With right side of work facing and using No. 10 (3¼ mm) needles, rejoin n. and pick up and k. 27 (28) (29) sts. round right front neck, k. 35 (37) (39) sts. across back, then pick up and k. 27 (28) (29) sts. round left front neck—89 (93) (97) sts.

Work 8 rows in rib as given for back.

Cast off in rib.

THE BUTTONHOLE BAND: With right side of work facing and using No. 10 (3¼ mm) needles, rejoin n. and pick up and k. 153 (153) (157) sts. evenly along right front edge, including row ends of neck band.

Work 3 rows in rib as given for back.

1st buttonhole row: Rib 4 (4) (6), * cast off 2, rib 15; repeat from * 7 times, cast off 2, rib 3 (3) (5).

2nd buttonhole row: Rib to end, casting on 2 sts. over each group cast off on previous row.

Rib 3 rows, then cast off in rib.

THE BUTTON BAND: Work as buttonhole band, omitting buttonholes.

TO MAKE UP THE CARDIGAN: Press with a warm iron over a dry cloth. Set in sleeves sewing row ends above markers to sts. cast off at underarms, then join sleeve and side seams. Add buttons.

Opposite *Norwegian-style Cardigan (page 127)*. Above *Wrap-over Jacket (page 132)*

Wrap-over Jacket
Illustrated on page 131

MEASUREMENTS	*in centimetres (and inches, in brackets)*									
To fit bust sizes	86	(34)	91	(36)	97	(38)	102	(40)	107	(42)
All round at underarms	95	(37¼)	100	(39¼)	105	(41¼)	110	(43¼)	115	(45¼)
Side seam	46	(18)	46	(18)	46	(18)	46	(18)	46	(18)
Length	71	(28)	72.5	(28½)	72.5	(28½)	74	(29)	74	(29)
Sleeve seam	40.5	(16)	40.5	(16)	40.5	(16)	40.5	(16)	40.5	(16)

MATERIALS: *Allow the following quantities in 50 g balls of Jaeger Gabrielle:* 11 *pink,* 4 *cream for* 86 *cm size;* 12 *pink,* 5 *cream for* 91 *cm and* 97 *cm sizes;* 13 *pink,* 5 *cream for* 102 *cm size;* 13 *pink,* 6 *cream for* 107 *cm size. For any one size: a pair each of No.* 4 (6 *mm) and No.* 7 (4½ *mm) knitting needles.*

TENSION: *Work at a tension of* 16 *stitches and* 15 *rows to measure* 10 × 10 *cm, over the pattern, using No.* 4 (6 *mm) needles to obtain measurements given.*

ABBREVIATIONS: To be read before working: *K., knit plain; p., purl; st., stitch; tog., together; inc., increase (by working twice into same st.); dec., decrease (by working* 2 *sts. tog.); up* 1, *pick up the loop lying between needles and k. or p. into the back of it; s.s., stocking st. (k. on the right side and p. on the wrong side); single rib is k.* 1 *and p.* 1 *alternately; pk., pink; c., cream; sl., slip; nil, meaning nothing is worked here for this size.*

NOTE: *The instructions are given for the* 86 *cm (34 inch) size. Where they vary, work the figures within the first brackets for the* 91 *cm (36 inch) size; work the figures within the second brackets for the* 97 *cm (38 inch) size, and so on.*

THE BACK: With No. 7 (4½ mm) needles and pk., cast on 68 (72) (76) (80) (84) sts. and work 7 rows in single rib.

Next (increase) row: Rib 8, up 1, * rib 13 (14) (15) (16) (17), up 1; repeat from * until 8 sts. remain, rib 8—73 (77) (81) (85) (89) sts. Change to No. 4 (6 mm) needles.

Join in c. and work the 2-colour pattern, which is worked entirely in s.s. beginning with a k. row, so only the colour details are given.

1st row: * 1 c., 1 pk. *; repeat from * to * nil (1) (2) (2) time(s), ** 4 c., 1 pk., 9 c., 1 pk., 9 c., 1 pk., 4 c. **, 1 pk., work from * to * 5 (5) (7) (7) (9) times, work from ** to ** once, * 1 pk., 1 c; repeat from this * nil (1) (1) (2) (2) time(s).

2nd row: 1 pk., * 1 c., 1 pk. *; repeat from * to * nil (1) (1) (2) (2) time(s), ** 2 c., 3 pk., 7 c., 3 pk., 7 c., 3 pk., 2 c., 1 pk. **, work from * to * 6 (6) (8) (8) (10) times, work from ** to ** once, work from * to * 1 (2) (2) (3) (3) time(s).

3rd row: * 1 c., 1 pk., *; repeat from * to * nil (1) (1) (2) (2) time(s), ** 2 c., 2 pk., 1 c., 2 pk., 5 c., 5 pk., 5 c., 2 pk., 1 c., 2 pk., 2 c. **, 1 pk., work from * to * 5 (5) (7) (7) (9) times, work from ** to ** once, * 1 pk., 1 c.; repeat from this * nil (1) (1) (2) (2) time(s).

4th row: 1 pk., * 1 c., 1 pk. *; repeat from * to * nil (1) (1) (2) (2) time(s), ** 2 c., 3 pk., 5 c., 3 pk., 1 c., 3 pk., 5 c., 3 pk., 2 c., 1 pk. **, work from * to * 6 (6) (8) (8) (10) times, work from ** to ** once, work from * to * 1 (2) (2) (3) (3) time(s).

5th row: * 1 c., 1 pk. *; repeat from * to * nil (1) (1) (2) (2) time(s), ** 4 c., 1 pk., 5 c., 3 pk., 3 c., 3 pk., 5 c., 1 pk., 4 c. **, 1 pk., work from * to * 5 (5) (7) (7) (9) times, work from ** to ** once, * 1 pk., 1 c.; repeat from this * nil (1) (1) (2) (2) time(s).

6th row: 1 pk., * 1 c., 1 pk. *; repeat from * to * nil (1) (1) (2) (2) time(s), ** 2 c., 3 pk., 3 c., 3 pk., 2 c., 1 pk., 2 c., 3 pk., 3 c., 3 pk., 2 c., 1 pk. **, work from * to * 6 (6) (8) (8) (10) times, work from ** to ** once, work from * to * 1 (2) (2) (3) (3) time(s).

7th row: * 1 c., 1 pk. *; repeat from * to * nil (1) (1) (2) (2) time(s), ** 2 c., 2 pk., 1 c., 2 pk., 1 c., 3 pk., 2 c., 3 pk., 1 c., 2 pk., 1 c., 2 pk., 2 c. **, 1 pk., work from * to * 5 (5) (7) (7) (9) times, work from ** to ** once, * 1 pk., 1 c.; repeat from this * nil (1) (1) (2) (2) time(s).

8th to 12th rows: As 6th row back to 2nd row in that reverse order.

These 12 rows form the pattern, work a further 50 rows – mark each end of last row with a coloured thread to denote end of side seams.

Pattern 30 (32) (32) (34) (34) rows.

To slope the shoulders: Cast off 7 (7) (7) (8) (8) sts. at the beginning of the next 2 (4) (2) (2) (6) rows, then cast off 6 (6) (7) (7) (7) sts. at the beginning of the following 6 (4) (6) (6) (2) rows.

Cast off remaining 23 (25) (25) (27) (27) sts.

THE POCKET BACKS (both alike): With No. 4 (6 mm) needles and pk., cast on 22 sts. and s.s. 20 rows, increasing 1 st. in centre of last row.

Leave these 23 sts. on a spare needle.

THE LEFT FRONT: With No. 7 (4½ mm) needles and pk., cast on 33 (35) (37) (39) (41) sts. and beginning odd-numbered rows with k. 1 and even-numbered rows with p. 1, work 8 rows in single rib, increasing 1 st. each end of the last row—35 (37) (39) (41) (43) sts.

Change to No. 4 (6 mm) needles.

Join in c. and work in pattern which is worked entirely in s.s. beginning with a k. row, so only the colour details are given. ***

1st row: * 1 c., 1 pk. *; repeat from * to * nil (1) (1) (2) (2) time(s), work from ** to ** as given on 1st pattern row of back, * 1 pk., 1 c.; repeat from this * 1 (1) (2) (2) (3) time(s).

2nd row: 1 pk., * 1 c., 1 pk. *; repeat from * to * 1 (1) (2) (2) (3) time(s), work from ** to ** as given on 2nd row of back, work from * to * 1 (2) (2) (3) (3) time(s).

These 2 rows set the position of the pattern for the left front, keeping continuity of pattern panel to match back, work 14 rows.

Next (pocket) row: Pattern 5 (7) (7) (9) (9), slip next 23 sts. on to a stitch-holder and leave at front of work, in their place pattern across 23 sts. of one pocket back, pattern 7 (7) (9) (9) (11).

**** Pattern 29 rows.

To slope front edge: Dec. 1 st. at end—read beginning here when working right front—of the next row and 3 following 4th rows—31 (33) (35) (37) (39) sts.

Work 3 rows, mark end—read beginning here when working right front—of the last of these rows.

Dec. 1 st. at the end—read beginning here when working right front—of the next row and 5 (6) (6) (7) (7) following 4th rows—25 (26) (28) (29) (31) sts.

Work 9 (7) (7) (5) (5) rows – work 10 (8) (8) (6) (6) rows here when working right front.

To slope the shoulder: Cast off 7 (7) (7) (8) (8) sts. at the beginning of the next row, 6 (7) (7) (7) (8) sts. at the beginning of the following alternate row, then 6 (6) (7) (7) (8) sts. at the beginning of the following alternate row.

Work 1 row.

Cast off remaining 6 (6) (7) (7) (7) sts.

THE RIGHT FRONT: Work as given for left front to ***.

1st row: * 1 c., 1 pk. *; repeat from * to * 1 (1) (2) (2) (3) time(s), work from ** to ** on 1st pattern row of back, * 1 pk., 1 c.; repeat from this * nil (1) (1) (2) (2) time(s).

2nd row: 1 pk., * 1 c., 1 pk. *; repeat from * to * nil (1) (1) (2) (2) time(s), work from ** to ** on 2nd pattern row of back, work from * to * 2 (2) (3) (3) (4) times.

These 2 rows set the position of the pattern for the right front, keeping continuity of pattern panel to match back, work 14 rows.

Next (pocket) row: Pattern 7 (7) (9) (9) (11), slip next 23 sts. on to a stitch-holder and leave at front of work, in their place pattern across 23 sts. of other pocket back, pattern 5 (7) (7) (9) (9).

Work as given for left front from **** to end, noting variations.

THE SLEEVES (both alike): With No. 7 (4½ mm) needles and pk., cast on 51 (55) (55) (59) (59) sts. and work 8 rows in rib as given for left front, increasing 1 st. each end of last row—53 (57) (57) (61) (61) sts.

Change to No. 4 (6 mm) needles, join in c. and working in s.s. beginning with a k. row, work in pattern as follows:

1st row: * 1 c., 1 pk. *; repeat from * to * 5 (6) (6) (7) (7) times, work from ** to ** on 1st pattern row of back, * 1 pk., 1 c.; repeat from this * 5 (6) (6) (7) (7) times.

2nd row: 1 pk., * 1 c., 1 pk. *; repeat from * to * 5 (6) (6) (7) (7) times, work from ** to ** on 2nd pattern row of back, work from * to * 6 (7) (7) (8) (8) times.

These 2 rows set the position of the pattern for the sleeves, keeping continuity of pattern panel to match back and working extra sts. into the side pattern as they occur, inc. 1 st. each end of the next row and 4 following 8th rows—63 (67) (67) (71) (71) sts.

Pattern 19 rows.

Cast off.

THE LEFT FRONT BORDER AND COLLAR: With No. 7 (4½ mm) needles and pk., cast on 147 (149) (149) (153) (153) sts.

***** **1st and 2nd turning rows:** * K. 1, p. 1; repeat from * 7 (8) (8) (10) (10) times for 1st row, turn, sl. 1, rib to end for 2nd row.

3rd and 4th turning rows: Rib 20 (22) (22) (26) (26) for 3rd row, turn, sl. 1, rib to end for 4th row.

5th and 6th turning rows: Rib 24 (26) (26) (30) (30) for 5th row, turn, sl. 1, rib to end for 6th row.

7th and 8th turning rows: Rib 28 (30) (30) (34) (34) for 7th row, turn, sl. 1, rib to end for 8th row.

9th and 10th turning rows: Rib 32 (34) (34) (38) (38) for 9th row, turn, sl. 1, rib to end for 10th row.

11th and 12th turning rows: Rib 3, * then p. 1, k. 1 and p. 1 all into next st., rib 3; repeat from * 7 times, rib 1 (3) (3) (7) (7) for 11th row, turn, sl. 1, rib to end for 12th row—163 (165) (165) (169) (169) sts.

13th and 14th turning rows: Rib 56 (58) (58) (62) (62) for 13th row, turn, sl, 1, rib to end for 14th row.

Continue in this way, working 4 sts. extra on next row and every alternate row for a further 20 rows.

Work 10 rows in rib across all sts.—work 9 rows here when working right front border and collar.

Cast off in rib.

THE RIGHT FRONT BORDER: With No. 7 (4½ mm) needles and pk. cast on 147 (149) (149) (153) (153) sts.

1st row: K. 1, * p. 1, k. 1; repeat from * to end.

Work as given for left front border from ***** to end, reading k. for p. and p. for k. and noting variation.

THE POCKET TOPS (both alike): With right side of work facing rejoin pk., and using No. 7 (4½ mm) needles k. across 23 sts. from stitch-holder, inc. 1 st. each end of row—25 sts.

1st row: K. 1, * p. 1, k. 1; repeat from * to end.

2nd row: K. 2, * p. 1, k. 1; repeat from * until 1 st. remains, k. 1.

Repeat these 2 rows, twice.

Cast off in rib.

THE BELT: With No. 7 (4½ mm) needles and pk., cast on 11 sts. and working in rib as given on pocket tops beginning with a 2nd row, work until belt measures 117 (122) (127) (132) (137) cm—46 (48) (50) (52) (54) inches.

Cast off in rib.

TO MAKE UP THE JACKET: Do not press. Join shoulder seams. Set sleeves between markers on back and fronts, then join sleeve and side seams. Stitch pocket backs to wrong side and row ends of pocket tops to right side. Join row ends of collar and place at centre back, then stitch cast on edge of front bands and collar all round front edge.

Above *Lacy Cardigan with Drop Shoulders (page 136)*   Opposite *Jacket with Diamond Panels (see page 137)*

Lacy Cardigan with Drop Shoulders

Illustrated on page 134

MEASUREMENTS					
To loosely fit bust sizes	*in centimetres (and inches, in brackets)*				
	86 (34)	91 (36)	97 (38)	102 (40)	107 (42)
Side seam	40 (15¾)	40 (15¾)	40 (15¾)	40 (15¾)	40 (15¾)
Length	61.5 (24¼)	62.5 (24½)	62.5 (24½)	63.5 (25)	63.5 (25)
Sleeve seam	45.5 (18)	45.5 (18)	45.5 (18)	45.5 (18)	45.5 (18)

MATERIALS: *Allow the following quantities in 50 g balls of Patons Beehive Shetland Chunky:* 10 for 86 and 91 cm sizes; 11 for 97 cm size; 12 for 102 cm size; 13 for 107 cm size. For any one size: a pair each of No. 4 (6 mm) and No. 7 (4½ mm) knitting needles; 3 buttons.

TENSION: *Work at a tension of 13 stitches and 17 rows to measure 9 × 9 cm, over the pattern, using No. 4 (6 mm) needles, to obtain measurements given.*

ABBREVIATIONS: To be read before working: *K., knit plain; p., purl; st., stitch; tog., together; inc., increase; dec., decrease (by working 2 sts. tog.); up 1, pick up loop lying between needles and k. or p. into back of it; y.r.n., yarn round needle to make a st.; sl., slip; p.s.s.o., pass the sl.st. over; single rib is k. 1, p. 1 alternately; nil, meaning nothing is worked for this size.*

NOTE: *The instructions are given for the 86 cm (34 inch) size. Where they vary, work figures within first brackets for 91 cm (36 inch) size; work figures within second brackets for 97 cm (38 inch) size, and so on.*

THE BACK: With No. 7 (4½ mm) needles cast on 60 (62) (66) (68) (72) sts. and work 19 rows in single rib.

Inc. row: Rib 7 (7) (9) (6) (6), up 1, * rib 15 (12) (16) (8) (10), up 1; repeat from * until 8 (7) (9) (6) (6) sts. remain, rib to end—64 (67) (70) (76) (79) sts.

Change to No. 4 (6 mm) needles and work the 4-row pattern as follows:

1st row: P. 1, * k. 2 tog., y.r.n., p. 1; repeat from * to end.

2nd row: K. 1, * p. 2, k. 1; repeat from * to end.

3rd row: P. 1, * keeping yarn at front so that it passes over needle before working next st., sl. 1, k. 1, p.s.s.o., p. 1; repeat from * to end.

4th row: As 2nd row.

Pattern a further 86 (88) (88) (90) (90) rows, marking each end of the 54th of these rows to denote end of side seams.

To slope the shoulders: Cast off 5 (5) (6) (6) (6) sts. at beginning of next 4 (2) (4) (4) (2) rows, then 6 (6) (6) (7) (7) sts. on the following 4 (6) (4) (4) (6) rows—20 (21) (22) (24) (25) sts. Cast off.

THE LEFT FRONT: With No. 7 (4½ mm) needles cast on 27 (29) (31) (31) (33) sts. and, beginning odd-numbered rows with k. 1 and even-numbered rows with p. 1, work 19 rows in single rib.

Inc. row: Rib 4 (7) (5) (3) (4), up 1, * rib 6 (14) (10) (5) (8), up 1; repeat from * until 5 (8) (6) (3) (5) sts. remain, rib to end—31 (31) (34) (37) (37) sts.

Change to No. 4 (6 mm) needles and work 18 rows in pattern as given on back.

To shape front edge: Dec. 1 st. at the end—read

beginning here when working right front—of the next row, then on the 4 (3) (4) (6) (4) following 8th (10th) (8th) (6th) (8th) rows—26 (27) (29) (30) (32) sts.

Pattern 7 (9) (7) (3) (7) rows, marking side edge on the last of these rows, to denote end of side seam.

Pattern nil (nil) (nil) (2) (nil) rows, the dec. 1 st. at front edge on the next row, then on the 3 (3) (4) (3) (4) following 8th (10th) (8th) (6th) (8th) rows—22 (23) (24) (26) (27) sts.

Pattern 7 (3) (1) (15) (3) row(s)—pattern 8 (4) (2) (16) (4) rows here when working right front.

To slope the shoulder: Cast off 5 (5) (6) (6) (6) sts. at beginning of the next row, 5 (6) (6) (6) (7) sts. on the following alternate row, then 6 (6) (6) (7) (7) sts. on the next alternate row—6 (6) (6) (7) (7) sts. remain.

Pattern 1 row, then cast off.

THE RIGHT FRONT: Work as left front, noting variations.

THE SLEEVES: With No. 7 (4½ mm) needles cast on 30 (32) (32) (34) (34) sts. and work 19 rows in single rib.

Inc. row: Rib 5 (5) (5) (6) (6), up 1, * rib 1, up 1; repeat from * until 4 (5) (5) (5) (5) sts. remain, rib to end—52 (55) (55) (58) (58) sts.

Change to No. 4 (6 mm) needles and work 68 rows in pattern as given for back.

Cast off.

THE FRONT BORDER: First join shoulder seams. With No. 7 (4½ mm) needles cast on 9 sts.

1st rib row: K. 2, * p. 1, k. 1; repeat from * twice, k. 1 more.

2nd rib row: K. 1, * p. 1, k. 1; repeat from * to end.

1st buttonhole row: Rib 3, cast off 3, rib to end.

2nd buttonhole row: Rib to end, casting on 3 sts. over those cast off on previous row.

Rib 14 rows.

Repeat the last 16 rows once, then the 2 buttonhole rows again.

Continue in rib until band fits up right front, round neck and down left front, casting off in rib when correct length is assured.

TO MAKE UP THE CARDIGAN: Press with a warm iron over a dry cloth. Set in sleeves between markers, then join sleeve and side seams. Sew front band into position, placing last buttonhole level with first front dec. Add buttons.

Jacket with Diamond Panels

Illustrated on page 135

MEASUREMENTS	*in centimetres (and inches, in brackets)*					
To fit bust sizes	86	(34)	91	(36)	97	(38)
Side seam	44.5	(17½)	44.5	(17½)	44.5	(17½)
Length at centre back	69.5	(27¼)	69.5	(27¼)	69.5	(27¼)
Sleeve seam, with cuff turned back	36.5	(14¼)	36.5	(14¼)	36.5	(14¼)

MATERIALS: *Allow the following quantities in 100 g balls of 3 Suisses Mayfair: 8 for 86 cm size; 8 for 91 cm size; 9 for 97 cm size. For any one size: a pair each of No. 5 (5½ mm) and No. 6 (5 mm) knitting needles.*

TENSION: *Work at a tension of 16 stitches and 24 rows to measure 10 × 10 cm, over the garter st. pattern, using No. 5 (5½ mm) needles, to obtain measurements given.*

ABBREVIATIONS: To be read before working: *K., knit plain; p., purl; st., stitch; tog., together; k. 2 tog.b., k. 2 tog. through back of sts.; g.st., garter stitch (k. plain on every row); y.fwd., yarn forward to make a st.; sl., slip; p.s.s.o., pass slipped st. over; dec., decrease (by taking 2 sts. tog.); inc., increase (by working twice into same st.); y.t.b., yarn to back of work; y.t.f., yarn to front of work.*

NOTE: *The instructions are given for the 86 cm (34 inch) size. Where they vary, work figures within first brackets for the 91 cm (36 inch) size; work figures within second brackets for the 97 cm (38 inch) size.*

THE MAIN PART (one piece to armholes): With No. 6 (5 mm) needles cast on 164 (174) (184) sts. and k. 9 rows.

Change to No. 5 (5½ mm) needles and work in g.st. with pattern panels.

1st pattern row: K. 22 (21) (20), * y.fwd., k. 2 tog.b., k. 18 (20) (22); repeat from * ending last repeat with k. 20 (19) (18) instead of k. 18 (20) (22).

2nd row: K. 20 (19) (18), * p. 3, k. 17 (19) (21); repeat from * ending last repeat with k. 21 (20) (19).

3rd row: K. 20 (19) (18), * k. 2 tog., y.fwd., k. 1, y.fwd., k. 2 tog.b., k. 15 (17) (19); repeat from * ending last repeat with k. 19 (18) (17).

4th row: K. 19 (18) (17), * p. 2, k. 1, p. 2, k. 15 (17) (19); repeat from * ending last repeat with k. 20 (19) (18).

5th row: K. 19 (18) (17), * k. 2 tog., y.fwd., k. 3, y.fwd., k. 2 tog.b., k. 13 (15) (17); repeat from * ending last repeat with k. 18 (17) (16).

6th row: K. 18 (17) (16), * p. 2, k. 3, p. 2, k. 13 (15) (17); repeat from * ending last repeat with k. 19 (18) (17).

7th row: K. 18 (17) (16), * k. 2 tog., y.fwd., k. 5, y.fwd., k. 2 tog.b., k. 11 (13) (15); repeat from * ending last repeat with k. 17 (16) (15).

8th row: K. 17 (16) (15), * p. 2, k. 5, p. 2, k. 11 (13) (15); repeat from * ending last repeat with k. 18 (17) (16).

9th row: K. 17 (16) (15), * k. 2 tog., y.fwd., k. 7, y.fwd., k. 2 tog.b., k. 9 (11) (13); repeat from * ending last repeat with k. 16 (15) (14).

10th row: K. 16 (15) (14), * p. 2, k. 7, p. 2, k. 9 (11) (13); repeat from * ending last repeat with k. 17 (16) (15).

11th row: K. 16 (15) (14), * k. 2 tog., y.fwd., k. 9, y.fwd., k. 2 tog.b., k. 7 (9) (11); repeat from * ending last repeat with k. 15 (14) (13).

12th row: K. 15 (14) (13), * p. 3, k. 7, p. 3, k. 7 (9) (11); repeat from * ending last repeat with k. 16 (15) (14).

13th row: K. 18 (17) (16), * y. fwd., k. 2 tog.b., k. 5, k. 2 tog., y.fwd., k. 11 (13) (15); repeat from * ending last repeat with k. 17 (16) (15).

14th row: K. 17 (16) (15), * p. 2, k. 5, p. 2, k. 11 (13) (15); repeat from * ending last repeat with k. 18 (17) (16).

15th row: K. 19 (18) (17), * y. fwd., k. 2 tog.b., k. 3, k. 2 tog., y. fwd., k. 13 (15) (17); repeat from * ending last repeat with k. 18 (17) (16).

16th row: K. 18 (17) (16), * p. 2, k. 3, p. 2, k. 13 (15) (17); repeat from * ending last repeat with k. 19 (18) (17).

17th row: K. 20 (19) (18), * y. fwd., k. 2 tog.b., k. 1, k. 2 tog., y.fwd., k. 15 (17) (19); repeat from * ending last repeat with k. 19 (18) (17).

18th row: K. 19 (18) (17), * p. 2, k. 1, p. 2, k. 15 (17) (19); repeat from * ending last repeat with k. 20 (19) (18).

19th row: K. 21 (20) (19), * y.fwd., sl. 1, k. 2 tog., p.s.s.o., y.fwd., k. 17 (19) (21); repeat from * ending last repeat with k. 20 (19) (18).

20th row: K. 20 (19) (18), * p. 3, k. 17 (19) (21); repeat from * ending last repeat with k. 21 (20) (19).

These 20 rows form the pattern. Repeat them a further 4 times.

To divide for fronts and back: Next row: Pattern 41 (44) (46), turn, and work on these sts. for right front.

The right front: 1st and 2nd turning rows: Pattern 25, turn for 1st row, then sl. 1, pattern until 2 sts. remain, k. 2 tog. for 2nd row.

3rd and 4th turning rows: Pattern 14, turn for 3rd row, then sl. 1 pattern until 2 sts. remain, k. 2 tog. for 4th row.

5th and 6th turning rows: Pattern 7, turn for 5th row, then sl. 1, pattern until 2 sts. remain, k. 2 tog. for 6th row.

Break yarn and leave remaining 38 (41) (43) sts. on spare needle for yoke.

With right side facing, rejoin yarn to inner end of remaining sts., cast off 4 sts. for underarm, pattern a further 73 (77) (83) sts., turn and work on these centre 74 (78) (84) sts. for back.

The back: Keeping continuity of the pattern, work 1 row, then dec. 1 st. each end of the next row and the 2 following alternate rows.

Break yarn and leave remaining 68 (72) (78) sts. on spare needle for yoke.

With right side facing, rejoin yarn to inner end of remaining sts., cast off 4 sts. for underarm, and work on remaining sts. for left front.

The left front: 1st and 2nd turning rows: Pattern a further 24, turn for 1st row, then sl. 1, pattern until 2 sts. remain, k. 2 tog. for 2nd row.

Continued on page 138

3rd to 6th turning rows: As 3rd to 6th turning rows of right front.

Do not break yarn, but leave remaining 38 (41) (43) sts. on spare needle for yoke.

THE SLEEVES (2 alike): With No. 6 (5 mm) needles cast on 54 (56) (58) sts. and k. 16 rows.

Change to No. 5 (5½ mm) needles and work in g.st with pattern panel.

1st row: K. 22 (23) (24), y.fwd., k. 2 tog.b., k. 5, k. 2 tog., y.fwd., k. 23 (24) (25).

2nd row: K. 23 (24) (25), p. 2, k. 5, p. 2, k. 22 (23) (24).

3rd row: K. 23 (24) (25), y.fwd., k. 2 tog.b., k. 3, k. 2 tog., y.fwd., k. 24 (25) (26).

4th row: K. 24 (25) (26), p. 2, k. 3, p. 2, k. 23 (24) (25).

5th row: K. 24 (25) (26), y. fwd., k. 2 tog.b., k. 1, k. 2 tog., y.fwd., k. 25 (26) (27).

6th row: K. 25 (26) (27), p. 2, k. 1, p. 2, k. 24 (25) (26).

7th row: K. 25 (26) (27), y.fwd., sl. 1, k. 2 tog., p.s.s.o., y.fwd., k. 26 (27) (28).

8th row: K. 26 (27) (28), p. 3, k. 25 (26) (27).

These 8 rows set the position of the pattern panel.

Keeping continuity of the panel to match main part, and working extra sts. in g.st. as they occur, inc. 1 st. each end of next row and the 3 following 20th rows—62 (64) (66) sts. Pattern 19 rows.

To shape sleeve top: Keeping continuity of the pattern, cast off 2 sts. at beginning of next 2 rows, then dec. 1 st. each end of next row and 2 following alternate rows—52 (54) (56) sts.

Break yarn and leave for yoke.

THE YOKE: With right side facing, return to left front and using No. 5 (5½ mm) needles, using yarn attached, k. across left front sts., turn, then with wrong side facing, k. these 38 (41) (43) sts., k. across 52 (54) (56) sts. of one sleeve, then increasing 1 st. in centre, k. across back sts., k. across 52 (54) (56) sts. of other sleeve, and finally, k. 38 (41) (43) sts. of right front—249 (263) (277) sts.

K. 10 rows.

1st pattern row: K. 6 for g.st. border, p. 6, * y.t.b., sl. 1 k. wise, y.t.f., p. 6; repeat from * until 6 sts. remain, k. 6 for border.

2nd row: K. 6 for border, k. 6, * p. 1, k. 6; repeat from * until 6 sts. remain, k. 6 for border.

3rd row: As 1st row.

1st dec. row: K. 8, * k. 2 tog., k. 2, p. 1, k. 2; repeat from * until 10 sts. remain, k. 2 tog., k. 8—215 (227) (239) sts.

Next row: K. 6, p. 5, * y.t.b., sl. 1 k. wise, y.t.f., p. 5; repeat from * until 6 sts. remain, k. 6.

Keeping pattern correct as set, work a further 8 rows.

2nd dec. row: K. 8, * k. 2 tog., k. 1, p. 1, k. 2; repeat from * until 9 sts. remain, k. 2 tog., k. 7—181 (191) (201) sts.

Pattern 9 rows keeping pattern correct as set.

3rd dec. row: K. 7, * k. 2 tog., k. 1, p. 1, k. 1; repeat from * until 9 sts. remain, k. 2 tog., k. 7—147 (155) (163) sts.

Pattern 7 rows keeping pattern correct as set.

4th dec. row: K. 7, * k. 2 tog., p. 1, k. 1; repeat from * until 8 sts. remain, k. 2 tog., k. 6—113 (119) (125) sts.

Pattern 7 rows keeping pattern correct as set.

5th dec. row: K. 6, * k. 2 tog., p. 1; repeat from * until 8 sts. remain, k. 2 tog., k. 6—79 (83) (87) sts.

Pattern 4 rows with sts. as set.

Change to No. 6 (5 mm) needles.

6th dec. row: K. 6, pattern 15 (16) (17), * sl. 1, k. 2 tog., p.s.s.o., pattern 14 (15) (16); repeat from * once, sl. 1, k. 2

tog., p.s.s.o., pattern 15 (16) (17), k. 6—73 (77) (81) sts.

1st rib row: K. 7, p. 1, * k. 1, p. 1; repeat from * until 7 sts. remain, k. 7.

2nd rib row: K. 6, p. 1, * k. 1, p. 1; repeat from * until 6 sts. remain, k. 6.

Repeat last 2 rows, 3 times more.

Change to No. 5 (5½ mm) needles and work for collar.

The collar: 1st pattern row: K. 6, y.t.b., sl. 1 k. wise, y.t.f., * p. 1, y.t.b., sl. 1 k.wise, y.t.f.; repeat from * until 6 sts. remain, k. 6.

2nd row: K. 6, p. 1, * k. 1, p. 1; repeat from * until 6 sts. remain, k. 6.

Repeat last 2 rows, 11 times more.

Change to No. 6 (5 mm) needles and k. 9 rows.

Cast off k.wise.

TO COMPLETE THE JACKET: Do not press. Join sleeve seams reversing seam at lower edge for cuff. Join tiny underarm seams. Fold 16 rows of g.st. to right side for cuff.

Finishing Touches

SEWING IN A SLIDE FASTNER

Lay the pieces of the garment in position on the flat (they should have been pressed if so instructed on the ball band). First pin and then tack the slide fastner into place. With the wrong side of the work facing you, back stitch close to the zip teeth using ordinary thread. Finally slip stitch the outer edges of the fastner flat to the garment.

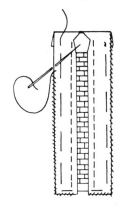

MAKING A FRINGE

Cut several strands of yarn of equal length, place them together and fold in half. Insert a crochet hook into the edge of the fabric and draw the looped ends of the strands through the fabric, thread the cut ends through the loops and draw up tightly to form the fringe. Repeat along the edge at regular intervals.

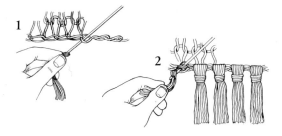

MAKING A POMPON

Cut two circles of card approximately the size of the pompon required, and cut a circle from the centre of each. Using several strands of yarn together, bind the cards together taking the strands through the centre hole and round the outer edge until the card is covered and the centre hole is filled. Cut through the outer edges of the yarn, insert a thread between the cards and tie tightly round the centre. Remove the cards and trim the pompon to shape and size.

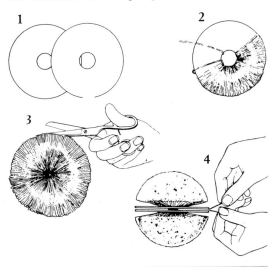

Knitting Needle Conversion Chart

ENGLISH	METRIC
14	2mm
13	$2\frac{1}{4}$mm
12	$2\frac{3}{4}$mm
11	3mm
10	$3\frac{1}{4}$mm
9	$3\frac{3}{4}$mm
8	4mm
7	$4\frac{1}{2}$mm
6	5mm
5	$5\frac{1}{2}$mm
4	6mm
3	$6\frac{1}{2}$mm
2	7mm
1	$7\frac{1}{2}$mm
0	8mm
00	9mm
000	10mm

Useful Addressess

For details of local stockists please write directly to the appropriate
manufacturer at the address below:

Emu Wools,
Leeds Road,
Greengates,
Bradford,
W. Yorks.

Tel: Bradford 614031

Lister/Lee Target,
P.O. Box 37,
Providence Mill,
Wakefield,
Yorkshire.

Tel: 0924 75311

3 Suisses,
Marlborough House,
Welford Road,
Leicester, LB2 7AA.

Tel: 0533 554713

Pingouin Wools,
French Wools Ltd.,
7–11 Lexington Street,
London, W.1.

Tel: 01 439 8891

Phildar (UK) Ltd.,
4 Gambrel Road,
Westgate Industrial Estate,
Northampton, NN5 5NF.

Tel: 0604 583111

Sirdar Wools,
Sirdar Press Office
  (Suite 507),
16 Berkeley Street,
London, W.1.

Tel: 01 499 0768

Wendy Wools Ltd.,
325 City Road,
London, E.C.1.

Tel: 01 837 7991

KingCole,
R.J. Cole Ltd.,
Rhone Mills,
Sun Street,
Keighley.

Tel: 0535 605249

Hayfield Press Office,
16 Berkeley Street,
  (Suite 508),
London, W.1.

Tel: 01 499 0928

Ladyship Wools,
Scarborough Mills,
Halifax,
W. Yorks.

Tel: 0422 58433

Argyll Wools,
P.O. Box 15,
Priestley Mills,
Pudsey,
W. Yorkshire, LS28 9LD.

Tel: 0532 573411

Patons & Baldwins,
& Jaeger Wools,
54 Gt. Marlborough Street,
London, W.1.

Tel: 01 437 9898

Robin Wools,
Golley Slater
  & Partners Ltd.,
42 Drury Lane,
London, W.C.2.

Tel: 01 240 5131

H.G. Twilley Ltd.,
Roman Mills,
Stamford,
Lincs.

Tel: 0780 52661

J. & P. Coats,
155 St. Vincent,
Glasgow,
Scotland.

Tel: 041 221 8711

Index

Page numbers in italics indicate illustrations